# TURNING POINTS

## Other Books by Damon Knight

### NOVELS

A for Anything
Beyond the Barrier
Hell's Pavement

The Other Foot
The Rithian Terror

### STORY COLLECTIONS

The Best of Damon Knight
Far Out
In Deep
Off Center

Turning On
Three Novels
World Without Children
*and* The Earth Quarter

### ANTHOLOGIES

Best Stories from *Orbit*, Vols. 1–10
Beyond Tomorrow
A Century of Great Short
    Science Fiction Novels
A Century of Science Fiction
Cities of Wonder
The Dark Side
Dimension X
First Contact
The Golden Road
Happy Endings
100 Years of Science Fiction
The Metal Smile
Nebula Award Stories One

Now Begins Tomorrow
Orbit, Vols. 1–19
Perchance to Dream
A Pocketful of Stars
A Science Fiction Argosy
Science Fiction Inventions
Science Fiction of the Thirties
The Shape of Things
A Shocking Thing
Tomorrow and Tomorrow
Tomorrow × 4
Toward Infinity
Westerns of the Forties
Worlds to Come

### TRANSLATIONS

Ashes, Ashes, by René Barjavel

13 French Science Fiction Stories

### BIOGRAPHY AND CRITICISM

Charles Fort: Prophet of the
    Unexplained

The Futurians
In Search of Wonder

# Essays on the Art of Science Fiction

Edited by
DAMON KNIGHT

HARPER & ROW, PUBLISHERS

NEW YORK  HAGERSTOWN  SAN FRANCISCO  LONDON

# ACKNOWLEDGMENTS

"Science Fiction: Its Nature, Faults and Virtues," by Robert A. Heinlein, copyright © 1959 by Robert A. Heinlein; reprinted by permission of the author and Lurton Blassingame.

"Social Science Fiction," by Isaac Asimov, copyright © 1953 by Coward-McCann, Inc.; reprinted by permission of the author.

"Pilgrim Fathers: Lucian and All That," by Brian W. Aldiss, copyright © 1973 by Brian W. Aldiss; reprinted by permission of the author.

"Science Fiction Before Gernsback," by H. Bruce Franklin, copyright © 1966, 1968 by Oxford University Press, Inc.; reprinted by permission of the publisher.

"The Situation Today," by Kingsley Amis, copyright © 1960 by Kingsley Amis; reprinted by permission of Harcourt Brace Jovanovich, Inc.

"On Science Fiction," by C. S. Lewis, copyright © 1966 by the Executors of the Estate of C. S. Lewis; reprinted by permission of Harcourt Brace Jovanovich, Inc.

*Continued on next page*

TURNING POINTS: ESSAYS ON THE ART OF SCIENCE FICTION. Copyright © 1977 by Damon Knight. All rights reserved. Printed in the United States of America. No part of this book may be used or reproduced in any manner whatsoever without written permission except in the case of brief quotations embodied in critical articles and reviews. For information address Harper & Row, Publishers, Inc., 10 East 53rd Street, New York, N.Y. 10022. Published simultaneously in Canada by Fitzhenry & Whiteside Limited, Toronto.

FIRST EDITION

*Designed by C. Linda Dingler*

---

**Library of Congress Cataloging in Publication Data**

Main entry under title:
Turning points.

Includes bibliographical references.

1. Science fiction—Addresses, essays, lectures.

I. Knight, Damon Francis, date

PN3448.S45T8   1977        809.3′876        75-5135

ISBN 0-06-012432-6

---

77 78 79 80 10 9 8 7 6 5 4 3 2 1

# CONTENTS

## VII.  CONFESSIONS

# INTRODUCTION

Science fiction passed through a long period when nobody was writing criticism of it—first because s.f. had not yet been recognized as a distinct field and therefore it was not perceived that there was anything to criticize; later (after Hugo Gernsback founded *Amazing Stories* in 1926) because the laborers in the new field were too busy watering it with praise. Not until the early 1950s did science fiction become sufficiently mature to begin examining itself, and until 1960 critics outside the field noticed it only in order to dismiss it with contempt. Thus there was a period of some ten years in which science fiction writers, unencumbered by outside help (or, in most cases, by any formal training in literature), joyfully invented s.f. criticism *ab initio*. As you will see, their work was highly partisan, narrow and individualist; each of them had his own principles and attitudes, which he asserted as self-evident, and the result was a glorious collision of credos.

I have chosen what seem to me to be the liveliest and most provocative of these essays, and have arranged them with a sampling of later criticism in a way which I hope will give a comprehensive view of this turbulent and perplexing field. I have written two new essays for this book, solely because the topics were not covered by anything I could find or get permission to use. I feel I should apologize for this, because it has always seemed to me that an anthologist who immortalizes his own work is hard to distinguish from a contest judge who awards himself a prize. Nevertheless, I don't regret the necessity that forced me to re-examine one of the most vexed questions in s.f. criticism—"What is science fiction?"—with results which I think are novel.

I hope this book will be useful to teachers and students of science fiction, as well as to aspiring s.f. writers; but, with one possible exception (Poul Anderson's "How to Build a Planet," which I put in to show just how technical science fiction can get), there is nothing here that can't be read for pure enjoyment as well as for information.

Notes in the text are the authors'; my own comments are in a separate section at the end of the book.

DAMON KNIGHT

# I.
# A WALK AROUND THE TOPIC

# SCIENCE FICTION:

## *Its Nature, Faults and Virtues*

## Robert A. Heinlein

First let us decide what we mean by the term "science fiction"—or at least what we will mean by it here. Anyone wishing a scholarly discussion of the etymology of the term will find one by Sam Moskowitz in the February, 1957, issue of *The Magazine of Fantasy and Science Fiction*. I shan't repeat what he has said so well but will summarize for our immediate purposes. The field now known as science fiction had no agreed name until about twenty-five years ago. The field has existed throughout the history of literature but it used to be called by several names: speculative romance, pseudo-scientific romance (a term that sets a science fiction writer's teeth on edge), utopian literature, fantasy—or, more frequently, given no name, simply lumped in with all other fiction.

But the term "science fiction" is now part of the language, as common as the neologism "guided missile." We are stuck with it and I will use it . . . although personally I prefer the term "speculative fiction" as being more descriptive. I will use these two terms interchangeably, one being the common handle, the other being one that aids me in thinking—but with the same referent in each case.

"Science fiction" means different things to different people. "When I make a word do a lot of work like that," said Humpty Dumpty, "I always pay it extra"—in which case the term science fiction has piled up a lot of expensive overtime. Damon Knight, a distinguished critic in this field,

FROM *The Science Fiction Novel*, Advent, 1959

argues that there is no clear distinction between fantasy and science fiction, in which opinion August Derleth seems to agree. I cannot forcefully disagree with their lines of reasoning—but I wonder if they have made their definitions so broad as to include practically all fiction? To define is to limit; a definition cannot be useful unless it limits. Certainly Mickey Spillane's murder stories could easily be classed as fantasies, as can many or most of the love stories appearing in the big slick magazines. But I feel sure that Mr. Knight and Mr. Derleth did not intend their definitions to be quite that unbounded and in any case my difference of opinion with them is merely a matter of taste and personal convenience.

Theodore Sturgeon, a giant in this field, defines a science fiction story as one in which the story would not exist if it were not for the scientific element—an admirably sharp delimitation but one which seems to me perhaps as uncomfortably tight as the one above seems to me unusefully roomy. It would exclude from the category "science fiction" much of Mr. Sturgeon's best work, stories which are to my mind speculative rather than fantastic. There are many stories that are lumped into the class "science fiction" in the minds of most people (and in mine) which contain only a detectable trace, or none, of science—for example, Sinclair Lewis' *It Can't Happen Here*, Fritz Leiber's great short story "Coming Attraction," Thomas F. Tweed's novel *Gabriel Over the White House*. All three stories are of manners and morals; any science in them is merely parsley trimming, not the meat. Yet each is major speculation, not fantasy, and each must be classed as science fiction as the term is commonly used.

Reginald Bretnor, author, editor and acute critic of this field, gives what is to me the most thoughtful, best reasoned, and most useful definition of science fiction. He sees it as a field of literature much broader than that often termed "mainstream" literature—or "non-science fiction," if you please—science fiction being that sort in which the author shows awareness of the nature and importance of the human activity known as the scientific method, shows equal awareness of the great body of human knowledge already collected through that activity, and takes into account in his stories the effects and possible future effects on human beings of scientific method and scientific fact. This indispensable threefold awareness does not limit the science fiction author to stories about science—he need not write a gadget story; indeed a gadget story would not be science fiction under this definition if the author failed in this threefold awareness. Any subject can be used in a science fiction story under this definition, provided (and indispensably required) that the author has the attitude comprised by the threefold awareness and further provided that he has and uses appropriately that body of knowledge pertinent to the scope of his story. I have paraphrased in summary Mr. Bretnor's comments and I hope he will forgive me.

Mr. Bretnor's definition gives the science fiction author almost unlimited freedom in subject matter while requiring of him high, rigorous, difficult and mature standards in execution.

In contrast to science fiction thus defined, non-science fiction—all other fiction including the most highly acclaimed "literary" novels—at most shows awareness of the byproducts of scientific method already in existence. Non-science fiction admits the existence of the automobile, radar, polio vaccine, H-bombs, etc., but refuses to countenance starships and other such frivolities. That is to say, non-science fiction will concede that water is running downhill but refuses to admit that it might ever reach the bottom . . . or could ever be pumped up again. It is a static attitude, an assumption that what is now forever shall be.

An example of the great scope of this definition is Sinclair Lewis' novel *Arrowsmith*, a story motivated by the human problems of a man aware of and consciously trying to practice the scientific method in medical research in the face of difficulties. *Arrowsmith* was not labeled science fiction by its publisher, it is not concerned with spaceships nor the year 3000; nevertheless it is science fiction at its best, it shows that threefold awareness to the utmost and is a rousin' good yarn of great literary merit.

Let's back off for a moment and compare science fiction with other forms of fiction. First: What is fiction?

Merriam-Webster: "Works of imagination in narrative form."

Funk & Wagnalls: "Imaginary narrative."

Thorndike-Barnhart: "Prose writings about imaginary people and happenings."

Fowler's *Modern English Usage* equates "fictitious" with "imaginary."

These reasonably equivalent definitions are all based on the common element "imaginary"—so let's put it in everyday words: Fiction is storytelling about imaginary things and people. These imaginary tales are usually intended to entertain and sometimes do, they are sometimes intended to instruct and occasionally manage even that, but the only element common to all fiction is that all of it deals with imaginary events.

Even fiction of the most sordid and detailed ashcan realism is imaginary —or it cannot be termed fiction.

But if all fiction is imaginary, how is realistic fiction to be distinguished from fantasy?

The lexicographers cited above are not quite so unanimous here. However, I find certain words used over and over again in their discussions of fantasy: "dream, caprice, whim, fanciful, conceit, figment, unreal, irrational." These descriptive words have a common element; they all imply imaginings which are not limited by the physical universe as we conceive it to be.

I therefore propose to define "fantasy" in accordance with the implication common to the remarks of these lexicographers. There have been many wordy and fruitless battles over the exact meaning of the word "fantasy"; I have no intention of starting another. I ask merely that you accept for the purpose of better communication during the balance of this essay a definition based on the above. When I say "fantasy fiction" I shall mean "imaginary-and-not-possible" in the world as we know it; conversely all fiction which I regard as "imaginary-but-possible" I shall refer to as "realistic fiction," i.e., imaginary but could be real so far as we know the real universe.

Science fiction is in the latter class. It is not fantasy.

I am not condemning fantasy, I am defining it. It has greater freedom than any other form of fiction, for it is completely independent of the real world and is limited only by literary rules relating to empathy, inner logic and the like. Its great freedom makes it, in the hands of a skilled craftsman, a powerful tool for entertainment and instruction—humor, satire, gothic horror, anything you wish. But a story is not fantasy simply because it deals with the strange, the exotic, the horrible, the unusual or the improbable; both fantasy and realistic fiction may have any of these elements. It is mere provincialism to confuse the wildly strange with fantasy; a fantasy story is one which denies in its premise some feature of the real world; it may be quite humdrum in all other respects, e.g., Eric Knight's *The Flying Yorkshireman*.

Conversely, a realistic story may be wildly strange while holding firmly to the possibilities of the real world—e.g., E. E. Smith's *Gray Lensman*. The science fiction author is not limited by currently accepted theory nor by popular opinion; he need only respect established fact.

Unfortunately there is never full agreement as to the "established facts" nor as to what constitutes the "real world," and definitions by intention are seldom satisfactory. By these two terms I mean the factual universe of our experience in the sense in which one would expect such words to be used by educated and enlightened members of the western culture in 1959.

Even this definition contains semantic and philosophic difficulties but I shall not attempt to cope with them in this limited space; I will limit myself to pointing out some stories which, in my opinion, deny some essential fact of the real world and therefore are, by the "imaginary-and-not-possible" definition, fantasy:

My story *Magic, Inc.*; E. R. Eddison's *The Worm Ouroboros*; the *Oz* books; stories using talking mules, or seacoast Bohemia, or astrology treated as if it were a science; any story based on violation of scientific fact, such as spaceship stories which ignore ballistics, stories which have the lizard men of Zlxxt crossbreeding with human females, stories which represent the surface conditions of Mars as being much like those of Earth. Let me emphasize: Assumptions contrary to fact such as the last one mentioned do not in themselves invalidate a story; C. S. Lewis' powerful *Out of the Silent Planet* is not spoiled thereby as a religious parable —it simply happens to be fantasy rather than science fiction.[1]

Very well—from here on "fantasy" will be considered identically equal to "impossible story."

All other fiction including science fiction falls into the category "imaginary-but-possible." Examples: Frederic Wakeman's *The Hucksters*, Dr. E. E. Smith's galactic romances, Daniel Defoe's *Moll Flanders*; stories about time travel, other dimensions, speeds faster than light, extrasensory perception; many ghost stories, ones about extraterrestrial life, John Steinbeck's *The Grapes of Wrath*.

You will have noted that I make the category "possible" very broad. Faster-than-light, time travel, reincarnation, ghosts, all these may strike some of you as impossible, contrary to scientific fact. No, they are contrary to present orthodox theory only and the distinction is extremely important. Such stories may be invalidated by their treatments; they cannot be ruled out today as impossible simply because of such themes. Speeds faster than light would seem to be excluded by Einsteinian theory, a theory which has stood up favorably under many tests, but such an exclusion would be a subjective one, as anyone may see by examining the equations; furthermore, Dr. Einstein's theories and related ones are now being subjected to careful re-examination; the outcome is not yet. As for time travel, we know almost nothing about the nature of time; anyone who has his mind made up either pro or con about time travel is confusing his inner opinions with objective reality. We simply don't know.

With respect to reincarnation, ghosts, ESP and many related matters concerning consciousness, the evidence concerning each is, in 1959, incomplete and in many respects unsatisfactory. We don't even know how consciousness anchors itself to mass; we are short on solid facts in this field and any opinion, positive or negative, can be no better than a tentative hypothesis today.

Hypotheses and theories are always expendable; a scientist modifies or discards them in the face of new facts as casually as he changes his socks. Ordinarily a scientist will use the convenient rule of thumb called "least hypothesis" but he owes it no allegiance; his one fixed loyalty is to the observed fact.[2] An honest science fiction writer observes the same loyalty to fact but from there on his path diverges from that of the scientist because his function is different. The pragmatic rule of least hypothesis, useful as it may be to orderly research, is as unfunctional in speculative fiction as a chaperone on a honeymoon. In matters incompletely explored such as reincarnation and time travel the science fiction writer need not be and should not be bound either by contemporary opinion or least hypothesis; his function is to speculate from such facts as there are and to do so as grandly and sweepingly as his imagination permits. He cannot carry out his function while paying lip service to the orthodox opinions or prejudices of his tribe and generation, and no one should expect it of him. It is difficult enough for him to bear in mind a multitude of facts and not wander inadvertently across into fantasy.

I have made perhaps too much of this point because it is a sore one with all science fiction writers; we are regularly charged with "violating facts" when all we have done is to disregard currently respected theory. Every new speculation necessarily starts by kicking aside some older theory.

To categorizing there is no end, and the field of prose fiction may be classified in many different ways: by length, plot, subject, period, locale, language, narrative technique; or by intent—satire, romance, burlesque, comedy, tragedy, propaganda. All these classes blend together and what categories a critic chooses to define depends upon his purpose. We have divided fiction into possible and impossible; now let us divide again by temporal scene:

*REALISTIC FICTION*
1. Historical Fiction
2. Contemporary-Scene Fiction
3. Realistic Future-Scene Fiction

*FANTASY FICTION*
I. Fantasy laid in the past
II. Fantasy laid in the present
III. Fantasy laid in the future

This arbitrary classification has advantages; on inspecting it several facts show up at once:

So-called mainstream literature fills most of class 1 and class 2.

Class 3 contains only science fiction; a small amount of science fiction may also be found in class 1 and class 2.

In the second division, good fantasy, conscientiously written and skilfully executed, may be found in all three classes. But a great quantity of fake "science" fiction, actually pseudo-scientific fantasy, will be found there also, especially in class III, which is choked with it.

But the most significant fact shining out from the above method of classifying is that class 3, realistic future-scene fiction, contains nothing which is not science fiction and contains at least 90% of all science fiction in print. A handy short definition of almost all science fiction might read: realistic speculation about possible future events, based solidly on adequate knowledge of the real world, past and present, and on a thorough understanding of the nature and significance of the scientific method.

To make this definition cover all science fiction (instead of "almost all") it is necessary only to strike out the word "future." But in fact most science fiction is laid in the future; the reasons for this are not trivial and will be discussed later.

As always, categories tend to overlap, or stories turn out to overlap the categories. We will not offer them Procrustean hospitality—a story is what it is, regardless of a critic's classifications. John Taine's novel *The Time Stream* is science fiction which spans past, present and future; Dr. Frank G. Slaughter's *Sangaree* is a fine historical novel which is also a science fiction novel; Lion Feuchtwanger's *Success* is an historical novel laid in the present and told as if the narrator were in the future; Maxwell Griffith's *The Gadget Makers*, Philip Wylie's *Tomorrow* and Pat Frank's *Forbidden Area* are examples of science fiction laid in a future no later than tomorrow morning. Some stories are such exotic creatures as to defy almost any method of literary taxonomy. A skillful writer could combine in one story an element of fantasy, some of science fiction, a contemporary story, an historical drama and a bit of the future, some comedy, some tragedy, some burlesque and a little straight hortatory propaganda —in fact I have seen one which includes all of these elements: Vincent McHugh's *Caleb Catlum's America.*

But realistic speculation—science fiction—is usually laid in the future, because it extrapolates from "what is" to "what might be." Some will say that this is the rankest form of fantasy, since the future is not "real." I deny that. We have the dead past, the dying moment and the ever-emerging, always-living future. Our lives always lie in the future; a casual decision to scratch oneself must be carried out at least an instant in the future. The future is all that we can change—and thank Heaven we can!—for the present has obvious shortcomings.

If the future were not real, no insurance company could stay in business. All our lives we are more deeply concerned with what we are going to do than with what we are now doing or have done. The poet who said that every child is the hope of the world understood that. This process is time-binding, the most human of all activities, observing the past in order to make plans for the future. This is the scientific method itself and is the activity which most greatly distinguishes man from other animals. To be able to grasp and embrace the future is to be human.

For this reason I must assert that speculative fiction is much more realistic than is most historical and contemporary-scene fiction and is superior to them both.

Are the speculations of science fiction prophecy? No.

On the other hand, science fiction is often prophetic. There was once a race-track tout who touted every horse in each race, each horse to a different sucker. Inevitably he had a winner in every race—he had extrapolated every possibility. Science fiction writers have "prophesied" (if you will excuse a deliberate misuse of the word) so many things and so many possible futures that some of them must come true, with sometimes rather startling accuracy. Having bet on all the horses we can't lose. But much has been made of the "successful prophecies" of science fiction—the electric light, the telephone, the airplane, the submarine, the periscope,[3] tanks, flamethrowers, A-bombs, television, the automobile, guided missiles, robot aircraft, totalitarian government, radar—the list is endless.

The fact is that most so-called successful prophecies are made by writers who follow the current scientific reports and indulge in rather obvious extrapolation of already known fact. Let me pick to pieces two cases which I know well because the "prophecies" are attributed to me. The first is from my story *Waldo*, and refers to remote-control manipulators described therein which I called "waldos" after the fictional inventor. Willy Ley calls this "one of the neatest predictions ever to come out of science fiction" and goes on to describe how nearly perfectly I had described the remote-control manipulators now used in atomic "hot" laboratories, even to the use of stereotelevision to conn them . . . even to the development of master and slave teams to permit one operator to do multiple tasks. Sounds pretty good, eh? Especially as the word "waldo" has since become engineering slang.

The second refers to my story "Solution Unsatisfactory." John W. Campbell, Jr., in an essay on this point, lists nine major prophecies in this story, seven of which he says have come true, and two of which, he notes, may very well come true soon. All of them refer to atomic weapons and their impact on history. I might even add that one of those predictions would have come true even more precisely had I not just finished writing another story on atomic power and wished to avoid repeating one of the incidents in it. All of these so-called prophecies were made early in 1940 and they have "come true," so to speak, during the ensuing nineteen years.

Sounds as if I own a crystal ball, doesn't it?

Now to pick them to pieces, the latter one first. At the time I wrote "Solution Unsatisfactory" there wasn't enough U-235 in pure state to blow the hat off a flea. But I had had my attention called to its explosive and military possibilities not only by technical reports but both by Mr. Campbell himself (who had maintained his connections at M.I.T.) and by Dr. Robert Cornog, atomic physicist from Berkeley who later helped develop the atomic bomb. Thus I had first-hand and most recent scientific knowledge to build on—all this was before security restrictions were placed on the matter, before the famous first pile was erected at the University of Chicago.

I had two more all-important data: a great world war was already going on, and the basic knowledge which made U-235 potentially an unbeatable weapon which could win that war was already known to scientists the world around—even though the public was unaware of it.

Given all this mass of fact could a careful fictionist fail to come up with something near the truth? As prophecies, those fictional predictions of mine were about as startling as for a man to look out a train window, see that another train is coming head-on toward his own on the same track—and predict a train wreck.

The other one, the waldos or remote control manipulators, was even simpler. Back in 1918 I read an article in *Popular Mechanics* about a poor fellow afflicted with myasthenia gravis, a pathological muscular weakness so great that even handling a knife and fork is too much effort. In this condition the brain and the control system are okay, the muscles almost incapable. This man—I don't even know his name; the article is lost in the dim corridors of time—this genius did not let myasthenia gravis defeat him. He devised complicated lever arrangements to enable him to use what little strength he had and he became an inventor and industrial engineer, specializing in how to get maximum result for least effort. He turned his affliction into an asset.

Twenty-two years after I had read about his inspiring example I was scratching my head for a story notion—and I recalled this genius. Now I myself am a mechanical engineer who once specialized in mechanical linkages and had worked in industrial engineering. Is it surprising that with so much real fact to go on and with my own technical background I could describe fictionally remote-control manipulators—"waldos"—which would multiply human muscle power and at the same time handle things with delicate precision? Television had already been invented years before—about twenty years before the public got it—and somebody had already built such linkages, even though they were not in common use. So I "prophesied" them—twenty years after the fact.

What I did miss was that the development of atomics would make waldos utterly indispensable; I predicted them for straight industrial use —now even that is coming true as industry is finding other uses for the manipulators developed for atomics.

But as a "prophecy" I was taking as much chance as a man who predicts tomorrow's sunrise.

These manipulators exist in the opposite direction, too—down into the very small . . . micromanipulators for microchemistry and microsurgery. I have never worked with such things but I learned their details from my wife, who is a microchemist and microsurgeon. Working with such and using a stereomicroscope a skilled operator can excise a living nucleus from a living cell, transplant it to another cell, and cause it to live—a powerful tool in biological research . . . and a beautiful example of re-search scientist and engineer working together to produce something new. The scientist wanted it—working under his direction, optician and mechanical engineers could make what he needed.

There are other obvious extrapolations from these facts. Put these four things together, the remote-control manipulator with the micromanipula-tor, television with microscopy. Use micromanipulation to make still smaller instruments which in turn are used to make ones smaller yet.[4] What do you get? A scientist, working safely outside a "hot" laboratory—perhaps with the actual working theater as far away as the Antarctic while the scientist sits in Chicago—seeing by stereomicroscopic television, using remote-control microscopic manipulation, operating not just on a cell and a nucleus, but sorting the mighty molecules of the genes, to determine the exact genetic effect of mutation caused by radiation. Or a dozen other things.

I give this prediction about twenty years, more or less. The basic facts are all in and soon we'll be needing such a technique. There may be a story in it for me, too—another easy dollar as a fake prophet. I'm afraid the itch to prophesy becomes a vice. Forgive me.

Sometimes the so-called prophecies are even less prophetic than these two I have just deflated. For example, in one story[5] I described a rather remarkable oleo-gear arrangement for handling exceedingly heavy loads. I was not cheating, the device would work; it had been patented about 1900 and has been in industrial use ever since. But it is a gadget not well known to the public and it happened to fit into a story I was writing.

Most so-called science fiction prophecies require very little use of a crystal ball; they are much more like the observations of a man who is looking out a train window rather than down at his lap—he sees the other train coming, and the ensuing "prophecy" is somewhat less remarkable than a lunar eclipse prediction.

However, science and science fiction do interact. There are close rela-tionships between scientists and science fiction writers—indeed some of them are both. H. G. Wells had a degree in biology and kept up with science all his life. Jules Verne worked very closely with scientists. Dr. E. E. Smith is a chemist, a chemical engineer, and a metallurgist. "Philip Latham" is a world-famous astrophysicist. Philip Wylie has a degree in physics, as has "Don A. Stuart." "Murray Leinster" is a chemist. Dr. Isaac Asimov teaches at the medical school of Boston University, does research in cancer, writes college textbooks on biochemistry, writes a junior series of science books as well—and somehow finds time to be a leading science fiction author. "John Taine" is the pen name of one of the ten greatest living mathematicians. L. Sprague de Camp holds three technical degrees. "Lee Correy" is a senior rocket engineer.[6] George O. Smith is a prominent electronics engineer. Chad Oliver is an anthropologist. Is it surprising that such men, writing fiction about what they know best, manage to be right rather often?

But science fiction not infrequently guides the direction of science. I had a completely imaginary electronics device in a story published in 1939. A classmate of mine, then directing such research, took it to his civilian chief engineer and asked if it could possibly be done. The researcher replied, "Mmm . . . no, I don't think so—uh, wait a minute . . . well, yes, maybe. We'll try."

The breadboarded first model was being tried out aboard ship before the next installment of my story hit the newsstands. The final development of this gadget was in use all through World War II. I wasn't predicting anything and had no reason to think that it would work; I was just dreaming up a gadget to fill a need in a story, sticking as close to fact and possibility as I could.[7]

*"Tout ce qu'un homme est capable d'imaginer, d'autres hommes seront capable de la réaliser."* ( M. Jules Verne—I am indebted to Willy Ley for the quotation.) "Anything one man can imagine, other men can make real." Or to put it in the words of Colonel Turner, first commanding officer of White Sands: "I'll go this far: Anything we want to do, we now can do, if we want to badly enough." As Oscar Wilde put it, "Nature mirrors art" . . . and it often does, in science fiction. If a writer knows that mankind wants to do something or needs to do something and that writer is reasonably familiar with current trends in research and development, it is not too hard for him to predict approximately what one of the solutions will be.

However, "in science fiction as in law, ignorance is no excuse," to quote L. Sprague de Camp. The man who has neglected to keep himself informed concerning the frontiers of science, or, even having managed that, fails to be reasonably knowledgeable about any field of human activity affecting his story, or who lacks a fair knowledge of history and current events—failing in any of these things, he has no business writing speculative fiction. It is not enough to interlard an old plot with terms like "space warp," "matter transmitter," "ray gun," or "rocket ship" with no knowledge of what is meant (if anything) by such terms, or how they might reasonably work. A man who provides Mars with a dense atmosphere and an agreeable climate, a man whose writing shows that he knows nothing of ballistics nor of astronomy nor of any modern technology would do better not to attempt science fiction. Such things are not science fiction—entertainment they may be; serious speculation they cannot be. The obligation of the writer to his reader to know what he is talking about is even stronger in science fiction than elsewhere, because the ordinary reader has less chance to catch him out. It's not fair, it's cheating.

Let's cite another example of the strong interconnection between true science fiction and scientific development itself. Back in 1931 a story by Edmond Hamilton was published called "The Sargasso of Space" which portrayed the first spacesuits I happen to be aware of. In 1939 I wrote a story, "Misfit," which made much use of spacesuits, and I remembered how Hamilton had visualized them—remembered with approval—I had done a little suit diving and had some knowledge of engineering and it seemed to me that Hamilton had a good idea; my spacesuits were elaborated versions of his. A former shipmate of mine, now Rear Admiral A. B. Scoles, was then engaged in aviation research and development. A long-time science fiction fan, Scoles read my story. When we got into the war he sent for me, put me in charge of a high-altitude laboratory of which one of the projects was the development of a spacesuit (then called a high-altitude pressure suit). I worked on it a short while, then was relieved by L. Sprague de Camp, who is an aeronautical and mechanical engineer as well as a writer; he carried on with this research all through the war, testing and developing many spacesuits. The war ended; I wrote a story involving spacesuits in which I applied what I had had opportunity to learn. The story eventually was made into a motion picture, so I sent for a photograph of one of the spacesuits Sprague de Camp had helped develop, and we copied it as closely as we could for the movie.

With this crossing back and forth between fiction and technology is it surprising that the present day spacesuit (or high-altitude pressure suit, if you prefer) now used by the U. S. Air Force strongly resembles in appearance and behavior the spacesuit visualized by Edmond Hamilton in 1931?[8]

A more startling example of the crossing back and forth between science fiction and technology occurs in space travel itself. I shall not go into it in detail as Arthur C. Clarke, the distinguished science fiction writer and scientist, has already done so—but I will mention some of the pioneers in rocketry who also have written fiction about the subject: Professor Hermann Oberth, Willy Ley, Wernher von Braun, Arthur C. Clarke, G. Harry Stine. This is by no means a complete list; it is illustrative only, and I use it to preface a quotation. I am indebted to Reginald Bretnor for this item; he found it in the pages of America's best known and possibly most respected journal of literary criticism:*

Even before the German inventors created the first navigable rocket at Peenemünde the writers of this somewhat crude form of entertainment had developed the rocket ships which cruised to the moon and the solar planets and then burst into outermost space and explored the galaxies of the Milky Way. Driven by atomic power these apparently mad devices were as well known to the devotees of science fiction as the liners that cross our oceans. Nevertheless, it [space travel] remained unadulterated fantasy until scientists contemplated the experiments with rockets that have proceeded since the last war.

And this entire quotation is unadulterated tosh!

In literary criticism, as in science fiction and in law, ignorance is no excuse. Let's take it bit by bit:

"—the German inventors created the first navigable rocket at Peenemünde—" The V-2 was not a navigable rocket; the first navigable rocket was developed in the United States long years after Peenemünde was destroyed.

"—this somewhat crude form of entertainment—" This critic is speaking of the writings of, among others, Dr. Olaf Stapledon, H. G. Wells, Jules Verne, C. S. Lewis, Philip Wylie, Edward Everett Hale, Johannes Kepler, Lucian of Samosata, Cyrano de Bergerac, Edgar Allan Poe. I readily concede that many stories about space travel are crude—but is there any field of literature in which most efforts are not crude? Take a look at any newsstand, any bookstall. Is the literary worth of the historical novel *Quo Vadis* gauged by the merits of dime novels and nickel shockers which purport to describe American history?

The examples I have given are a few of the writers of some claim to literary reputation who wrote about space travel prior to the time the first

* *The Saturday Review*, July 17, 1952: "Escape Into Space" (editorial) by "H.S.," presumably Harrison Smith.

V-2 from Peenemünde fell on London. I submit that a critic who refers to Poe, Wells, Edward Everett Hale, *et al.*, as writers of a "somewhat crude form of entertainment" is spiritually akin to the Hollywood producer who is alleged to have condemned *Hamlet* as "just a moldy old plot strung together with a bunch of familiar quotations." This critic really should familiarize himself with the literature he claims to be judging.

Let us see if he knows any more about science than he appears to know about literature. "—rocket ships which . . . burst into outermost space and explored the galaxies of the Milky Way—"

Any science fiction writer (and almost any twelve-year-old boy) knows that rocket ships are not appropriate for interstellar travel. Obviously this man knows nothing of rocket engineering . . . but his notions of astronomy are even more disheartening. "Galaxies of the Milky Way" indeed! This is about as mixed up concerning the elementary facts of descriptive astronomy as one can get. One could as reasonably call London a borough of New York. I won't take up your time setting him straight; instead I refer him to any boy scout.

We are not through with him. "—these apparently mad devices—" Dear literary critic, the telephone is a "mad device" to a Congo pygmy and flying machines were "apparently mad devices" to ignorant minds in the early part of this century.

"—remained unadulterated fantasy until scientists contemplated the experiments with rockets that have proceeded since the last war."

This is so filled with nonsense that I must take it to pieces almost word by word. In the first place, why does he pick this date (around 1944 or '45; he's vague though emphatic) as being the date on which space travel ceased to be "unadulterated fantasy"? Surely not because space travel has already been achieved, for it has not been [1959]. But, while space travel is as certain as anything in the future can be, it is not yet here.

In the second place, this critic seems totally unaware that many of the fiction writers about space travel and many of the rocket experimenters who are the true space travel pioneers are, in many important instances, the very same people.

In the third place, he seems just as totally innocent of the history of rocketry—he seems to think that it started at Peenemünde sometime during World War II. Rockets as military missiles (which is what they still are today) date with certainty back through the 18th century and their actual first use is lost in the mists of Chinese history. Mathematical investigation of the problems of space travel and rocketry, and experimentation with rocket prototypes consciously intended to be developed into spaceships, both began early in this century. The basic mathematical physics on which a reaction-propelled vehicle capable of moving itself through airless space depends has been available to any educated man since Sir Isaac Newton published his famous Third Law of Motion nearly three hundred years ago. Yet this person seems not even aware of the pioneer work of Professor Oberth and our own Dr. Goddard.

The progress toward space travel has been unbroken and the basic knowledge underlying it has been available to anyone for almost three centuries. The imminence of space travel has been staring in the face of anyone who can read for at least thirty years. I submit that a man who can label all that has gone before as "unadulterated fantasy" is logically as likely so to label any research and development project, in progress but not completed, at Bell Laboratories or Westinghouse. Progress is always accompanied by the wiseacres who stand sneering on the sidelines, always unbelieving before the fact and always without wonder after the fact.

If one were to inflate a toy balloon, release it and allow it to flutter to a stop . . . There it is, ladies and gentlemen—the self-contained, reaction-propelled vehicle, the prototype of the spaceship . . . known to mathematical physics since the time of Newton and now being realized on the drawing boards and in the proving grounds of our fabulously science-fictional nation. Yet to ignorant and unimaginative critics it is just a child's balloon. There are none so blind as they who will not see.

Yet this is precisely the sort of "literary criticism" to which science fiction is all too often subjected. I have quoted a gross but not outstanding example.

But what is the literary merit of speculative fiction? By what standards should it be judged?

By precisely the same standards which apply to any other field of fiction. I myself prefer fiction which is entertaining, although some critics do not seem to care about this point. Rules of unity, plot structure, characterization, consistency and all other rules which may fairly be applied to any piece of fiction also should be applied to science fiction; it is not exempt from any of them. It is also subject to another rule which I can best explain by analogy with respect to contemporary-scene fiction and historical fiction. If a man does a story about the meat-packing industry of

Chicago, as Upton Sinclair did in *The Jungle*, he owes it to the public first to study the meat-packing industry carefully. If a man writes a novel about Henry VIII he is obligated to know 16th-century England as well as he knows his own back yard—and by the same token a man writing about rocket ships is morally obligated to the public to be up on rocket engineering. Since a science fiction writer cannot possibly know all about anthropology, law, history, cybernetics, biochemistry, psychology, mathematics, nucleonics, ballistics and four dozen more major subjects, he is obligated to do just as a competent historical novelist does—make good use of public libraries and other reference sources and seek the advice and help of specialist experts in the fields he touches on. The science fiction writer is especially obligated to do this because many of the subjects he treats are even more esoteric to the average reader than are the facts of 16th-century England. Furthermore, his task is both more crucial and more difficult because he is extrapolating, speculating. The historical novelist has a solid and readily accessible framework of known fact to fall back on; the man who speculates about the future has only his knowledge and his reason to guide him.

In other words, all the usual criteria of literature apply to science fiction . . . only more severely.

But, by the same token, I think we who practice it are entitled to be judged only by critics well enough educated to be capable of judging. I do not think that a critic who takes his profession seriously would attempt to judge a novel about Henry VIII without knowing something or learning something of the historical background. At least he should not. But apparently almost any bloke who can read without moving his lips considers himself qualified to take a roundhouse swipe at a speculative novel.

How well does the field of speculative fiction measure up to these conventional literary standards?

Not very well, I am afraid, in most cases. However, there are extenuating circumstances and the accused now throws himself on the mercy of the court. A goodly number of us who write it have had no formal training in writing; we are self-taught and the fact often shows. Regrettably, not too many people have both extensive scientific training and intensive literary training—and good speculative fiction calls for both. However, many excellent writers in many fields have been self-taught; this alone is not sufficient excuse.

A second and more important extenuating circumstance is that speculative fiction is the most difficult of all prose forms. Not only does it require greater knowledge to do it well, greater imagination to make it rational and consistent—these are not easy; almost anyone can write at least one autobiographical novel fairly well; he knows his material, life itself has shaped its consistency and the editor will prune the surplusage —good speculation comes harder. But also, a speculative novel, to be entertaining, must accomplish something which is necessary to all fiction but which is technically very much more difficult in science fiction, i.e., a writer must create the scene and the culture and make it come alive. In historical and contemporary-scene fiction the writer is greatly assisted in this by the fact that the reader is already somewhat familiar with the scene, either through personal experience or through common reading. The speculative story, laid in the future, or on another planet, or possibly in another dimension, cannot use this convenient assumption. The science fiction writer must build up a scene strange to the reader, perhaps a wholly new culture, and he must make it convincing, else he will not simply lose empathy with his reader, he will never gain it in the first place—and there is nothing more dead than a story in which the writer fails to bring his reader into that feeling of belief.

A writer of Western stories may say, "The lone rider topped the rise— spingow!—a shot rang out." Trite perhaps, but the reader knows where he is; he's been there a hundred times before. An historical writer may say: "General Washington stepped outside his headquarters and gazed sadly at the ragged figure of a gaunt private soldier standing barefoot in the snow"—rather trite again, but we know where we are—Valley Forge.

But it is not enough to say, "With a blast the spaceship took off for Mars." Oh, it may do for comic books and for pulp magazines aimed at ten-year-olds, but not for serious literature; the writer must fill in this strange scene clearly enough to create empathy.

It's not easy. In the first place he must do it without slowing up the story; neither reader nor literary critic can be expected to hold still for long engineering discussions, or tedious sociological sermonizing. He must get his gadgets in, if he is using gadgets, without getting them in the way of his human characters and their human problems—yet get them in he must, else the story takes place in a literary vacuum and suffocates at once.

This is much harder than the other difficult problems of finding time to do adequate research and then blending that research into a consistent human story. But it must be solved; it is a *sine qua non* in any story involving a strange scene—the scene and all necessary postulates of the story must be made convincing without cluttering up the story. I will not attempt to explain how to do it; I have been studying the problem by trial and error for years and it still gives me headaches with each new story I write.

This difficulty alone is sufficient to account for the fact that there are very few really good science fiction short stories—solving this problem usually calls for more elbow room than a short story allows. Most short science fiction stories are aimed at the regular reader of the field who has learned to accept certain shorthand assumptions unfamiliar to the general reader (just as the regular reader of the "Western" accepts a complex of assumptions about the American Old West). The valid science fiction short story acceptable to the general reader is not an impossible art form, but it is so excruciatingly difficult that it is quite rare.

But the primary reason that there is so little good science fiction is that there is so little science fiction of any sort.

This may sound preposterous in view of the growing popularity of the field, the large number of trade books so labeled since the war, and the plethora of specialist magazines; nevertheless it is literally true. For every person now writing speculative fiction today there are a dozen writing historical fiction and at least fifty writing contemporary-scene fiction of one sort and another. The editors in any other field have an enormously greater mass of wordage to choose from. I believe that I know, personally or through his work, every regular writer of speculative fiction in the United States today. There are less than a hundred of us all told, both those of us who work at it full time and those of us who give it only part time. There are less than ten of us who make our livings through full-time, freelance writing of speculative fiction—ten is probably too high; I can think of only six by name—and I am sure that I know all the full-timers.

With such a corporal's guard to draw from, how can we be expected to turn out very many great works of literature? We can't and we don't.

As a result of the excess of demand over supply a great many poor speculative novels have reached hard covers these past few years. Anything readable and even moderately entertaining could be sure of publication—it has been a classic case of "We don't want it good; we want it Wednesday."

This great demand has frequently resulted in authors with well-established literary reputations in other fields attempting to turn an easy dollar by whipping off a "science fiction" story or two. In most cases they have fallen flat on their scholarly faces, for this is not an art to be practiced successfully without hard and prayerful preparation. No man in his right mind would attempt a novel concerning the era of the Emperor Justinian without tedious research; the corollary is still more emphatically true when the "mainstream" writer tackles speculative fiction. He simply can't do it, despite finished narrative technique, unless he already has, or painfully acquires, the necessary special knowledge.

Unfortunately, for these reasons, I do not think that we are likely to have a large volume of competent, literate speculative fiction in the foreseeable future. Those of you who are addicted to it in quantity must perforce resign yourselves to reading much that is second-rate. The situation can be expected to improve slowly as demand eventually results in a larger number of competent writers in this field—but only slowly.

There is not space to discuss in detail the competent, literate speculative fiction which has been written, but I will give a list of speculative novels which I consider to be competent, and of literary merit by any standards. It is not a definitive list and represents simply a sample of my own taste, but these are examples of what I mean by good works in this field: *General Manpower*, by John S. Martin; *Not This August* and *Take-off*, both by C. M. Kornbluth; *Man's Mortality*, by Michael Arlen; *Woman Alive*, by Susan Ertz; *It Can't Happen Here*, by Sinclair Lewis; *1984*, by George Orwell; *The War with the Newts*, by Karel Čapek; *Pebble in the Sky* and *The Caves of Steel*, both by Isaac Asimov; *Needle*, by Hal Clement; *Nerves*, by Lester del Rey; *Seven Famous Novels*, by H. G. Wells; *To Walk the Night*, by William Sloane; *Odd John*, by Olaf Stapledon; *The Doomsday Men*, by J. B. Priestley; *Brave New World*, by Aldous Huxley; *Lest Darkness Fall*, by L. Sprague de Camp; *I Am Thinking of My Darling*, by Vincent McHugh; *The World Below*, by S. Fowler Wright, and *Prelude to Space*, by Arthur C. Clarke.

For comparison, let me list a few fantasies, good by any criteria: *The Sword in the Stone*, by T. H. White; *Alice in Wonderland*, by Lewis Carroll (Charles L. Dodgson); *The Wind in the Willows*, by Kenneth Grahame; *The Wizard of Oz*, by L. Frank Baum; *Out of the Silent Planet*, by C. S. Lewis, and the collections *Thirteen O'Clock*, by Stephen Vincent Benét, and *Fancies and Goodnights*, by John Collier.

Again for comparison, two good contemporary-scene novels, in my opinion, are Herman Wouk's *The Caine Mutiny* and Pat Frank's *Hold Back the Night,* and examples of good historical novels by contemporary authors are Paul Wellman's *The Female* and McKinlay Kantor's *Long Remember.* I think that science fiction, to be worthy of critical literary praise, should approximate the standards of these four novels and of the fantasies mentioned just above.

I had hoped to discuss the history of science fiction. However, there is in print one comprehensive history covering the field from the distant past to about 1935: J. O. Bailey's *Pilgrims Through Space and Time.* This is Dr. Bailey's dissertation for his Ph.D. and it is amazing to me that any university accepted the subject in view of the low esteem in which speculative fiction is held in most departments of English.

Of what use is science fiction? I have already said that it is not prophecy, that most of it is not very good from a literary standpoint . . . and now let me add that much of it is not even very entertaining in my opinion. Good heavens! Does it have any virtue?

Yes. It is the most alive, the most important, the most useful, and the most comprehensive fiction being published today. It is the only fictional medium capable of interpreting the changing, headlong rush of modern life. Speculative fiction is the mainstream of fiction—not, as most critics assume, the historical novel and the contemporary-scene novel.

On behalf of all my science fiction colleagues I have no intention of being modest about this. The speculative novel is both more important and more difficult than the so-called mainstream novel. Speculative fiction has been expected to stand, hat in hand, a barely recognized illegitimate cousin of the "respectable" forms of literature. I claim for speculative fiction the prior place, the head of the table, even if I have to step on some tender feelings to seat it there.

The historical novel will always have an important place in literature and I have no criticism to make of historical fiction now being written save to note that plunging necklines and bedroom scenes are not in themselves a substitute for honest research. On the other hand the conscientious and competent historical novelist (of whom there are many) is assisted in creating a true picture of times past by the recent increase in freedom to describe in frank terms customs differing from ours.

But historical fiction can never be as useful to the human race as speculative fiction can be (and sometimes is) for the very reason that historical fiction concerns the past. The past can be instructive and very interesting—but the future is far more important . . . to us, to our children, to our children's children. We cannot drive safely by looking only in the rear-view mirror; it is more urgent to watch the road ahead. Too much emphasis on historical fiction partakes of the attitude of the fabulous bird who flew backwards because he didn't care where he was going but liked to see where he had been. Nevertheless, historical fiction has its proper and useful place.

But as for contemporary-scene literature, it is sick with a deep sickness —in its present state it cannot possibly interpret this fast-changing world. Time was when the novel of contemporary life could satisfy most reasonable needs of the spirit, back in a quieter, less rapidly changing day, back when the advancing front of human knowledge was not turning the whole world topsy-turvy every few years. But those quiet days are gone, not to return in your lifetime nor mine, nor in the predictable future. Most novels of contemporary life today tragically fail to live up to the needs of our times.

I am not speaking now of the detective story, the adventure story, or any other genre intended solely as entertainment. Nor am I condemning every novel offered as a serious interpretation of the contemporary scene —there are a number of fine ones. But I am condemning the overwhelming majority.

A very large part of what is accepted as "serious" literature today represents nothing more than a cultural lag on the part of many authors, editors and critics—a retreat to the womb in the face of a world too complicated and too frightening for their immature spirits. A sick literature. What do we find so often today? Autobiographical novels centered around neurotics, even around sex maniacs, concerning the degraded, the psychotic, or the "po' white trash" of back-country farms portrayed as morons or worse, novels about the advertising industry or some other equally narrow area of human experience such as the personal life of a television idol or the experiences of a Park Avenue call girl.

Ah, but this is "realism"! Some of it is, some of it decidedly is not. In any case, is it not odd that the ashcan school of realism, as exemplified by Henry Miller, Jean-Paul Sartre, James Joyce, Françoise Sagan and Alberto Moravia, should be held up to us as "high art" at the very time when all other forms of art are striving to achieve more significant and more interesting forms of expression? Can James Joyce and Henry Miller and their literary sons and grandsons interpret the seething new world of atomic power and antibiotics and interplanetary travel? I say not.[9] In my opinion a very large portion of what is now being offered the public as serious, contemporary-scene fiction is stuff that should not be printed, but told only privately—on a psychiatrist's couch. The world, the human race, is now faced with very real and pressing problems. They will not be solved by introverted neurotics intent on telling, in a tedious hundred thousand words, that they hate their fathers and love their mothers.

In any case, I, for one, am heartily sick of stories about frustrates, jerks, homosexuals and commuters who are unhappy with their wives— for goodness' sake! Let them find other wives, other jobs—and shut up!

True, some of this sick literature does shine some light into dark corners of the human soul. Even a sordid, narrow novel such as James Jones' *From Here to Eternity* can sometimes manage that. But is this enough? Does it meet the challenge of our century? At best such a novel shows only one frame of a complex and rapidly moving picture.

"I am a stranger and afraid in a world I never made."

Not true! "I am not a stranger and I am not afraid in a world I am helping to make . . . and I am 'damned from here to eternity' only if I abandon my human intelligence and, sheeplike, give up the struggle!"— that is the answer of science fiction, that is why it is alive when most of our current literature is sick and dying. Change . . . change . . . endless change—that is the keynote of our times, whether we face it or run away from it. The mature speculative novel is the only form of fiction which stands even a chance of interpreting the spirit of our times. Most literature has cut itself out of the competition by refusing to deal with the all-too-evident facts—most writers in other fields could not deal properly with the world today even if they tried; their education is too limited, their private world too narrow. They wear blinders.

Speculative fiction is the only form of fiction which does not exclude any area of human experience . . . and in particular it does not exclude that most truly human of all human activities, the one that sets us above animals: the exercise of the scientific method and the sober consideration of the consequences thereof. This is an era when the scientific method, its meaning and use, is indispensable to the mature man—we either use it, or we and our free democratic culture will go under. And yet most modern novelists find no need for it, are even afraid of it. True, they reflect a sickness in the culture, not alone a sickness in themselves. I refer to the increasingly strong trend toward anti-intellectualism, anti-science, demands for a "moratorium" in science, screwball cults and philosophies such as Zen Buddhism (Gautama Buddha must be spinning in his grave!), existentialism, astrology—I once counted more than a dozen different astrology magazines on a newsstand which had not one magazine on astronomy and only one on science in general.

But it is so much easier to consult the stars! So it is. It makes life simple to blame failures on a horoscope. It is much harder to study ballistics, study engineering, try to reach those stars—but it is a much more mature activity. It is always hard to face up to a complex world, try to figure out what makes it tick, try to cope with it, survive and triumph over it.

But this is precisely what science fiction strives toward . . . and what most so-called mainstream literature does not even attempt. It used to be that mature men discussed the world and its meaning through the speculative essay. The speculative essay is almost extinct today; it is rarely written, still more rarely published. Its place has been taken by speculative fiction, a tool which, properly handled, is more subtle and more versatile than is the speculative essay. By means of science fiction one can (as one does in mathematics) examine the extremes of a social problem, search it for inflexures, feel out its changing slopes. Nearly all stories in the "mainstream," by their very frameworks, are forever self-excluded from this important form of analysis. Through science fiction the human race can try experiments in imagination too critically dangerous to try in fact. Through such speculative experiments science fiction can warn against dangerous solutions, urge toward better solutions. Science fiction joyously tackles the real and pressing problems of our race, wrestles with them, never ignores them—problems which other forms of fiction cannot challenge. For this reason I assert that science fiction is the most realistic, the most serious, the most significant, the most sane and healthy and human fiction being published today.

I must add that some interlopers have sneaked in under the back of the tent and are masquerading as science fiction. I refer to the "anti-science fiction" which sometimes appears labeled as science fiction, both in books and magazines. This stuff is still another symptom of the neurotic, sometimes pathologic, anti-intellectualism all too common today; it is the wail of the grown-up infant unwilling and perhaps unable to bring reason and reasoned action to bear on our pressing problems. Instead it offers a "devil theory" in which "science" is something outside of and inimical to the human race and "scientists" the inhuman high priests thereof. It reminds me of a plaint attributed (perhaps unjustly) to one United States senator: "Why in the world were those scientists ever trusted with the secret of the A-bomb in the first place?"

I cannot sympathize with this hatred of science. Scientists are human beings, not devils and they are engaged in that most typically human of all human activities, the attempt to understand the laws of nature. I myself am satisfied with the laws of nature as they are and I think it is virtuous to try to understand them. I do not believe that the Lord God Almighty made a stupid error when He created uranium.

But you will recognize anti-science fiction when you see it. Its childish, screaming, afraid-of-the-dark hysteria is easy to spot.

I claim one positive triumph for science fiction, totally beyond the scope of so-called mainstream fiction. It has prepared the youth of our time for the coming age of space. Interplanetary travel is no shock to youngsters, no matter how unsettling it may be to calcified adults. Our children have been playing at being space cadets and at controlling rocket ships for quite some time now. Where did they get this healthy orientation? From science fiction and nowhere else. Science fiction can perform similar service to the race in many other fields. For the survival and health of the human race one crudely written science fiction story containing a single worthwhile new idea is more valuable than a bookcaseful of beautifully written non-science fiction.

In a broader sense, all science fiction prepares young people to live and survive in a world of ever-continuing change by teaching them early that the world does change. Since that is the only sort of world we have, science fiction leads in the direction of mental health, of adaptability. In a more specific sense, science fiction preaches the need for freedom of the mind and the desirability of knowledge; it teaches that prizes go to those who study, who learn, who soak up the difficult fields of knowledge such as mathematics and engineering and biology. And so they do! The prizes of this universe go only to those able and equipped to reach out for them. In short, science fiction is preparing our youngsters to be mature citizens of the galaxy . . . as indeed they will have to be.

Where does science fiction go from here?—remembering that much of it is crude and not too competent. We can expect it slowly to increase in amount and quality. We should not expect it ever to become mass entertainment, as it is directed primarily at the superior young person and secondarily at his thoughtful elder. But serious and mature literature has never been mass entertainment; most fiction in all fields in all ages has been trivial and even trashy. Most people read classics of literature only under classroom compulsion and never touch them again. I see no reason to think that this will change in the foreseeable future and certainly no reason why the growth of a mature science fiction should be expected to change it.

I do expect to see some decrease in the neurotic and psychotic fiction now being palmed off on us as "serious literature"; I expect, perhaps too optimistically, that both editors and critics will someday begin to catch up with the real world and quit nursing such nonsense.

In the meantime, to that extent to which science fiction influences its readers toward greater knowledge, more independence of thought, and wider intellectual horizons, it serves its prime function.

While I alone am accountable for the opinions and assertions contained in this discussion I would be remiss were I not to say that my thoughts have been strongly influenced by others. Among these others are Willy Ley, Reginald Bretnor, Dr. E. E. Smith, Dr. E. T. Bell, Arthur C. Clarke, John W. Campbell, Jr., William A. P. White, G. Harry Stine, Damon Knight, L. Sprague de Camp and Dr. Isaac Asimov. In particular, anyone who has had the pleasure of reading Mr. Bretnor's critical writings will see at once the extent of my indebtedness to him. The above is an incomplete list of the living; I could not list the dead, but among them are T. H. Huxley (*Essays*), Socrates (*Apologia*), and A. Korzybski (*Science and Sanity*).

# SOCIAL SCIENCE FICTION

## Isaac Asimov

Science fiction is an undefined term in the sense that there is no generally agreed-upon definition of it. To be sure, there are probably hundreds of individual definitions but that is as bad as none at all. Worse, perhaps, since one's own definition gets in the way of an understanding of the next man's viewpoint.

I should stress that my own definition is not necessarily better than the next man's or more valid or more inclusive or more precise. It simply expresses my way of thinking and will serve to lend a framework to this essay.

About a year ago, I wrote an article for *The Writer* which I called "Other Worlds to Conquer." In it, I defined science fiction as follows: *Science fiction is that branch of literature which is concerned with the impact of scientific advance upon human beings.*

I intend to stick to that definition here, with a single slight modification which I will come to in a moment. I find intellectual satisfaction in the definition because it places the emphasis not upon science but upon human beings. After all, science (and everything else as well) is important to us only as it affects human beings.

The modification I wish to make in the definition is made necessary by the fact that it narrows the boundaries of science fiction to a greater

FROM *Modern Science Fiction, Its Meaning and Its Future*, ed. Reginald Bretnor. Coward-McCann, 1953 extent than most people are willing to see it narrowed. For that reason, I would like to say that my definition applies not to "science fiction" but to a subdivision of the field which I find it convenient to speak of as "social science fiction."

It is my opinion that social science fiction is the only branch of science fiction that is sociologically significant, and that those stories which are generally accepted as science fiction (at least to the point where skilled editors accept them for inclusion in their science-fiction magazines) but do not fall within the definition I have given above, are *not* significant, however amusing they may be and however excellent as pieces of fiction.

This is a broad statement and may even sound a bit snobbish. But then the general purpose of this essay is to give my opinions on the influence of society upon science fiction and science fiction upon society, so I am prepared to explain my stand at considerable length.

I

It is rather fashionable among some connoisseurs of science fiction to stress its age. This is partly the result of a thoroughly natural desire to lend an air of respectability to a class of literature that is often the target of laughter and sneers from those who picture it in terms of comic strips and horror movies.

August Derleth, for instance, one of the most able and indefatigable anthologists in the entire field of fantasy, has collected a volume called *Beyond Time and Space* (Pellegrini and Cudahy, 1950), which he has subtitled *A Compendium of Science-Fiction Through the Ages*. In it, he traces back his own conception of science fiction some 2400 years to Plato. The Platonic selection is, of course, the Atlantis story from the dialogue, "Critias." Selections are also included from More's *Utopia*, Rabelais' *Gargantua*, and Swift's *Gulliver's Travels*.

The anthology is one of the best and most fascinating in the field. Nevertheless, I think that Derleth is overzealous. The attraction of great names notwithstanding, science fiction, even at its broadest, cannot logically be traced farther back in time than the period in which the western world became aware of the significance of the Industrial Revolution.

What about Plato's Atlantis, then? What about More's Utopia and Swift's Lilliput, Brobdingnag and Laputa? They represent superlative feats of imagination, but they do not have the *intent* of science fiction.

They are social satires. The societies they describe are not intended to have meaning in themselves but are a reflection, usually a derogatory one, of the societies in which the authors lived.

Let's give this type of literature a name for convenience's sake. Let's call it *social fiction*, and define it in this way: *Social fiction is that branch of literature which moralizes about a current society through the device of dealing with a fictitious society.*

This is really an inevitable category of fiction if we consider that at most periods of human history, it was more than a little dangerous to analyze the then-prevalent society with too probing a finger and too curious an eye. It was far safer to show the reader his own image in a distorting mirror, hoping that sooner or later he would turn from the grotesque reflection to himself with the sobering thought that it *was* a reflection and, after all, not such an inaccurate one.

There is nothing in the definition of social fiction which limits the nature of the fictitious society. It can be a very realistic one, or it can be a fantastic one involving men on the moon, six-inch-high pygmies or intelligent horses. The presence of these *outré* overtones does not of itself convert social fiction into science fiction. It is, I repeat, a question of intent.

Social fiction, whatever the nature of its fictitious society, has its eye fixed on the current society. It pictures life not as it will be or as it might be or as it could be, but as it *should* be or as it *should not* be.

Science fiction, on the other hand, is really concerned with the fictitious society it pictures. It becomes not merely a lesson to us, a text from which to draw a moral, but something that bears the possibility of importance in its own right. When does science fiction become conceivable then? When the minds of mankind are so oriented by circumstance that it becomes reasonable to them that any society other than the one in which they live can be conceived of, if not in the present, then at least in the future.

This may sound startling. Surely it is obvious that more than one kind of society is possible. You have only to look about you to see India, China, the South Seas; only to look back in time to see pagan Rome and Pharaonic Egypt.

But that is only because we live in an era of widespread education, rapid transportation and universal communication. Go back two hundred years and Earth expands into a tremendous, shadowy unknown while the horizon of the average individual shrinks to the village in which he is born, lives and dies.

Until the middle of the eighteenth century, the dominant factor in human history was stasis. Empires rose and empires fell. Conquerors flashed across the world stage. Barbarians thundered in from the steppes. To the peasant on his farm, generally speaking, it all meant nothing. The generations went on.

The "changes" that seem so impressive in the history books, the rise of this city or that, the fall of this empire or that, are really not changes to the average man. A given individual might have the current of his life turned awry if a war band clattered through his patch of farming ground, or if pestilence struck, or famine ground him. If he survived, however, he was back in the old place, and if in a large city a hundred miles away, a new king reigned, he heard it only by rumor and it meant nothing.

To a man who lived his life as his father had done and all his father's fathers as far back as his knowledge went, it would inevitably seem that there was a "natural order" of things. This natural order was prescribed either by the innate qualities of the human being and his world (if we listen to the Greek thinkers) or it was imposed by the greater wisdom of some supernatural being (if we listen to the Judean thinkers). In either case, it could neither be fought nor changed.

In such a world, science might exist, but its potentialities for social change would be understood only by a few, and that with difficulty. To the ancient Greeks, for instance, science was not the study of the blind laws that governed the motions of matter and its components. Instead, it was simply an aspect of beauty. Its final aim was purely and statically intellectual. By greater understanding, the educated Greek hoped to appreciate the design of the universe, almost as though it were a geometric figure conceived by a divine mathematician, rather than a handy device which impious man could seize and use to increase his own comfort.

Greek science was abstract geometry; Pythagorean studies of the mystical values of number; Platonic and Aristotelian speculations on the existence of "ideals," on the true nature of "virtue." Beautiful it was, but sterile, also.

To have viewed science as a means by which mankind could control his environment and deliberately change social structure would have made a marked man of one, a crackpot, a possible blasphemer. Plato, on being asked by an aspiring student as to the usefulness of geometry, gave him a coin that he might not feel he had gained nothing from the study, and ordered him to begone. A man who wanted practical applications was no true scientist.

It was the lack of social insight and not the lack of scientific ability that prevented Greece from initiating the Industrial Revolution two thousand years early. L. Sprague de Camp, in a brilliant commentary on the science of the Hellenistic age ("The Sea-King's Armored Division," *Astounding Science Fiction*, September–October, 1941), describes how close to it they were.

This is not to say that there was *no* change in human society until the mid-eighteenth century. Obviously mankind advanced continuously from the stone axe to gunpowder and from a hollowed-out tree trunk to the full-rigged ship. But the advance was slow in comparison to the passing of the generations.

Probably the first single event in history which affected the general population in a fundamental manner with sufficient quickness and intensity to be unmistakable to all was the French Revolution of 1789–1799. This phenomenon differed from previous rapid changes, such as Alexander's blitzkrieg against the Persian Empire, in that the alterations that resulted applied not to a thin Macedonian aristocracy, but to the entire French population from King Louis to Jacques Bonhomme.

It seemed like the end of the world to most of Europe. By the time the Revolution and its Napoleonic sequel had come to an end, the social structure of Europe had been changed radically in the space of *less than one generation*. The statesmen at the Congress of Vienna did their best to wipe out those changes, to restore the "natural order" of things, to replace the omelet within the eggshell. They failed, of course.

It is obvious then, that if science fiction is to deal with fictitious societies as possessing potential reality rather than as being nothing more than let's-pretend object lessons, it must be post-Napoleonic. Before 1789 human society didn't change as far as the average man was concerned and it was silly, even wicked, to suppose it could. After 1815, it was obvious to any educated man that human society not only could change but that it did.

Before passing on to the post-Napoleonic world, however, it might be well to forestall certain doubts that may exist in the reader's mind as to the true priority of the French Revolution as a recognizable rapid-fire social disintegrator. There have, for instance, been numerous religious revolutions in world history. Usually they are slow, but the Lutheran Reformation, two centuries before the French Revolution, was certainly rapid enough. In one generation, the religious map of Europe changed and was never the same again. Despite a series of wars, as vicious as any in history, the Reformation was another omelet that would not re-enter the egg.

Nevertheless, religious revolutions, important though they are, cannot be creators of nonstatic societies. Each new religion, however scornful of the claims to absolute knowledge and absolute authority on the part of the older faith, is firm in the belief that now, at least, the truth *has* been found, and that there is no ground for any further innovations.

Politico-economic revolutions are only slightly less emotion-ridden than are religious revolutions and there is little to choose in bitterness between them, but there is this important difference. A religious stasis is accepted by its devotees as having been ordained by a god or gods, and therefore not to be questioned by man. Not one jot or tittle of the law may be changed till all is fulfilled. Political stases, however, are ordained by men; none of their devotees can deny that. And it is easier to gainsay men, however great, than gods, however small.

Nevertheless, this difference does not seem sufficient to support my argument. Is there another difference between the time of Luther and Calvin and the times of Robespierre and Napoleon? The answer is, yes, the centuries involved—the sixteenth in one case and the eighteenth in the other.

Actually, the French Revolution itself was not primary. Underlying it lay centuries of slow changes in the fabric of society—changes of which most men were unaware. But from the nadir of western society—the tenth century—and through the Renaissance the *rate* of change had been steadily and continuously increasing. In the eighteenth century, the rate bounced forward tremendously. With the French Revolution, it became completely obvious.

To start the era of change with the French Revolution is therefore merely a handy way of pegging a date. The fundamental consideration is that about 1800, the tide of hastening change due to the scientific and industrial development of western society had become a colossal current that swept all other competing factors into discard.

In the eighteenth century, the Industrial Revolution began in England. It not only began, it was drastically stimulated by events on the Continent. The necessity of fighting France, then twice as populous, heavily militarized, and, eventually, the controller of all Europe from Madrid to Moscow, forced England's economy into hothouse growth. In 1815 after twenty years of continuous warfare, she was stronger and richer in relation to the rest of the world than ever before or since.

II

Even today it is not entirely plain to many people that scientific-economic change is the master and political change the servant. From 1789 to 1900, we changed from Louis XVI to the Third French Republic; from George III to Victoria; from George Washington to William Mc-Kinley; but we also changed from the stagecoach to the railroad; from the sailboat to the steamboat; from Buffon to Darwin and from Lavoisier's discovery of the nature of oxidation to Becquerel's discovery of the fact of radioactivity.

You may wonder how one can balance the Emancipation Proclamation against the electric light and the Bill of Rights against the X-ray tube, but we are not making moral judgments or comparisons here. We are trying to look the facts of social change in the face. Consider the political changes in our own generation. The rise and fall of Nazi Germany, with its World War II enclosure, took place in a round dozen years. Forty years ago the word "Fascism" did not exist. In less than forty years, Communism grew from a splinter group in the Socialist left to the predominant code of thinking of one third of the world. And today we live surrounded by a cold war of a type few could have anticipated ten years ago.

Tremendous! It seems more cosmic, more world-shaking than the scientific and technological changes in the same period of time: things like the rise and decline of radio, the growth of the automobile, the coming of television and sound movies, jet planes and radar. The only scientific innovation that perhaps really impresses us is the atomic bomb.

Yet consider! Imagine a world in which Communism suddenly ceased to be. It would be a different world, wouldn't it? Your life would be changed, perhaps drastically (if you were an aeronautical engineer, for instance). Now imagine a world in which the automobile ceased to be. I feel certain that your life would experience a greater *immediate* change in that case. In other words, while changes in political affairs often hit us at an abstract and rarefied level, technological changes always hit home, right in the breadbasket.

Then, too, technological changes lie at the root of political change. It was the developing Industrial Revolution that placed western Europe so far ahead of the rest of the world, that it could control all of it from China to Patagonia, either by outright political rule or by indirect economic mastery. Even the railroads of the United States were built as the result of the investments of European capitalists. And it is the Industrial Revolution spreading outward to America first, then to Russia, and now to China and India, that has shaken and is destroying European hegemony. Forty years ago, Russia couldn't build its own railroads without help. Today it is building jet planes we suspect of being better than ours. The world wags away, and these days the wagging is so rapid as to be a blur.

How did this new factor of social change enter western literature? In three ways, which we may list.

1) Through adoption in the field of social fiction. After all, the social satirists were describing fictitious societies. Why not one in which the obviously advancing technology advanced still further? Bellamy wrote *Looking Backward* and Wells wrote *The Shape of Things to Come*. But these were still social fiction.[10] The writer's eye was still on the present. He was using science to help him point his moral, to shape his warning, or to help point the way. We might, if we wished to be whimsical about it, call this sort of thing enriched social fiction, since a moribund literary form was revitalized through the addition of a sprinkling of science, much as white flour is "enriched" with various vitamins. This type of literature is still with us today and the authors who engage in it are far from being unrespected. I point to Huxley's *Brave New World* and the quite recent *1984* of Orwell. But it is a blind alley. We cannot forever face the future only as the present's object lesson; we must look at it as the future, something as valid as the present. We may not like it, but there it is.

2) Through adoption in the field of Gothic horror fiction. The terrifying tale of the supernatural (or, usually, subnatural) is as old as literature, and to adopt the mysteries of science as an aid to horror was an inevitable development. *Frankenstein* is one of the first and certainly one of the most successful of its kind. That genre has lived through the decades also. Its recent representatives include the works of Merritt and Lovecraft.

3) Finally, around scientific advance there developed—there *had* to develop—a new and specialized literature, peculiar to itself. Let us now, therefore, make a new and very broad definition of science fiction. *Science fiction is that branch of literature which deals with a fictitious society, differing from our own chiefly in the nature or extent of its technological development.*

This is a very broad definition. Since nothing is said about whether or not this fictitious society is intended to be a possibly real one or is merely composed as a lesson to present humanity, it even includes "social fiction plus science." (My personal impulse is to add a clause to the definition to the effect that the fictitious society is not advanced for the purpose of conscious moralization—but such a limitation would conflict with the ideas of those science-fiction enthusiasts who consider the works of Stanton A. Coblentz, for instance, as science fiction.)

We have now reached the point of the foundation of science fiction. Before we pass on to a new section in which we consider the development and differentiation of science fiction, I would like to rephrase briefly the reason for its beginnings. I can do it in one sentence.

Technological advance, rapid with respect to the passing of the generations, is a new factor in human history, a factor that marks off the last few generations of mankind from all the generations that preceded, and science fiction is the literary response to that new factor.

### III

The history of science fiction can be divided into four eras: 1) 1815–1926; 2) 1926–1938; 3) 1938–1945; and 4) 1945–present.

The first era, a long, amorphous one, may be termed "primitive." It was a primitive era because although the concept of science fiction had been born, the economic basis for the support of science-fiction writers did not yet exist. It may seem a detestably commercial attitude to take toward art, but before any extensive literature can exist, some method must be found for feeding, clothing, and sheltering the practitioners while they create the literature.

Until 1926, science fiction possessed no regular outlet. Individual science-fiction stories had to find a literary home in periodicals devoted to general literature. Such periodicals could absorb only a limited quantity of experimental material. Individuals of towering stature, a Jules Verne or

an H. G. Wells, might publish these fantastic stories about trips to the
moon but no young writer, still clumsy with his words, could think of
specializing in science fiction unless he were quite content to make his
living some other way while doing so. No large class of science-fiction
specialists, such as exists today, could possibly have existed before 1926.
The economic basis for it was lacking.

In 1926, Hugo Gernsback founded *Amazing Stories*. He had edited
magazines previously which published science fiction among other things,
but *Amazing Stories* was devoted exclusively to science fiction. What this
meant, put in its baldest terms, was this: allowing six stories per issue,
seventy-two science-fiction stories could be published each year. A corollary was that with the success of *Amazing Stories*, other publishers would
take the risk. Within five years two more magazines, *Science Wonder
Stories* and *Astounding Stories*, were out.

It is quite reasonable, therefore, to call the second era of science
fiction from 1926 to 1938, the "Gernsback Era."

It is interesting that in the very early days of *Amazing Stories*, the
poverty of the field was such that Gernsback devoted himself to reprint-
ing H. G. Wells. It was only gradually that young authors developed to
whom science fiction was the primary and, sometimes, exclusive means of
literary expression; authors such as Edmond Hamilton and Jack Williamson, to name two who, a quarter of a century later, are still publishing.

But now we have a fundamental change. Social fiction (which may be
considered a sort of ancestor of science fiction, as alchemy is to chemistry) was essentially an extremely mature fiction. Only men of mature
thought would be expected to appreciate either the satire or the moralization. (What does a youngster make of *Gulliver's Travels*? He considers it
an English *Sindbad*.)

Science fiction, on the other hand, entered a domain that belonged
almost exclusively to the young at that time, even to the adolescent. This
*had* to be. A new literature, devoted to the principle that change was
continuous, inevitable and even desirable, had to find its devotees among
those to whom change was not something frightening; to the young, in
other words.

To the youngster, born in the midst of this change, more change was
only natural. They could hardly wait for it. The airplane had been invented; it was already old stuff; the next step is the rocket-ship; what are
we waiting for? Well, we have radio; where's television; what's the delay?

This meant that science fiction had to lose most of its adult qualities, which were already well developed in the work of such a primitive master as Wells. (The word "primitive" is by no means to be taken as a derogatory term. I am merely placing Wells in time, setting him down as belonging to the "primitive era" because he wrote his science fiction before 1926.)

As most of the readers and many of the writers were in their teens, it was not reasonable to expect many stories containing social and economic complexities to be written, and even less reasonable to expect the few that were to be appreciated. In the place of such things there came again the epic individual who is the hallmark of primitive literature; the hero of infinite resource and daring, lacking completely the imaginative intellect that can conjure up horror and produce terror. The d'Artagnan sword and the Hickok six-shooter were thrown away and discarded and, in their place, there came the Hawk Carse-Richard Seaton hero with his raygun and spaceship.

The "adventure science fiction" dominated science fiction during the Gernsback Era. Please do not think that by this I imply that there are sharp boundaries in anything I discuss. Adventure science fiction existed before 1926 and it continued to exist after 1938. The point is that never has it dominated the field as it did between those two dates.

Among the connoisseurs of today, adventure science fiction is spoken of, with a certain flavor of disapproval, as "space opera"—the term being analogous to the contemptuous "horse opera" applied to the run-of-the-mill "western." There is perhaps a little unjust snobbery in this.

In the first place, space opera within the limitations of its own field can reach a high pitch of excellence. Edward E. Smith and John W. Campbell brought this type of story to its heights. With the entire cosmos as their field they streaked their heroes from star to star and from galaxy to galaxy. No homesickness intruded, no fear, no human weaknesses, no petty quarrels, no passion—only gigantic wars and conquests, tremendous victories and gargantuan dangers boldly disposed of.

Make no mistake. They were exciting reading.

Even today, many magazines specialize in adventure science fiction, and this is not an evil thing, or even particularly undesirable. The youngsters of today can't plunge head first into a complex adult story. They must begin with adventure, i.e., space opera. But space opera, unlike horse opera, is not a dead end. The youngster may grow out of the science-fiction habit altogether as he almost invariably grows away from Hopalong Cassidy, but he may also graduate into the more complex varieties of science fiction.

Another kind of science fiction that was important during the Gernsback Era was the reverse of adventure science fiction. If the youngsters wanted their blood and thunder they also wanted their science, and so story after story came out in which that stock character, the irascible, eccentric (or even mad) scientist explained his inventions and discoveries in interminable double-talk.

We might call this "gadget science fiction," and dismiss further consideration of it here, since it becomes more important in the next era of science fiction.


IV


In 1938, John W. Campbell became editor of *Astounding Stories*. If Gernsback is the father of science fiction, Campbell is the father of "social science fiction"; that is, the branch of science fiction which really lives up to my original definition: (*Social*) *science fiction is that branch of literature which is concerned with the impact of scientific advance upon human beings.*

It would be wise to pause at this point. I have mentioned three varieties of science fiction now: adventure science fiction, gadget science fiction, and social science fiction. Definitions are all right but it won't hurt, and it would probably help considerably, if I come up with a few examples.

Let us suppose it is 1880 and we have a series of three writers who are each interested in writing a story of the future about an imaginary vehicle that can move without horses by some internal source of power; a horseless carriage, in other words. We might even make up a word and call it an automobile.

Writer X spends most of his time describing how the machine would run, explaining the workings of an internal-combustion engine, painting a word-picture of the struggles of the inventor, who after numerous failures, comes up with a successful model. The climax of the yarn is the drama of the machine, chugging its way along at the gigantic speed of twenty miles an hour between a double crowd of cheering admirers, possibly beating a horse and carriage which have been challenged to a race. This is gadget science fiction.

Writer Y invents the automobile in a hurry, but now there is a gang of ruthless crooks intent on stealing this valuable invention. First they steal the inventor's beautiful daughter, whom they threaten with every dire eventuality but rape (in these adventure stories, girls exist to be rescued and have no other uses). The inventor's young assistant goes to the rescue. He can accomplish his purpose only by the use of the newly perfected automobile. He dashes into the desert at an unheard of speed of twenty miles an hour to pick up the girl who otherwise would have died of thirst if he had relied on a horse, however rapid and sustained the horse's gallop. This is adventure science fiction.

Writer Z has the automobile already perfected. A society exists in which it is already a problem. Because of the automobile, a gigantic oil industry has grown up, highways have been paved across the nation, America has become a land of travelers, cities have spread out into suburbs and—what do we do about automobile accidents? Men, women, and children are being killed by automobiles faster than by artillery shells or airplane bombs. What can be done? What is the solution? This is social science fiction.

I leave it to the reader to decide which is the most mature and which (this is 1880, remember) is the most socially significant. Keep in mind the fact that social science fiction is not easy to write. It is easy to predict an automobile in 1880; it is very hard to predict a traffic problem. The former is really only an extrapolation of the railroad. The latter is something completely novel and unexpected.

In any case, it was this social science fiction that Campbell encouraged. A new group of writers grew up about him: Robert A. Heinlein, L. Sprague de Camp, A. E. van Vogt, Theodore Sturgeon and many others. Older writers such as Jack Williamson and Henry Kuttner changed their styles to suit the times. (I might mention as an aside that I sold my first story to Campbell only a few months after he became editor.)

What, specifically, did Campbell do? First and foremost, he deemphasized the nonhuman and nonsocial in science fiction. Science fiction became more than a personal battle between an all-good hero and an all-bad villain. The mad scientist, the irascible old scientist, the beautiful daughter of the scientist, the cardboard menace from alien worlds, the robot who is a Frankenstein monster—all were discarded. In their place,

Campbell wanted businessmen, space-ship crewmen, young engineers, housewives, robots that were logical machines.

He got them.

Again the dividing line is not sharp. Science fiction with real characters existed before Campbell, notably in the stories written by Stanley G. Weinbaum in his short, meteoric career. His first story, *A Martian Odyssey*, is, in my opinion, the first example of modern social science fiction. It dealt with an alien race not inferior to Earthmen; not superior; merely different. He got across that sense of difference. His environment was not merely grotesque or merely horrible. It was different, naturally different. The scene was Mars and it felt like Mars, not like a horror movie. Most of all, his people talked like people and acted and felt like people. *A Martian Odyssey* appeared in 1934 in *Wonder Stories*. The editor—give him credit—was Charles D. Hornig.

The importance of Campbell is that he was not content to let Weinbaums spring up accidentally. He looked for them. He encouraged them. It is that which makes the years 1938–1945 the "Campbell Era."

Campbell also brought to the field an increasing rigor as far as scientific background was concerned. In the cut, thrust, and slash style of adventure science fiction, science which was inaccurate or even ridiculous in terms of what was actually known at the time frequently found a place. The better writers of the type, the aforementioned E. E. Smith and Campbell himself, were too well-trained in science (Smith has a doctorate in chemistry and Campbell is a physics-major graduate of M.I.T.)[11] to offend badly in this way, but hordes of lesser lights dealt with such things as a hollow Earth, inhabited within; atoms that were really miniature solar systems and inhabited; Mars that was pictured as having Earth gravity, atmosphere and temperature, with Earthlike inhabitants.

Although the stories written about such central ideas are often vastly entertaining, they remain completely fallacious. The Earth is *not* hollow. The atom is *not* a miniature solar system. Mars is very different from Earth and could not support Earth life.

The reader may seriously question my concern over such discrepancies. Does not all science fiction involve the fantastic? Yes, but there is a great difference between taking liberties with the unlikely and taking liberties with the impossible. The liberties allowed legitimate science fiction are so great that there is no need to drag in outright impossibilities, and there is an important social reason why it should not.

Science fiction aspires now to be more than a literature for youngsters. To appeal to adults, to gain serious consideration in our society, it must not offend reason. It must be coherent with the life we know in the sense that it does not contradict that which is known to be uncontradictable. A historical novel, to take an example from another field, might include a dozen thoroughly fictitious characters from the Civil War era, but it can't describe Stephen A. Douglas as president of the United States. It can make General Grant do many things he never did, but it can't make him surrender at Appomattox.

I will give my reasons later in this essay for thinking it important that science fiction be accepted with respect by society in general for the good not only of science fiction, but of society.

Two qualifications to my last argument must be made. It must not be thought that all writers of adventure science fiction are necessarily given to bad science. I have already mentioned Smith and Campbell. I want to emphasize the point and advance L. Sprague de Camp as an example. De Camp is one of the best, perhaps *the* best of the contemporary practitioners of the derring-do-and-swordplay school of science fiction. He is also one of the most meticulous men in the field when it comes to excluding known scientific impossibilities. Much more meticulous, for instance, than myself, though I do more preaching about it.

The second qualification has a name. That name is Ray Bradbury. Bradbury has written scores of stories about Mars. He gives Mars an Earthlike temperature, an Earthlike atmosphere and Earthlike people, sometimes down to tuxedos and pocket-handkerchiefs. His stories reek with scientific incongruity. But he gets away with it. Not only does he get away with it, but, among the general population, he is by far the most popular science-fiction writer and regularly appears in such magazines as *The Saturday Evening Post*.

In my opinion, Bradbury gets away with it because he does not really write science fiction. He is a writer of social fiction. His "Mars" is but the mirror held up to Earth. His stories do not depict possible futures; they are warnings and moral lessons aimed at the present. Because Bradbury believes that our present society is headed for chaos and barbarism unless it changes its present course (he may well be right), his warnings are jeremiads. This has led some critics to the superficial belief that the man is simply "morbid" or that he has a "death wish." Nonsense! He is simply writing social fiction.

It is not my wish to imply that the creation of social science fiction was a complete tour de force on the part of Campbell. It was true that he had the wisdom to see and respond to a new demand, but the fact of fundamental importance is that the demand existed.

After all, twelve years had passed. The boy of fifteen who had read *Skylark of Space* in 1928 and was overwhelmed by it was now twenty-five and longing for the "good old days." He no longer enjoyed science fiction and remembered the past with nostalgia because he thought the stories were better. They weren't. He had merely been ten years younger. To satisfy the veterans of science fiction, to take into account the steadily increasing average age of the readers, to prevent the older enthusiasts from falling away as similar grownups fell away from Edgar Rice Burroughs and Zane Grey, science fiction had to mature with its readers. Fortunately, it did.

V

In 1945, the atom bomb was dropped on Hiroshima and a fourth stage of science fiction was ushered in.

Why? Primarily because the atom bomb put a new light on science fiction. Until 1945, it was only too easy to dismiss science fiction as "weird stuff," as "horror stories," as "comic-strip things."

"Do you read that stuff?" people would say.

The great popularity of such strips as *Buck Rogers, Flash Gordon* and *Superman* made it easy for people to categorize all science fiction as juvenile. The lurid covers of many of the science-fiction magazines did not help. As a result, many adults who would have enjoyed and appreciated science fiction did not, because it never occurred to them to try it.

And then a weapon right out of science fiction ends World War II and changes the balance of power on Earth. It is time for a sober look at the crackpots, so-called, who have been talking about atom bombs at a time when no one but a few specialists in nuclear physics even thought they were possible.

The result was that more people tasted science fiction and found they liked it. As the reading public suddenly grew larger, science fiction became "respectable." Publishing houses such as Doubleday and Simon & Schuster began putting out science-fiction books regularly and with no attempt at "diluting" them in any mistaken belief that the book-buying public was not yet ready for the straight stuff. In addition, science-fiction magazines other than Campbell's *Astounding Science Fiction* (both newcomers and old reliables) began shifting their story policy in the direction of Campbell's.

In 1950, Horace L. Gold brought out *Galaxy Science Fiction* which, from the very beginning, published only advanced social science fiction so that with the first issue it was accepted by most fans as sharing top honors with *Astounding*.

Campbell is still editor of *Astounding* [1953] and still a tremendous force in the field, but because he is no longer the lone champion of social science fiction, the era since 1945 cannot be tabbed with his name, or any name. It must simply be called the "atomic era."

VI

Now it is time to look closely at social science fiction. Having isolated it as one of three types of science fiction, and the *one* type with social significance, the question next comes up whether social science fiction is a precise term or whether within it there are also subdivisions.

Neither alternative, in my opinion, is quite correct. Social science fiction is not a precise term but neither is it old enough to have developed a clear-cut subdifferentiation. Instead it consists of a broad continuous spectrum. If we consider the two extremes of the spectrum, we will seem to be treating two widely different types of story, but we will have to keep it continuously in mind that one extreme shades imperceptibly into the other and no man can point and say, "Here is the dividing line." (To a lesser extent this is true of the broader categories of adventure, gadget, and social science fiction; also of the still broader categories of social fiction and science fiction.)

Despite what I have just said, I cannot resist the temptation to give the two extremes names. Names are dangerous because they imply neat categories. Nevertheless, I hope you will humor me in this respect. I could call the extremes conservative and radical; realistic and romantic; simple and complex. I'll use none of these. Instead, I'll use the terms "chess game" and "chess puzzle" which are more picturesque than any of these but, in my opinion, more accurate as well.

A chess game has the following important characteristics: 1) it begins with a fixed number of pieces in a fixed position, and 2) the pieces change their positions according to a fixed set of rules.

A chess puzzle differs from a game in that although the second point holds, the first breaks down. A chess puzzle begins with any number of pieces (up to and including the full amount used in a game) placed in any arrangement that does not break the fundamental rules of chess.

It is important to remember that in the case of the puzzle, the original position is not necessarily one that is likely to be arrived at in the ordinary course of a game. In fact, in the vast majority of cases, a pair of chess players would have to be most ingeniously insane to arrive at the sort of position that would make a good puzzle.

How is this analogous to the spectrum of social science fiction? Point 2, which is held in common by games and puzzles, i.e., the rules by which the pieces move, may be equated with the motions and impulses of humanity: hate, love, fear, suspicion, passion, hunger, lust and so on. Presumably, these will not change while mankind remains Homo sapiens. Stories can be written about "supermen" or intellectual mutants. They may even be written about alien species or robots that do not share these fundamental human drives. However, they must still be written by a very human author and addressed to a very human audience. If the characters are not recognizably human in these respects it is difficult or impossible to treat them adequately or to please the audience with them.

(One exception—and virtually any generalization about science fiction has a dozen exceptions—is Olaf Stapledon's *Odd John*. This is the story of a superman who is so skilfully drawn that he really seems both nonhuman and superhuman. Being only human myself, I didn't like Odd John—the character, that is, not the story, which I thoroughly enjoyed—any more than a chimpanzee could like a human being if he were capable of really understanding the gulf of mental difference that separated himself from man.)

Point 1 of the chess-game–chess-puzzle dichotomy can be equated with the fundamental socio-economic environment of humanity. The type of story that corresponds to the chess game with its fixed starting position is that which assumes the socio-economic environment we now possess. That is: a city culture as opposed to a village culture; an agricultural economy as opposed to a nomadic or hunting economy; a family system as opposed to a tribal system. Add to these certain newer fashions which have become so ingrained in our own ways of thinking that any deviation has become abhorrent. For instance: heterosexual relationships as the sexual norm; monogamy; a mild, formal and passionless monotheism; taboos against cannibalism and incest; and so on.

With this starting position fixed, it is then only necessary to play the "chess game" according to the rules. The only modification from our own society is that certain technological innovations are allowed. Atomic power may have replaced coal and oil as these once replaced wood. Robots may have been developed. Interstellar travel may be commonplace. But people are still our kind of people with our way of thinking about things.

In the purest form of the chess-game type of social science fiction it is frequently found convenient to take advantage of the fact that "history repeats itself." Why shouldn't it? Given the same rules and the same starting position, the element of repetition must obtrude.

As a result, a whole class of "Galactic Empire" stories has arisen. The Galactic Empire, or its equivalent, is usually simply the Roman or British Empire written large, and the events that transpire can be equated without too much difficulty with analogous events that took place in past history.

I have a personal leaning toward this type of story and have written a few myself. My first novel, *Pebble in the Sky* (Doubleday, 1950), dealt with an Earth, ravaged by radioactivity, despised by its neighbors, but dreaming of its glorious past and certain of its special mission in the future. Most thoughtful readers had no difficulty in recognizing the fact that I was retelling the history of Rome and Judea. I even had Earth governed by an Imperial Procurator.

I wrote other stories, the germs of whose ideas I derived from the histories of Justinian and Belisarius, Tamerlane and Bajazet, John and Pope Innocent III. Naturally they were told in my own way and departed from their historical counterparts whenever it pleased me to have them depart. It was simply that I was following the chess-game theory in which all games start from the same point.

(I do not wish to imply that I am the only writer of such stories, or even the most important such writer. Robert A. Heinlein has specialized in this field and is widely considered to be the most proficient. Of the younger writers, one name which I pick at random is Poul Anderson who did an excellent job of chess-gaming in "The Helping Hand.")

Not everyone approves of this sort of thing. Damon Knight, one of the best and brightest of our postwar crop of social science fiction writers, and a devotee of the chess-puzzle variety, took particular issue with it in an article he wrote for an amateur science-fiction "fan magazine." His thesis was that history did *not* repeat itself.

Whether it does or does not repeat itself depends, of course, on what you mean by repetition. The same people never live twice, the same wars are never fought twice, the same conditions never occur *exactly* twice. Nevertheless, similar broad responses frequently occur under similar broad stimuli. If you stand far away from the great and variegated story of man and squint your eyes so that you drown out the details and see only the broad blocks of color, various repetitive patterns do appear.

We have, for instance, the alternation of city domination and nomad domination in the early days of Near-Eastern civilization; the pattern by which a dynasty or a nation or an empire establishes itself under a strong individual (usually destroying, in the process, a more aristocratic dynasty, a wealthier nation, a more civilized empire), maintains itself through a few harsh reigns or centuries, reaches a peak of luxury and magnificence and then declines to fall victim to another dynasty, nation, or empire.

However, I shall not try to repeat in detail what Toynbee has said in six volumes.

But, after all, how useful are these repetitions of extremely broad sweeps? Fiction to have a real interest must deal with specific happenings —and how specifically can history repeat? The answer is, in my opinion, that it can repeat with surprising specificity.

If you don't mind, now, I would like to present some examples. I have wanted to do this for years and now that the opportunity has come I do not intend to wait for a second knock. I will present, in bare outline, a certain passage of history, in which key words or phrases will be represented by dashes. I invite the reader to fill in the dashes before he looks at my own "solution" at the end of the passage.

VII

Sample: *The Revolution*

In the —(1)— Century, the European nation of  —(2)— was in a shaky state. In the previous century, it had reached a peak of military glory under the monarch —(3)—, under whose leadership the nation defeated the attempts of —(4)— to gain hegemony over Europe. Since then, the fortunes of the nation had declined, military defeats had been suffered and finances had grown nearly impossible.

The current king —(5)— was not noted for either firmness of character or brilliance of intellect. He was noted chiefly for the fact that, in a dissolute court, he maintained a spotlessly moral private life. He was well-meaning and amiable and had none of the sexuality and despotic instinct of his illustrious predecessor —(6)— who had a long and successful reign.

The king was, at least in the beginning, liked by the people who, however, bitterly distrusted Queen —(7)— who was of foreign extraction and, indeed, was of the —(8)— nation whom the people had thought of as enemies for generations. The queen was the stronger personality of the two, the less willing to compromise with the people and the more contemptuous of them.

Despite the resources of the nation, which were ample, and the taxes, which were ample, the government lacked money, partly because of waste and inefficiency and partly because of the —(9)— war.

Although the nation had been notoriously loyal to its sovereigns in previous centuries, it now rose in violent revolt. At first mildly radical policies prevailed under the influence of such personalities as —(10)—. As the revolution proceeded, however, it grew more violent. Some of the original architects of the revolution were forced into exile, for example, —(11)—. Others, as the revolution grew more violent, paid with their lives. Two of these, among numerous examples, are —(12)— and —(13)—. Eventually, a strong government was formed under —(14)—. The king was eventually executed, an act which shocked all of Europe.

What shocked some people even more were the measures taken against the established —(15)— church of the nation.

Although the rest of Europe would gladly have intervened to put down this dangerous new government and re-establish legitimacy and order, they were not in a position to do so efficiently. There was difficulty in coming to a common decision as to a means of action. In addition, much of Europe was disorganized because of the great —(16)— which was just coming to a conclusion.

Half-hearted attempts at intervention failed though they aroused the bitter resentment of the revolutionary government which was quick to respond. Its people became suddenly formidable. Against its foreign foes

—(17)— it won unexpected victories that, for a time, established its government securely, and, in fact, made of it a menace to the rest of Europe. Eventually, however, the revolution came to an end and after an interlude of domination under General —(18)— the heir of the executed king returned to his kingdom as —(19)—.

I doubt that any reader will not have definite ideas as to which nation and what period in its history I am talking about. Some, perhaps, are thinking that I may be talking of either of two nations. Actually, I am thinking of three. This is the way the blanks could be filled in:

|  | A | B | C |
|---|---|---|---|
| (1) | 17th | 18th | 20th |
| (2) | England | France | Russia |
| (3) | Elizabeth I | Louis XIV | Alexander I |
| (4) | Philip II of Spain | (not applicable) | Napoleon I of France |
| (5) | Charles I | Louis XVI | Nicholas II |
| (6) | Henry VIII | Louis XIV | Peter I |
| (7) | Henrietta Maria | Marie Antoinette | Alexandra |
| (8) | French | Austria | German |
| (9) | (not applicable) | American Revolution | World War I |
| (10) | Pym | Mirabeau | Kerensky |
| (11) | (not applicable) | Lafayette | Trotsky (later) |
| (12) | (not applicable) | Desmoulins | Zinoviev (later) |
| (13) | (not applicable) | Danton | Bukharin (later) |
| (14) | Cromwell | Robespierre | Lenin |
| (15) | Anglican | Roman Catholic | Orthodox |
| (16) | Thirty Years' War | (not applicable) | World War I |
| (17) | Holland | Austria | Germany |
| (18) | Monk | Bonaparte | (not applicable) |
| (19) | Charles II | Louis XVIII | (not applicable) |

I maintain that this is not bad. To be sure the comparisons can only go so far. Lafayette and Trotsky are in no way comparable except that both went into exile and, more strongly still, General Monk and General Bonaparte are completely different except insofar as one succeeded Richard Cromwell and preceded Charles II, and the other succeeded the Directorate and preceded Louis XVIII.

Now does this prove that history always repeats itself? No, but it shows that it is legitimate to extrapolate from the past because sometimes such extrapolations are fairly close to what happens. Suppose that in 1910 a science-fiction writer wished to lay a story of the future in Russia and, after a shrewd consideration of the conditions then prevailing, decided to have its social background one of revolution. If he were a believer in the chess-game theory he would have used the French Revolution as a framework to keep himself from overstepping the rules of the game.

And he would have done pretty well, if he had done so. Of course, he might have had the Tsarevich Alexius returning to his throne in 1930, and he might have had the ragged Red Army *not* defeated at Warsaw in 1920, but advancing to the Seine before it could be stopped by combined Anglo-American forces (a contingency that may have been premature rather than entirely wrong). Otherwise, it would sound well.

Is this a freak case? Have I just picked out the one case of duplication (or rather triplication) in history, in order to back up my own argument? Not at all. I could find many others. This example could itself have been almost indefinitely extended with parallels all along the line. I might even have, as a particular tour de force, attempted a five-way correlation between Philip II of Spain, Louis XIV of France, Napoleon of France, William II of Germany and Hitler of Germany. But it is time to leave the chess-game variety of social science fiction and pass on to the chess puzzles.

## VIII

In chess puzzles the starting position can be adjusted to the will of the puzzle composer. Analogously, in chess-puzzle social science fiction, the initial society in which the characters move can be as the author pleases. Ordinarily, the society is distinct from our own in one or more fundamental ways, though usually it can be viewed as possibly having originated from our society by some radical development or overgrowth of some aspect of our way of life. The heterogeneity of this type of literature is such that it can be explained satisfactorily only by examples.

Fritz Leiber, in an extraordinarily powerful story, "Coming Attraction," postulates an American society in which social disintegration is nearly complete. America is covered with patches of radioactive destruction as a result of a recently concluded atomic war. Women wear masks in public since sexual fixation has traveled from the breasts and hips to the face. Women wrestlers have become a recognized social caste and are more proficient than their male counterparts. The society reeks with a semi-accepted sadomasochism.

The reader is at once repelled by the story and strongly attracted. He is horrified at the society, moved by its reality and profoundly disturbed at the realization that it is an extrapolation of some of the worst features of our present way of life.

Another imagined society occurs in Wyman Guin's "Beyond Bedlam." Here we have a society in which schizoid personality is the accepted form. It is, in fact, the compulsory norm. Each body is controlled by two minds and personalities, not simultaneously, but alternately for five-day periods. The two mind-controlled bodies bear no relationship to each other. A single person in alternate five-day periods may have two different occupations, two different wives, two different statuses in society and so on. The postulation states further that by forcing split personality on humanity, the eternal struggle between the half-formed personalities within men and women can no longer find its outlet in war and destruction. The two personalities are released, freed of one another, and may go their way in peace.[12]

Guin goes further in this story than a mere statement of a schizoid society. He writes about a situation that is natural, perhaps inevitable, in such a society, but which is alien to us. He gives us an insight into life in a changed society that, in an abstract sense, is very valuable to those of us who expect inevitable change. The story deals with a man who has fallen in love with his wife's alter ego, who has in turn fallen in love with him. In the society of "Beyond Bedlam" this is evil, disgusting and immoral. The struggles and dilemmas of the two star-crossed lovers are followed to the inevitable tragic ending.

It is as though a Roman writer of the Augustan age told a story of a future society in which color distinctions were important, and in which a man found himself hopelessly in love with a girl whose skin tinge was slightly different.

Both "Beyond Bedlam" and "Coming Attraction" appeared in *Galaxy Science Fiction*. This is not to imply that chess-puzzle social science fiction does not appear in *Astounding Science Fiction*. In that magazine, I can cite William Tenn's "Firewater" as an excellent recent example. Nevertheless, due perhaps to the differing personalities of the two editors, the chess-game variety is slightly more prominent in *Astounding*, and the chess-puzzle variety in *Galaxy*.

Two more examples. (It is difficult to know where to stop.) Eric Frank Russell's story "—And Then There Were None" in *Astounding Science Fiction* dealt with a society in which individualism was carried to its logical extreme. Each man did exactly what he wished and no more. Efforts to persuade him to do otherwise were met with a grim, and effective, passive resistance. The other is *Rogue Queen* by L. Sprague de Camp, which has appeared in book form only (Doubleday), and which deals with a quasi-human society whose manner of living is akin to that of the bees, i.e., one functioning female per economic unit, a relatively small number of functioning males, and a large majority of non-functioning females.

I have now followed the divisions and subdivisions of science fiction as far as I can and I must pause to remind the reader of a statement I made at the very beginning of this chapter. All that you have read represents a strictly personal organization of the subject. I do not pretend that there is any objective truth in it or even that any sizable portion of science-fiction readers agree with me. It may well be that almost all disagree with me.

Even if we can suppose that in some way I can persuade most or all readers to accept my classification of the field, there would still be wide disagreement as to which story belongs where. To me, for instance, the stories of A. E. van Vogt are gadget science fiction since van Vogt uses Korzybskian semantics as a "mental-variety" gadget around which to build his story, much as George O. Smith used his "physical-variety" gadgets to build his Venus Equilateral stories. To others A. E. van Vogt is social science fiction.

Again, some readers are beginning to take the attitude that any story dealing in Galactic sweeps is automatically "space opera." They will include in the category such examples of adventure science fiction as *Galactic Patrol* by E. E. Smith, gadget science fiction such as *Weapon Shops of Isher* by A. E. van Vogt, and social science fiction of the chess-game variety, such as *The Stars, Like Dust* . . . by myself. To my own way of thinking that broadens the term, space opera, to the point where it is almost co-extensive with science fiction. I therefore disapprove of this tendency. To others this may seem very logical and right, on the other hand.

Since there is no way for any of us to establish absolute truth, if, indeed, such an animal exists, our only alternative is to consider the various classifications presented to us and make that decision among them which pleases us most. The one that pleases me most is the one I've presented here.

IX

Having until now considered the effect of society upon science fiction, its genesis and development, it remains to consider the reverse of the proposition: the effect, actual or potential, of science fiction upon society.

This may seem rather bumptious of me. Can a literary form such as science fiction seriously be considered to have any likely effect upon society? Is it not simply a form of escape literature, simply a kind of entertainment?

If it were, that would be no disgrace. Any human being has the right to relax and get his mind off his dreary surroundings, particularly today, when dreariness is a universal factor. As the tailor said, when reproached for taking a month to make a suit when God had created the world in only six days: "Feel the material of this suit and then come to the window and take a look at this phooey world."

The world today certainly does seem phooey, and it would be a harsh and self-righteous man indeed who could quarrel with the natural desire of an individual to look the other way. Unfortunately, the fact remains that we've got to face our problems at least part of the time. We have to live in the world and be part of it. Worse still, our children will have to also.

But is science fiction *only* escape literature? Is it similar in this respect to the western story which describes a world that has not existed these fifty years and probably never existed in the manner made familiar to our cap-pistol-toting children? Is it similar to the love story that lifts our typists and housewives into an imaginary world of synthetic passion purified by the Post Office Department of any trace of true-to-life sex? Is it similar to the mystery story designed to present the *aficionado* with incredible amounts of make-believe danger and violence within the safe confines of an easy chair?

Superficially, science fiction is similar to these. In one way, however, it is vitally different. It treats not of a make-believe past or a make-believe present. It treats of a make-believe future.

The importance of this difference rests in the fact that a make-believe past or present must exist side-by-side with a known and actual past or present. A make-believe future has no known competitor. It can serve as a nucleus for serious thought without the distracting thought that it is a *known* falseness.

But is there a value in considering make-believe futures? I think so. For the first time in history, the future is a complete puzzle even in its most general aspects. There used to be the consolation, that even though we, as individuals, might die, life would continue, spring would come, flowers would bud. But now we have brought ourselves to such a pass that we wonder whether the planet itself might not die with us.

We've *got* to think about the future now. For the first time in history, the future cannot be left to take care of itself; it must be thought about.

But what can science fiction do about it? It can first, and most important, accustom the reader to the notion of change. The force of change is all about us, it is the essence of our society. Science fiction is the literature of social change, and it treats social change as the norm.

This is important. Resistance to change is, next to the desire for self-preservation, perhaps the most deeply ingrained behavior pattern in the human being. A child will not sleep in a strange crib. A man's digestion is upset if he eats at an unusual time.

In broader terms, you cannot reasonably expect any individual who has attained years of maturity and a place in society which seems natural to him (whether that place be stockbroker or dishwasher) to accept cheerfully any change that alters his place into a new and unaccustomed one.

I once did some library work for a sociology professor (in those days I had to work my way through college) who was writing a book on social resistance to technological change. It was a fascinating and frustrating experience. The priestly caste of primitive civilizations, for instance, fought any attempt to establish a system of writing. Once writing was established, they used all their influence to resist any simplification that would make writing more available to the general population. Naturally, that would weaken their own influence as the repositories of tribal wisdom. The introduction of the iron plow was met with the cry that iron would poison the soil. The use of coal for fuel purposes was opposed by the theory that the fumes would poison the air. Fulton's steamboat, the observers said, would never start. Once started, they knew it would never stop. The airplane, as Simon Newcombe (an eminent astronomer) proved mathematically, was an impossibility. No engine could be designed strong enough to lift a machine aloft which was capable of carrying a man. The Wright brothers flew at Kitty Hawk, and Newcombe changed his mind. All right, he said, *one* man. But no airplane, he insisted, would ever carry more than one man.

The dislike for technological innovations that upset the even comfort of a carefully designed rut extends with even greater force to social customs. Even the skeleton of a custom of which the pith has long since rotted away remains untouchable.

But is change valuable? Is it even necessary?

In the study of evolution, it turns out that organisms which do not change to meet a changing environment become extinct. Organisms, on the other hand, which find themselves an unchanging environment, find themselves also in blind alleys with no possibility of future advancement.

Human societies, history shows, must also grow and develop or they will suffer. There is no standing still.

Examples can be presented. Two occur to me. In the eighteenth and nineteenth centuries, Europe was presented with the necessity of change. A new industrialism was upsetting the old peasant culture, bringing to the fore two new classes: the industrial employer and the industrial employee. The former became more important than the old landowning aristocracy; the latter, more important than the generally inarticulate peasantry.

Nowhere in Europe was this gathering change popular among those who were getting along perfectly well under the old system. On the continent of Europe, the landowners resisted the change manfully. They would not and did not give in to change. They *fought* change.

Did they *stop* change? They did not. Resistance welled further and further up the dam formed by the unyielding breasts of the old aristocracy. Then when the dam buckled, the flood was infinitely worse than it would have been had it never been built. From 1789 to 1917 a series of revolutions shook and convulsed Europe.

In England, however, the landowning squirearchy retreated (often unwillingly, it is true) step by step, inch by inch, giving in here, giving in there. The result? Where in Europe, outside of England, is there such a secure throne, such a secure peerage?

Much the same may be said of the small Scandinavian countries and of Switzerland. Here, however, it is not so remarkable. Small countries may vegetate, unaffected by the stress of large world movements, except where it is forced upon them by invading armies. England, however, was subject at all times to the pressures and risks devolving upon a great power. (How much of her fortune is due to the twenty-two miles separating Dover and Calais?)

Another example! Our western culture hit the Far East with a thunderous roar one hundred years ago. The Far East, with a civilization of its own that was superior in many respects to ours, fought it bitterly and unsuccessfully, since our own civilization happened to possess one advantage worth all the rest—a superior technology. China rejected the technology along with all the rest of our culture. She would not compromise. She would not yield. She would not change.

The result? She lost anyway and what she would not give was taken by force.

Japan also retained her culture, but she had the wisdom to bow to the necessity of change. She accepted our technology. The result was that in fifty years she not only became a great power in her own right, respected by all the other great powers, but she was even able to join in the exploitation of China, and outdo all the rest.

Now a fictitious example! Suppose that in the 1840's, the American South had come to the conclusion that the world tide was against chattel slavery and had decided to make the best of a bad bargain by selling its slaves to the government and then rehiring them on the open labor market. Suppose that the North had decided that if matters went as they were, things would only end in a big catastrophe, and that they might as well contribute to the buying of the slaves and their subsequent liberation.

It might have cost money—but not one percent of what the Civil War cost. The South would still have its labor supply, as it has now. Without the memory of a costly war and a costlier reconstruction, without the sense of a regional humiliation, without the sense of being picked on and kicked about, the South eventually might have come to feel less lordly about the color line.

What am I advocating? A doctrine of an irresistible wave of the future, à la Anne Morrow Lindbergh? Not at all.

I am saying this: It is useless to attempt to solve the tremendous problems of our times by adopting one of only two attitudes. Either to resist change, any change, and hold savagely to the status quo, or to advocate change, a certain change, and no other change. Neither of these views is flexible. Both are static. The result of a collision of such views is almost always disastrous.

I say there must be a third group, one which realizes that the status is not and cannot be quo forever, but which also realizes that the exact nature of the change which will best suit the currently changing social and economic forces may not be guessed at very far in advance.

Franklin Delano Roosevelt's New Deal represented such a third group. He broke with the brute capitalism of the twenties, yet did not accept a doctrinaire socialism. Roosevelt frankly and unashamedly experimented. He stated in one of his fireside chats that he liked to try *something*. If it worked, fine; if not, he tried something else.

I cannot help but wonder if a maturely developed sense of social experimentation may not some day bear as much fruit for society as physical experimentation has done for science.

Certainly, there is a good deal of this notion in science fiction. Its authors, as a matter of course, present their readers with new societies, with possible futures and consequences. It is social experimentation on paper; social guesses plucked out of air.

And this is the great service of science fiction. To accustom the reader to the possibility of change, to have him think along various lines— perhaps very daring lines. Why not? In the world, as it wags today, there is precious little to lose. We face the atom. . . .

X

So far, the contribution of science fiction seems to be an entirely passive one. It says "Change!" but it doesn't say how. It says "Go!" but it doesn't say where.

As I have already pointed out, it is service enough merely to say "change" and "go." It would be nice, however, if science fiction could be said to point actively in a worthwhile direction. It would seem that it cannot. It presents a thousand possible futures and there is no way of telling which of these will resemble the real future or even whether any of them will resemble the real future.

Unless, that is, we can find any way in which most of the futures presented resemble one another. There is such a way. The large majority of the futures presented in science fiction involve a broader stage for the drama of life. The one world of Earth is expanded to a whole series of worlds, sometimes to millions of worlds. Other intelligences may exist or they may not, but at least the inanimate universe with which man struggles is stupendously expanded.

The result of this is that to science-fiction readers Earth becomes small and relatively unimportant. A subdivision smaller than Earth becomes even harder to focus upon.

There was some tendency, for instance, during World War II, to write science-fiction stories in which Nazis or Japanese were the villains. Such stories don't tend to be successful. They're too topical.

It is as though science fiction, dealing, as it does, with solar systems, cannot adjust itself conveniently down the scale to the villainies of a single country on this small world.

This is not because science-fiction writers are internationalists as a group, or because they have a more enlightened and all-inclusive outlook, are less patriotic or less given to sectional passions and race prejudice. They are human, as human as other people. I do not wish to imply that any effect science fiction has upon society is the result of conscious effort on the part of those who write it.

Using this present case as an example, writers ignore the subdivisions of mankind because the nature and scope of science fiction is such that anything less than the "Earthman" doesn't make much sense.

Whatever the reason for it, science fiction is serving a specific and important function. By ignoring "racial" divisions among men it is moving in a direction the rest of our culture must move in out of sheer self-defense.

There has always been hostility between the "us guys" and the "you guys." This hostility, however, need not flare into violence. I was brought up in Brooklyn, but for some reason I was a New York Giant fan. (I still am.) I hated the Dodger fans and they hated me, but it was a business hate. When we weren't discussing baseball, we were friends.

My state is better than your state, my city than your city, my block than your block, and my father can lick your father. It's all very normal. When your own group shines, you shine by reflected glory. When dear old Siwash wins a football game, all the Siwash alumni get drunk— although their only connection with their alma mater might have been a dismal four-year record of rejected education.

Where does this me-you rivalry stop being exhilarating and start being dangerous? When it coincides with a fixed belief that "you" are an inferior human being and "I" am a superior human being.

Just at the time that the western European powers began to expand across land and sea and to collide with societies other than their own, they also began to develop their superior material technology. Not only were the American Indians, the African Negroes, the Asiatic Indians and Chinese, the South Sea Malays and the Australian aborigines heathen and therefore inferior by divine fiat; they were unable to stand up to our gunfire and therefore inferior by natural law.

This division of mankind into whites (particularly Nordic whites) and everybody else was safe only as long as western Europe (and its cultural appendages in America and Australia) maintained their technological superiority.

But the superiority is no longer being maintained. In 1905, the Russians suffered the humiliation of being defeated by the yellow-skinned Japanese. But the rest of the white world took it calmly enough; after all, the Russians were half-Tartar and very backward for a theoretically white nation.

Then, in 1941 and 1942, Japan inflicted defeats upon British, French, Dutch, and American troops, the pick and cream of the white world. Even Japan's final defeat did not abolish the shock her initial victories communicated to the entire nonwhite world.

So times have changed and race prejudice is becoming a dangerous anachronism. We are treating with an outmoded emotional attitude a group of humans who outnumber us badly and who are drawing abreast of us technologically. For selfish reasons alone we should be wiser than we are. (And on moral grounds we never did have a leg to stand on.)

Science fiction, insofar as it tends to think of humanity as a unit and to face humanity, white, black, and yellow alike, with common dangers and common tasks, which must be pushed to a common victory, serves the world well, and America particularly well.

## XI

I have written longer than I intended and more circuitously. I would like to make up for that by ending with a three-point summary:

**1.** For the first time in history mankind is faced with a rapidly changing society, due to the advent of modern technology.

**2.** Science fiction is a form of literature that has grown out of this fact.

**3.** The contribution science fiction can make to society is that of accustoming its readers to the thought of the inevitability of continuing change and the necessity of directing and shaping that change rather than opposing it blindly or blindly permitting it to overwhelm us.

# WHAT IS SCIENCE FICTION?

## Damon Knight

Once at a Milford Science Fiction Writers' Conference I said a colleague's punctuation was wrong; he replied that he didn't agree with me. I failed to ask him why he thought punctuation was a matter of opinion, but I brooded over this later, and finally realized that he was talking about what the rules of punctuation ought to be, while I was talking about what they are. One is arguable, the other not.

In a similar way, science fiction writers and critics have been trying without success for forty years to define science fiction, because each of them has been talking about his own idea of what the field ought to be, never about what it is. Intent on distinguishing the true s.f. from the false, they invariably find that most of it is false; thus Heinlein casts out "space opera," Bailey "scientific romance," Asimov social satire. De Camp divides fiction into imaginative stories (including science fiction) and realistic stories; Heinlein insists that s.f. is a branch, and the most important branch, of realistic fiction.

Here are some other attempts:

"Science fiction is the search for a definition of man and his status in the universe which will stand in our advanced but confused state of knowledge (science), and is characteristically cast in the Gothic or post-Gothic mode."—Brian W. Aldiss. (This admits *The Fountainhead*, by Ayn Rand, but excludes Hal Clement's *Mission of Gravity*.)

"The more powers above the ordinary that the protagonist enjoys, the closer the fiction will approach to hard-core science fiction. Conversely, the more ordinary and fallible the protagonist, the further from hard-core."—Aldiss. (This admits *Dracula* as hard-core science fiction, but excludes "Night," by John W. Campbell.)

"A handy short definition of almost all science fiction might read: realistic speculation about possible future events, based solidly on adequate knowledge of the real world, past and present, and on a thorough understanding of the scientific method. To make this definition cover all science fiction (instead of 'almost all') it is necessary only to strike out the word 'future.' "—Robert A. Heinlein. (This admits *Arrowsmith*, by Sinclair Lewis, but excludes the collected works of Robert Sheckley.)

"There is only one definition of science fiction that seems to make pragmatic sense: 'Science fiction is anything published as science fiction.' " —Norman Spinrad. (This admits Spinrad's "The Last Hurrah of the Golden Horde," but excludes the book version of Walter Miller's *A Canticle for Leibowitz.*)

Taken together (if anyone were idiot enough to try), these definitions would narrow the field of science fiction almost to invisibility. Yet nearly every critic claims an intuitive knowledge of what s.f. is, and I claim it myself. We do know the difference between stories that are perceived as science fiction and those that are not: the question is, how do we know?

In an attempt to find out, I wrote a list of promising definitions and checked them against works published as science fiction to see how well they matched. This is the list:

1. Science. (Gernsback.)

2. Technology and invention. (Heinlein, Miller.)

3. The future and the remote past, including all time travel stories. (Bailey.)

4. Extrapolation. (Davenport.)

5. Scientific method. (Bretnor.)

6. Other places—planets, dimensions, etc., including visitors from the above. (Bailey.)

7. Catastrophes, natural or manmade. (Bailey.)

I discarded other definitions, for instance Campbell's dictum that s.f. is predictive, which I thought were impossible to evaluate. (To find out how many s.f. stories contain accurate predictions I would have to wait until the results are all in, i.e., to the end of the universe.) I also discarded all negative definitions, e.g., that any story that contains fantasy elements is not s.f. (because that excludes Heinlein's "Waldo"), or that any story that is literature is not s.f. (because that excludes Le Guin's *The Left Hand of Darkness*).

For source material I used *Nebula Award Stories Eight, The Hugo Winners, Volume Two*, and *The Science Fiction Hall of Fame, Volume One*, in the belief that any defect in the hypothesis would show up here first. I added recent issues of the three leading s.f. magazines, and recent volumes of three hardcover series, plus a one-shot anthology, Spinrad's *The New Tomorrows*, which I chose because it is devoted to "New Wave" s.f.*

On the basis of the results (see tables), I conclude that a story containing three or more of the elements listed above is usually perceived as science fiction; with two, it is perceived as borderline; with one or none, it is non-science fiction.

I had better emphasize that these scores say nothing about the quality of the stories, or about the quality of the science, the extrapolation, etc. If an element was present in a story, no matter how perfunctory or feeble, I scored it.

I also ran some test cases. The system held up well for these, with the single exception of *Gulliver's Travels*, which scored 4, although it is not usually perceived as s.f. To cure this, I would have to add the negative definition that nothing published before 1860 is science fiction, a perception due partly to tradition and, I think, partly to the desire to get rid of all the Lucians and Cyranos who have been dragged in by overanxious scholars.

In the course of this study my own perceptions were altered. At the end of it I found that I agreed with C. S. Lewis when he said that not all romances laid in the future are science fiction. I lost some (not all) of my dedication to a very broad definition of s.f., one which would include any work of fiction informed by a scientific attitude toward nature and man. I became more aware of the sleights practiced by commercial s.f. writers to ensure that their work will be perceived as science fiction, and to get work published which could as well have been written as mundane adventure fiction. I also became more aware of the number of non-s.f. stories regu-

---

* I omit these from the tables because they will be out of date by the time this book is published, but, for the record, *Galaxy* scored an average of 3.8, *Analog* 3.2, *New Dimensions* 3.2, *Orbit* 3.2, *Universe* 3.2 (like a sampling of near beers), *F&SF* 1.4, and *The New Tomorrows* 1.3.

larly published in nearly all the magazines and hardcover series, including my own.

I offer this study as an extended definition of what science fiction is. Like other people, I have an opinion about what it should be. I would like to see less dependence on conventional stage furniture and more on honestly worked out extrapolations. I am inclined to agree with Alexei and Cory Panshin when they say that s.f. and fantasy as we know them are two filled-in areas in a broad, largely empty field. I believe more strongly than before that science fiction has not yet found its limits.

"Science fiction" and "literature" are not mutually exclusive terms. I propounded this as a heresy in 1952, and it is still so regarded, not only by hostile critics but by many of s.f.'s defenders. The proposition "If it's s.f., it isn't literature" is self-proving: " 'But this looks good.' 'Well then, it's not s.f.' " And around we go again.

There is general agreement that science fiction has some essential attraction which is not easy to capture in words but which is unmistakable to a receptive reader. Kingsley Amis refers to this when he gives excerpts from two s.f. novels, and then remarks, ". . . anybody encountering such passages who fails to experience a peculiar interest, related to, but distinct from, ordinary literary interest, will never be an addict of science fiction." Basil Davenport, noting the argument as to whether *Arrowsmith* should be considered science fiction, says that he read the book at a time when he was avidly searching for s.f., and yet it never crossed his mind that this might be it. Isaac Asimov says that Plato, More and Swift are works of imagination, "but they do not have the *intent* of science fiction." I don't know what Isaac's version of the intent of s.f. is, but probably it has something to do with giving the same essential thrill of difference that Amis is talking about, and that Davenport failed to find in *Arrowsmith*.°

To say that this quality is characteristic of science fiction is not to say that it is always present, however, or that s.f. can have no other quality, no other way of appealing to its readers.

---

° I read *Arrowsmith* for the first time recently, and concluded that in an odd way it is the antithesis of science fiction. In a realistic novel set in the past or present, nothing can happen that would conspicuously alter the real world as we know it: therefore Lewis's hero, although he develops a new serum, has no place in history because someone else (a real person) beats him to it. This is just the opposite of what happens in a science fiction story, where the *consequences* of the invention or discovery are all-important.

### Nebula Award Stories Eight

| | science | technology, invention | future, past | extrapolation | scientific method | other places | catastrophes | total |
|---|---|---|---|---|---|---|---|---|
| A Meeting With Medusa, Clarke | • | • | • | • | | • | • | 6 |
| Shaffery Among the Immortals, Pohl | • | • | | | • | | | 3 |
| Patron of the Arts, Rotsler | | | • | • | • | | | 3 |
| When It Changed, Russ | • | | • | • | | • | • | 5 |
| On the Downhill Side, Ellison | | | | | | | | 0 |
| The Fifth Head of Cerberus, Wolfe | • | • | • | • | | • | • | 6 |
| When We Went to See the End of the World, Silverberg | • | • | • | • | | | • | 5 |
| Goat Song, Anderson | • | • | • | • | | | | 4 |

average: 4.0

### The Hugo Winners, Volume Two

| | science | technology, invention | future, past | extrapolation | scientific method | other places | catastrophes | total |
|---|---|---|---|---|---|---|---|---|
| The Dragon Masters, Vance | • | | • | • | | | • | 4 |
| No Truce With Kings, Anderson | | | • | • | • | • | • | 5 |
| Soldier, Ask Not, Dickson | | | • | • | • | • | | 4 |
| "Repent, Harlequin!" Said the Ticktockman, Ellison | | | • | • | • | | | 3 |
| The Last Castle, Vance | • | • | • | • | | | • | 5 |
| Neutron Star, Niven | • | • | • | • | | | • | 5 |
| Weyr Search, McCaffrey | • | • | • | • | | | • | 5 |
| Riders of the Purple Wage, Farmer | | | • | • | • | | | 3 |
| Gonna Roll the Bones, Leiber | | | | | | | | 0 |
| I Have No Mouth, and I Must Scream, Ellison | | | • | • | • | | | 3 |
| Nightwings, Silverberg | • | | • | • | • | | | 4 |
| The Sharing of Flesh, Anderson | • | • | • | • | | • | | 5 |
| The Beast That Shouted Love at the Heart of the World, Ellison | | • | | | | • | | 2 |
| Time Considered as a Helix of Semiprecious Stones, Delany | • | • | • | • | | | • | 5 |

average: 3.8

### The Science Fiction Hall of Fame, Volume One

| | science | technology, invention | future, past | extrapolation | scientific method | other places | catastrophes | total |
|---|---|---|---|---|---|---|---|---|
| A Martian Odyssey, Weinbaum | • | • | • | • | | • | • | 6 |
| Twilight, Campbell | • | • | • | • | | • | • | 6 |

| | science | technology, invention | future, past | extrapolation | scientific method | other places | catastrophes | total |
|---|---|---|---|---|---|---|---|---|
| **The Science Fiction Hall of Fame, Volume One** (cont'd) | | | | | | | | |
| Helen O'Loy, del Rey | | • | • | • | | | | 3 |
| The Roads Must Roll, Heinlein | | • | • | • | | | | 3 |
| Microcosmic God, Sturgeon | • | • | • | | | • | | 4 |
| Nightfall, Asimov | • | | | | • | • | • | 4 |
| The Weapon Shop, van Vogt | | • | • | • | | • | | 4 |
| Mimsy Were the Borogoves, Padgett | | • | • | | | • | | 3 |
| Huddling Place, Simak | | • | • | • | | • | • | 5 |
| Arena, Brown | | • | • | • | • | • | | 5 |
| First Contact, Leinster | | • | • | • | • | • | | 5 |
| That Only a Mother, Merril | | • | • | • | | | | 3 |
| Scanners Live in Vain, Smith | | • | • | | | • | | 3 |
| Mars Is Heaven! Bradbury | | • | • | • | | • | | 4 |
| The Little Black Bag, Kornbluth | • | • | • | • | | | | 4 |
| Born of Man and Woman, Matheson | | | | | | | | 0 |
| Coming Attraction, Leiber | | • | • | • | | | • | 4 |
| The Quest for Saint Aquin, Boucher | | • | • | • | | | • | 4 |
| Surface Tension, Blish | • | • | • | • | | • | | 5 |
| The Nine Billion Names of God, Clarke | | • | | • | | | • | 3 |
| It's a *Good* Life, Bixby | | | | | | • | | 1 |
| The Cold Equations, Godwin | | • | • | • | | • | | 4 |
| Fondly Fahrenheit, Bester | | • | • | • | | | | 3 |
| The Country of the Kind, Knight | | • | • | • | | | | 3 |
| Flowers for Algernon, Keyes | • | | • | | • | | | 3 |
| A Rose for Ecclesiastes, Zelazny | | • | • | | | • | • | 4 |

average: 3.7

**Test Cases**

| | science | technology, invention | future, past | extrapolation | scientific method | other places | catastrophes | total |
|---|---|---|---|---|---|---|---|---|
| *Gulliver's Travels*, Swift | • | • | | • | | • | | 4 |
| *Walden Two*, Skinner | • | | | | • | | | 2 |
| *1984*, Orwell | | | • | • | • | | | 3 |
| *Watch the North Wind Rise*, Graves | | | | • | | | | 1 |
| The Metamorphosis, Kafka | | | | | | | | 0 |
| *Winnie the Pooh*, Milne | | | | | | • | | 1 |
| *The Wind in the Willows*, Grahame | | | | | | | | 0 |
| *Alice in Wonderland*, Carroll | | | | | | • | | 1 |
| *The Sword in the Stone*, White | | | • | | | | | 1 |
| *Robinson Crusoe*, Defoe | | | | | • | | | 1 |

Science fiction, as C. S. Lewis points out, is not all one thing. Even in its commercial history in the United States, dating from the early years of the century, it has undergone repeated infusions from other kinds of fiction—dime-novel fiction beginning about 1900, pulp adventure fiction in the early thirties, slick fiction in the late thirties and forties, women's-magazine and little-magazine fiction in the early fifties, avant-garde fiction in the sixties and seventies.

Every one of these transformations has provoked cries of outrage from old-guard editors and writers, but not one of them has obliterated previous forms—the latter are all still alive, even the Gernsbackian story (see Isaac Asimov's "Take a Match" in *New Dimensions II*). Adventure s.f., now more than forty years old, accounts for more than half the science fiction on the newsstands.

Brian Stableford, in "Science Fiction: a Sociological Perspective" (*Fantastic*, March 1974), makes the interesting suggestion that "the identity of SF—the identity of the social phenomenon called SF—is not to be found in its content; it is to be found in the way people *use* it, the way people orient themselves towards it, and in the way which it orients *them* to matters external to it." What Stableford appears to overlook is that different people use s.f. in different ways. He identifies himself as a writer of trash, says that many such writers make a living at their trade, and therefore that s.f. must be "*useful* at a trash level." So far he is on safe ground, but he errs when he says that "with few exceptions, books labeled as SF tend to sell the same number of copies, regardless of literary merit or seriousness of intent." By and large, the first printings of s.f. books sell within a very narrow range. For the pure article of commerce, the kind of thing Stableford is talking about, that's the end—the book has had its one printing and will never be seen again. Science fiction books of unusual merit are reprinted over and over.

Earlier, Stableford argues that Verne and Wells are not part of "the same social phenomenon as science fiction," because the phenomenon did not exist when they wrote. "When *The Time Machine*—the Wells story which seems to live most meaningfully within the SF paradigm—was written, the paradigm did not exist. It did not then belong to the same subculture which SF belongs to, even to the same type of subculture. . . . It is now possible for us to *use The Time Machine* as SF, and to meaningfully speak of it as SF. We may also *use* as SF the works of Verne, of Cyrano de Bergerac, of Voltaire and of Lucian of Samosata, but

. . . it is a conceptual mistake to think that because I, in 1973, can read *The Time Machine* as science fiction, H. G. Wells, in 1895, *wrote The Time Machine* as science fiction."

This curious statement needs some interpretation. Let me approach it from the rear. During the recent wave of permissiveness, several paperback publishers put out lines of well-written erotic novels. They didn't sell. Hardcore pornography fans don't want good writing, characterization, vividness, insight, or any other literary quality—not only don't want it, but are actively annoyed by it. So with the lowest class of s.f. readers, and I think we ought to have a term for the crude, basic kind of s.f. that satisfies the appetite for pseudo-scientific marvels without appealing to any other portion of the intellect: I propose that we call it "sci-fi."*

Substitute this for "science fiction" in Stableford's essay: the argument then reads that since there was no audience of sci-fi readers when Wells wrote *The Time Machine*, it was not sci-fi when he wrote it. This makes perfect sense.

What is alarming is the suspicion that not only Stableford but other and more literate critics of the field are really sci-fi readers. Some of the most industrious promoters of science fiction, when they announce that s.f. is good, may only mean it is good junk. This is hardly more comforting than being told it is bad junk. Of the flock of pop culture enthusiasts who have descended on s.f. lately, how many are crypto-sci-fi-sniffers?

* Pronounced "skiffy."

# II.
# HISTORY WITHOUT TEARS

# PILGRIM FATHERS:

## *Lucian and All That*

## Brian W. Aldiss

"If this is the best of all possible
worlds, what can the rest be like?"
Voltaire: Candide

In this chapter we launch ourselves on the mysterious early seas of speculative fiction, letting down a bucket now and again. Our finest catches will
be in the eighteenth century, following a quick inspection of earlier times.
Since we shall deal with periods before the Romantics, we shall find little
or nothing that resembles either Poe's works or *Frankenstein* in feeling, or
in what we have called Inwardness, but much that in content prefigures
science fiction.

Poe, as we have seen, had trouble with the *form* of his science fiction.
In most of his forays into the genre, we witness him abandoning his usual
Gothic-fiction narrative line, employing instead a sort of straightforward
didacticism only thinly disguised as fiction, or served up as dialogue;
examples are *Mellonta Tauta, The Colloquy of Monos and Una*, and *The
Conversation of Eiros and Charmion*. And in this, he shows kinship with
his literary ancestors, the utopianists, the marvellous-voyagers, and the
moralists who use the fantastic to make their point. These older writers do
not seek to involve us in the sufferings of their heroes by tricks of sus-
pense and character-drawing, as do Ann Radcliffe and her heirs; their
intentions lie elsewhere. This holds true even when we look back towards
the beginning of the Christian Era to Lucian of Samosata.

FROM *Billion-Year Spree*, Harper & Row, 1973

The dialogue form of his *Icaro-Menippus* reminds us that Lucian had something of the Socratic spirit. In the *True History*, some of the episodes —particularly the ones in which the adventurers are swallowed, ship and all, by a whale—look forward to Baron Munchausen, as well as back to the tall stories in Homer; while the spirit of Aristophanes' comedies presides fitfully over the whole.

Mention of Socrates and Aristophanes must suffice to recall the truism that much is owed to the Greeks, in science fiction as in science and civilisation generally. Many of the staple themes of science fiction were familiar to the Greeks.

Plato's *Republic*, cast in the form of Socratic conversation, is the first utopia. Aristophanes' comedies sprout utopian ideas and fantastic notions; in his play *The Birds*, war-weary citizens join the fowls of the air in making a Cloudcuckooland between heaven and earth, and the birds become masters of the universe; in the *Lysistrata* we find a theme which has proved still viable in this century, where the women refuse to let their men have sexual intercourse with them until the war is brought to a close; in *The Frogs*, Aristophanes takes his audience on an excursion into another world—to Hell; in *Peace*, performed first for an Athens that had been ten years at war, Trygaeus rides up to heaven on the back of a giant beetle to see Zeus. (Perhaps Lucian was thinking of this flight when his Menippus also ascends.) But such flights of fantasy, permissible in comedy, were forbidden in tragedy; and so it still is today.

In the *True History*, waterspouts and winds carry a Greek ship to the Moon, which proves to be inhabited. The travellers find that the king of the Moon and the king of the Sun are at war over the colonisation of Jupiter. Fantastic monsters are employed in the battles; and the minions of the Sun build a double wall between Sun and Moon, so that the Selenites live in permanent eclipse. They surrender.

One of the clauses of the peace treaty is that both sides shall send a colony to the Morning Star (Venus). The travellers sail their ship to the new colony and then steer for the Zodiac, leaving the Sun to port, until they reach Lycnopolis, a city inhabited by lamps that speak. They also see Cloudcuckooland, witness a battle of giants, and visit a city built of gold and precious stones. Later, they come to the Isle of Dreams, where Antiphon invents dreams, of different kinds:

Some long, beautiful, and pleasant, others little and ugly; there are likewise some golden ones, others poor and mean; some winged and of an immense size, others tricked out as it were for pomps and ceremonies, for gods and kings; some we met with that we had seen at home; these came up to and saluted us as their old acquaintance, whilst others putting us first to sleep, treated us most magnificently, and promised that they would make us kings and noblemen; some carried us into our own country, showed us our friends and relations, and brought us back again the same day. Thirty days and nights we remained in this place, being most luxuriously feasted, and fast asleep all the time . . .°

Thus the first appearance of a Dream Palace, which has made several appearances in the fiction of our day.

Many translators of Lucian, wisely anxious to preserve the pure Anglo-Saxon world from dirty Mediterranean habits, have omitted the more titillating passages from his text—for instance his description of the custom of Lunar inhabitants to wear artificial private parts, which apparently work quite well. The rich have them made of ivory, the poor ones of wood. This disgusting information establishes Lucian's claim to be, not only the first writer of interplanetary fiction, but the first writer to describe prosthetic limbs and cyborgs.

Lucian's tales now read like pure fantasy, although for centuries they were highly regarded as speculative fiction. A charming example of this change in attitude taking place occurs in a little Victorian edition of Lucian's two trips to the Moon, published in Cassell's National Library. This edition contains the following footnote with supplement by later editor, inserted at the point where Earth is seen hanging in the lunar sky like a Moon: "Modern astronomers are, I think, agreed that we are to the moon just the same as the moon is to us. Though Lucian's history may be false, therefore his philosophy, we see, was true (1780). (The moon is not habitable, 1887)." The disappointments of progress.

We no longer expect anything but entertainment from Lucian, and that he provides, though he somewhat spoils his joke by launching on it with the remark that he expects that the reader "will not only be pleased with the novelty of the plan, and the variety of lies, which I have told with an air of truth, but with the tacit allusions so frequently made, not, I trust, without some degree of humour, to our ancient poets, historians, and philosophers, who have told us some most miraculous and incredible stories . . ."

Under the drift of centuries, interplanetary voyages were forgotten. Spiritual voyages were another matter; the progression of mankind in his

° Translation by Dr. Thomas Franklin.

frail coracle of civilisation is itself a spiritual voyage, which naturally finds its embodiment in tales of difficult journeyings. But the finest mediaeval minds were in quest for a unity between life on Earth and the Heavenly Father. In the words of Sir Kenneth Clark, "Behind all the fantasy of the Gothic imagination there remained, on two different planes, a sharp sense of reality. Mediaeval man could see things very clearly, but he believed that . . . appearances should be considered as nothing more than symbols or tokens of an ideal order, which was the only true reality."*

Perhaps the form of those times closest to science fiction was the bestiary, derived from Greek sources, in which animals were endowed with human attributes and enacted moral or satirical tales, just like aliens in today's science fiction. The history of Reynard the Fox is the best known of these tales in English-speaking countries, thanks to a translation printed by Caxton in 1481. Reynard and Chanticleer the Cock also figure in Chaucer's "Nun's Priest's Tale" in *The Canterbury Tales*.

Another popular beast was *The Golden Ass* of Apuleius, a contemporary of Lucian. This is a satire in which a man is turned into an ass and tells the tale of the follies and vices of his various owners. The transformation takes place accidentally, through the carelessness of an enchantress's servant. Such tales, always plentiful, take us too close to magic and too far from science fiction.

With the dawn of the Renaissance, men developed new ways in which to think and feel. They rediscovered the classical past and, among the great tally of its treasures, the writings of its poets, historians, and philosophers, including Lucian.

Lucian's writings in Greek and Latin ran through several editions in the late fifteenth and sixteenth centuries, and in 1634 were translated into English by Francis Hickes. The translation was widely read; the influence on later writers, both of the *True History* and *Icaro-Mennipus*, was considerable. Lucian is said to have inspired Rabelais' *Voyages of Pantagruel*, Cyrano de Bergerac's *Voyage dans la Lune*, and Swift's *Gulliver's Travels*, and no doubt all those eminent authors read their great predecessor avidly, for writers instinctively seek out others of their own persuasion; but there is a great deal of difference between imitation and emulation,

---

* Kenneth Clark, *Civilisation: A Personal View*, Harper & Row, 1969.

and the most original authors often begin on premises laid down by others.* Great authors borrow; little authors steal.

The early seventeenth century was a fantastic age, an age of great voyages and discoveries; of the writing of utopias and death-enriched plays; of a widening universe and the first use of the decimal point; of the sailing of the Pilgrim Fathers; of the discovery of the circulation of the blood and the invention of cribbage; of the founding of colleges and universities, the establishment of colonies and the perfection of the flint-lock; and the findings of Galileo, Kepler, and Van Leeuwenhoek. Exploration clearly had an appeal, and the times, rather than literary influence, may be blamed for the increase in fictitious Moon voyages.

Coincidentally, Kepler's *Somnium* (or *Dream*) was published in the same year as Hickes' translation of Lucian, in Frankfurt; Kepler had then been dead four years. Johannes Kepler (1571–1630) was a German mathematician, astrologer, and astronomer who helped lay the foundations of modern astronomy. Kepler's narrative is cast as a dream, and his observer, Duracotus, ascends to the Moon by supernatural means. Once we are on the Moon, however, science takes over, and Duracotus expatiates on that globe as recently revealed by telescope. Cold and heat are more extreme than on Earth; there are dreadful nights a fortnight long, unrelieved by moonlight. As the climate differs from Earth, so does the landscape: mountains are higher, valleys deeper. The ground is perforated by caves and grottoes. Cloud cover and rain prevail over the near side of the lunar globe.

Kepler introduces life to the Moon, but the living things are made to conform to the lunar environment. Although they are not drawn in detail, an impression of variety and grotesquery is given. One sentence gives us a foretaste of Wells' *First Men on the Moon:* "Things born in the ground— they are sparse on the ridges of the mountains—generally begin and end their lives on the same day, with new generations springing up daily."†

We acknowledge this as fantasy now. But Kepler conformed to or formed the science of his own day. That claim of scientific accuracy was

---

* Thus, Lucian himself conceived the *True History* as a parody of those Greek historians who magnified every detail into something grander than it began; while Swift's *Gulliver's Travels* began as a minute lampoon of the politics of Queen Anne's reign.

† The translation is Rosen's. The *Somnium* is very short. After it was written, Kepler added notes, almost one per sentence, which run to many more pages than the *Dream* itself. Kepler's *Somnium: The Dream, or Posthumous Work on Lunar Astronomy,* translated with a commentary by Edward Rosen, Madison, 1967.

made on behalf of Jules Verne, two centuries later, as if it were a great novelty.

Kepler had a scientific vision of the Moon; his *Somnium* is straightforwardly astronomical exposition. He established no utopias there. But utopias were still being built. A confusion of wonderful voyages with utopias is of long standing; once a writer has got his travellers to his obscure region on Earth, or to another world, or to the future, he must find something for them to do, and on the whole writers divide fairly sharply between those who have their protagonists lecture and listen to lectures, and those who have them menaced by or menacing local equivalents of flora, fauna, and Homo sapiens.

If this division of interest is still with us, at least the vexing problem of how to reach the Moon has been solved. It has in actuality proved far more costly than any storyteller ever dared guess. Lunar-voyage devices come very inexpensively until we reach the days of Verne and Wells and, even then, the Baltimore Gun Club finances their vehicle, while Cavor has comfortable private means. Before those days, nature, or a balloon, can be relied on to do the trick at a minimum of expense.

Supernatural means of travel were the cheapest of all. Athanasius Kircher, in his *Itinerarium Exstaticum* of 1656, produces an angel who takes the chief protagonist on a Grand Tour of the heavens to complete his education—a pleasant idea that could still be made to work fictionally today.

The next method requiring least human modification was to ascend with the aid of birds. Bishop Francis Godwin's *Man in the Moone: or A Discourse of a Voyage Thither by Domingo Gonsales* appeared in 1638 and remained popular for something like two centuries. Godwin's Gonsales trains some swans until, by degrees, they learn to carry him through the air. The swans or "gansas," twenty-five of them teamed together, save Gonsales from shipwreck. Unfortunately, Gonsales has overlooked the migratory habits of gansas, and his team heads for the Moon, where they hibernate, taking him with them.

Gonsales finds the lunar world a utopia inhabited by giants. The giants are long-lived and any wounds they receive quickly heal again; even if you get your head cut off, apply a certain herb and it will be joined together once more. But murders are unknown, and all other crimes; while the women are so beautiful that (claims Gonsales) no man ever wants to leave his wife. This peaceful state comes about because the

Moon-dwellers detect potential sinners at birth and ship them off to Earth, where most of them are deposited in North America (the first appearance of an idea to enjoy fresh currency in twentieth-century fiction).

Despite these delights, and the beautiful colours on the Moon, Gonsales wants to get back to his family. The Prince Pylonas gives him jewels, and he sets off for Earth with his gansas—landing in China, where he is imprisoned as a magician.

In the same year that this pleasant fiction was published, John Wilkins' *Discovery of a New World* appeared. This is a speculative book concerning the possibilities of travelling to the Moon, with discussions of what life there might be like—what we would call popular science. And, like Godwin's book, it was popular. The times were ripe for it and, with many a reference back to Daedalus, the more *au fait* citizens of the seventeenth and eighteenth centuries began to discuss the possibilities of flight. Although this eagerness to extend man's dimensions of experience has often been mocked, it lies deep in many hearts, and is summed up in John Keats' words, "Ever let the fancy roam, Pleasure never is at home"— though in present context, Milton perhaps puts it better: "Headlong joy is ever on the wing."

From imagining wings that would assist flight it is a short step to imagining humans with wings. Robert Paltock's *The Life and Adventures of Peter Wilkins* appeared in 1751, and remained popular for many years. After being shipwrecked, Peter Wilkins discovers the country of flying men and women; he marries one of them, Youwarkee, and the loving pair have seven children, some winged, some not.

Also in 1751, *The Life and Astonishing Transactions of John Daniel,* by Ralph Morris, was published, in which human flight is achieved by a veritable "engine," a platform on which two can stand and work the wings by means of levers; John Daniel and his son Jacob take themselves up to the Moon in this machine.

The corniest way of getting to the Moon was the one chosen by Cyrano de Bergerac, in *Voyage dans la Lune*, a comic history first published in 1657, and followed later by *L'Histoire des États et Empires du Soleil*. The two are known together as *L'Autre Monde*.*

---

* The best English translation of the two books is *Other Worlds*, translated and with an introduction by Geoffrey Strachan, 1965.

Bergerac makes himself his own hero, and fastens a quantity of small bottles filled with dew to his body. The Sun sucks him up with the dew, and he lands on the Moon in a couple of paragraphs.

So begins the jolliest of all lunar books, with Cyrano spouting unlikely explanations for amazing phenomena for all the world like a modern sf writer. He does the same in the second book, when he lands on the Sun, glibly explaining why he has no appetite in space, why the Sun's heat does not burn, what causes sleep, how he became invisible, how the inhabitants of the Sun grow from the ground in a sort of spontaneous generation, and so forth.

Cyrano meets Campanella, author of *The City of the Sun,* and together they encounter a woman whose husband has committed a curious crime.

"Since you are a philosopher," replied the woman, addressing Campanella, "I must unburden my heart to you before I go any further.

"To explain the matter that brings me here in a few words, you must know that I am coming to complain of a murder committed against the person of my youngest child. This barbarian, whom I have here, killed it twice over although he was its father."

We were extremely puzzled by this speech and asked to know what she meant by a child killed twice over.

"You must know that in our country," the woman replied, "there is, among the other Statutes of Love, a law which regulates the number of embraces a husband may give his wife. That is why every evening each doctor goes the rounds of all the houses in his area, where, after examining the husbands and wives, he will prescribe for them, according to their good or bad health, so many conjunctions for the night. Well, my husband had been put down for seven. However, angered by some rather haughty remarks I had addressed to him as we were getting ready to retire, he did not come near me all the time we were in bed. But God, who avenges those who are wronged, permitted this wretch to be titillated in a dream by the recollection of the embraces he was unjustly denying me, so that he let a man go to waste.

"I told you his father had killed him twice over, because by refusing to make him come into existence, he caused him not to be, which was the first murder, but subsequently he caused him never to be able to be, which was the second. A common murderer knows that the man whose days he cuts short *is no more,* but none of them could cause a man *never to have been.* Our magistrates would have dealt with him as he deserved if the cunning wretch had not excused himself by saying that he would have fulfilled his conjugal duty, had he not been afraid (as a result of embracing me in the height of the rage I had put him in) to beget a choleric man."

All writers of fantastic tales feed on their predecessors. Swift took a pinch of wit from Cyrano—about whose book Geoffrey Strachan, its translator, justly says, it "is a poem from an age when poetry, physics, metaphysics, and astronomy could all still exist side by side in one book." There is no need to detail further flights of fancy to the Moon. In any case, Marjorie Hope Nicolson has already produced a first-rate account, readable and scholarly, of the subject,\* which is not likely to be bettered; while Philip Grove has defined the genre and provided a list of two hundred and fifteen such voyages published in the eighteenth century alone.† These exemptions spare us much that is tedious now or has had time to allow its tediousness to mature.

The great utopias have better claim to our attention, for utopianism or its opposite, dystopianism, is present in every vision of the future—there is little point in inventing a future state unless it provides a contrast with our present one. This is not to claim that the great utopias are science fiction. Their intentions are moral or political. Often they are in dialogue form, as is the great exemplar, Thomas More's *Utopia*, first published in Latin in 1516 and translated into English in 1551—itself indebted to Plato's *Republic*.

> "Now am I like to Plato's city
> Whose fame flieth the world through"

The idea of utopianists, like our town-planners, is to produce something that is orderly and functions well. Citizens have to fit into this pattern as into a town plan. More's Utopia is quite a friendly and sensible place, yet some of its restrictions sound chilly to readers who live in a world of flourishing police states.

When More's Utopians go outdoors, they all wear the same kind of cloak, of one colour. There are a number of cities in Utopia, but all are alike; "whoso knoweth one of them knoweth them all." The citizens must get a licence to travel from one city to another. Furthermore, "dice-play and such other foolish and pernicious games they know not." Farewell,

---

\* Marjorie Hope Nicolson, *Voyages to the Moon*, New York, 1949.
† Philip B. Grove, *The Imaginary Voyage in Prose Fiction*, 1941.

Earth's bliss! Good-bye, Las Vegas! It is of small consolation to learn that they "use two games not much unlike the chess."

More offers higher things. His little world has sane laws and is wisely ruled. The citizens have fine gardens and hospitals. Bondmen perform all the drudgery, mercenaries fight all the wars. Conversation, music, and banquets are welcome, although ale houses and stews are forbidden, as is astrology. Many passages show the human side of More, not least in the question of courtship.

> For a sad and honest matron sheweth the woman, be she maid or widow, naked to the wooer. And likewise a sage and discreet man exhibiteth the wooer naked to the woman . . . The endowments of the body cause the virtues of the mind more to be esteemed and regarded, yea, even in the marriages of wise men.

It is a useful precaution—breakers of wedlock are sternly dealt with in Utopia. For this is a religious land and, although one's own faith may be followed without persecution, only the pious are allowed to teach children and adolescents.

Such sober and worthy plans as More's for a better life on Earth have become remote from us nowadays; our belief in the perfectibility of man and the triumph of altruism over self-interest is less strong than was the case in earlier centuries; a desperate environmentalism has become the new utopianism.

We have seen the noble line of utopias—such as Johann Valentin Andreae's *Christianopolis* (1619), Francis Bacon's *The New Atlantis* (1627), Tommaso Campanella's *Civitas Solis* (1623) (for which Campanella was faced with the Spanish Inquisition), James Harrington's *Commonwealth of Oceana* (1656), and those of the nineteenth century, such as Samuel Butler's *Erewhon* (1872), W. H. Hudson's *A Crystal Age* (1887), and Edward Bellamy's *Looking Backward* (1888)—we have seen this noble line of utopias slide down like sinking liners into such depths of dystopianism as Eugene Zamyatin's *We* (1920) and Orwell's *1984* (1949). Morality, the system whereby man controls himself, has become another weapon in the state armoury, whereby it controls its citizens.

A decline in the general belief in political systems; a profound questioning of the effects of technology; even the retreat from so much as lip service towards established religion; these are some of the factors that render the construction of utopias in the immediate future unlikely.

Aldous Huxley's *Island* (1962)—in common with its distinguished predecessors, more a polemic than a novel—may be the last considerable utopia
we shall see until the world climate alters; and even on Huxley's well-
favoured island, the people sustain themselves with drugs and acknowledge how transient is the status quo, threatened with immediate collapse
by the end of the book. Had this collapse been threatened by a polluted
ocean and broken chains of the life cycle, rather than by invasion by
enemy forces, then the message might have seemed more prophetic.

The trouble with utopias is that they are too orderly. They rule out the
irrational in man, and the irrational is the great discovery of the last
hundred years. They may be fantasy, but they reject fantasy as part of
man—and this is a criticism that applies to most of the eighteenth-century
literature with which we deal in this chapter. However appealing they
may be, there is no room in them for the phenomenon of a Shakespeare—
or even a Lovecraft.

And yet, among the distinguished seventeenth-century utopias, there
is one which could almost contain Shakespeare and Lovecraft, and even
E. E. Smith for that matter. Of course, we have to stretch our terms
somewhat wide to think of John Milton's *Paradise Lost* (1667) as a
utopia, but of the influence of this great poem there is no doubt. Particularly appealing are its vistas of an unspoilt Earth, while the passages
which deal with Hell, and Satan's lonely flight from Hell across the gulfs
of space to God's new world, still retain their magnificence. Satan in
particular is as puissant as a present-day Apollo when he

> Springs upward like a pyramid of fire,
> Into the wild expanse, and through the shock
> Of fighting elements, on all sides round
> Environ'd, wins his way . . . (Book 2)

Like his near contemporary, John Donne, Milton infuses his poetry
with "the New Philosophy."

From Milton's imagined worlds and exalted poetry, we bring ourselves
back to Earth with the aid of Peter Wilkins, the adventurer who married
a winged lady and had seven children by her.

For Wilkins' adventures encompass another science fictional device at
which we should look; the subterranean journey which discovers human
beings living underground. Later—and not much later—this will develop
into journeys to the centre of the Earth.

Wilkins' ship gets into trouble near Africa. A strong and remorseless current draws it towards the South Pole and eventually through an archway under an island, into a strange underground world. "I could perceive the boat to fall with incredible violence, as I thought, down a precipice, and suddenly whirled round and round with me, the water roaring on all sides, and dashing against the rock with a most amazing noise." The boat drifts in complete darkness down a subterranean river, delivering Wilkins into an immense cavern, where flying people live.

Here is more than one incident to be found later in Poe. The subterranean descent also carries reminders of a book published ten years before *Peter Wilkins*—Holberg's *Journey to the World Underground*. Holberg's is one of the books, together with Campanella's utopia *The City of the Sun*, which Poe lists as being in Roderick Usher's library—"the books which, for years, had formed no small portion of the mental existence of the invalid."

In turn, Holberg's work owes much to *Gulliver's Travels*, as well as to such earlier subterranean voyages as Athanasius Kircher's *Mundus Subterraneus* of 1665. But Holberg has some curious ideas of his own.

Baron Ludvig Holberg was born in Bergen, Norway, in 1684. He was a great traveller, and his writings, particularly his plays, brought him fame. *Nicolai Klimii Iter Subterraneum* (Holberg wrote it in Latin) was first published in Germany in 1741. It won immediate popularity and was translated and published—and is still being translated and published—into many languages.

Niels Klim is potholing in the mountains near Bergen when he falls down a steep shaft, and keeps falling for some time, for all the world like Alice. He emerges into a wonderland no less remarkable than Alice's, tumbling into the space at the centre of the Earth and becoming one more heavenly body circling about a central Sun.

Klim lands unhurt on the planet Nazar, which proves to be amazingly like Earth as far as the environment is concerned, except that night is almost as light as day. "Nay, the night may be thought more grateful than the day, for nothing can be conceived more bright and splendid than that light which the solid firmament receives from the sun and reflects back upon the planet, insomuch that it looks (if I may be allowed the expression) like one universal moon." Another difference from Earth is that the intelligent species on Nazar is perambulating trees.

This novelty is rather a distraction than otherwise, since, apart from their arboreality, the creatures are there for the same reason as Swift's Lilliputians and Brobdingnagians: to make reasonable man reflect on his own unreasonableness, to make what appears natural seem topsy-turvy. Trees resist serving didactic purposes.

The trees show local differences from land to land, and their paradoxes are paraded for Klim in a series of what might be called mini-utopias: farmers are most highly regarded of all citizens in one land; in another the more honour the state piles on a citizen, the more he acts with humility, since "he was the greatest debtor to the commonwealth"; in another, only the young are allowed to govern, for the older people grow, the more wanton and voluptuous they become; and so on. In one of the most curious countries, the inhabitants never sleep; as a result, they are always in a hurry and confusion, and are obsessed by details—for example, Klim looks into a local bookshop and notices a *Description of the Cathedral* in twenty-four volumes, and *Of the Use of the Herb Slac* in thirteen volumes. But none of these curious situations are developed— Holberg flicks them past our eyes like colour slides—involving Klim in them, for the most part, merely as observer.

Klim does have some adventures. He is banished by birds to the Firmament, which he finds full of monkeys; is wooed by an attractive lady monkey ("I thought it better to be exposed to the vengeance of disappointed love than to disturb the laws of human nature by mixing my blood with a creature not of the human species"); is sent for a galley slave; gets shipwrecked; wins a war; becomes Emperor of the Quamites, Niels the Great; grows overbearing; suffers revolution; escapes; and falls back up the same hole down which he fell twelve years previously!

Klim's journey is now little more than a curiosity. Overshadowing it are the two great books of fake-travel which preceded it, Defoe's *Robinson Crusoe* and Swift's *Gulliver's Travels*. Both books include shipwrecks in remote parts of the globe, both are honourable precursors of the science fiction genre, both are written in the sound style of their age which has guaranteed them wide readership even in ours.

Often when talking of science fiction and the ur-science fiction preceding it, one is like a traveller walking down an unkempt lane, over the other side of the hedge from which lie the cultivated gardens of Literature. But occasionally lane and garden become one, and then the prospect widens out, to the benefit of both wild and sown. So it is in the age of

Defoe and Swift, when the enormous advances in pure science of the previous century, the findings of Galileo and Isaac Newton, were still providing speculative fuel.

Swift and Defoe are writers very different in character. Swift belongs to the mandarin tradition of his friend Pope, the great Augustan poet; Defoe is much more of the people. We must resist the temptation here to discuss them and their tremendous variety of writings, Defoe's especially, and concentrate on what we may call the science fictional element in their books.

Daniel Defoe (1659–1731) was the son of a butcher in Cripplegate. His life was filled with cross currents of religion, politics, and economics. He was a Puritan, born on the eve of the Restoration, who lived through the bursting of the South Sea Bubble. All these influences are apparent in his best novel. As for literary influence, this is the place to mention, belatedly, that wonderful journey which was to be found in almost every English home from its first appearance in the sixteen-seventies until the end of the Victorian times: Bunyan's *Pilgrim's Progress*.

After a crowded life, enormously productive as a journalist, Defoe in his sixties took to writing novels, or rather fake memoirs, such as *Moll Flanders* and—a book which Poe surely knew and cherished—*The Journal of the Plague Year*.

*The Life and Strange Surprising Adventures of Robinson Crusoe, of York, Mariner* was published in 1719. It was an immediate success. Popularity seems to have been a test of merit, for the book has never been out of print since, despite all changes of taste in the past two hundred and fifty years. Crusoe on his lonely island at the mouth of the Orinoco (and he was there for twenty-five years before setting eyes on his man Friday) has as perennial a fascination as Prospero on his island, also marooned in the same quarter of the world.

It is conceivable that if some kind of global ballot were taken to determine the best-known incident in all English literature, then Crusoe's discovery of the solitary footprint in the sand would be voted first, or at least very soon after the apparition of the ghost of Hamlet's father, Oliver Twist's asking for more, and the death of Little Nell! That alien imprint has proved indelible.

The science-fictional attractions of *Robinson Crusoe* are obvious: the desert-island theme is eternal, whether transposed to William Golding's island in *Lord of the Flies* or to another planet (as was expertly done by

Rex Gordon, paying eponymous tribute to sources, in *No Man Friday*, set on Mars). But beyond this lies a deeper attraction.

In the slow plodding of Crusoe's mind, as he creates in the wilderness of his island a model of the society he has left, and as solitude forces him to come to terms with himself, Defoe builds up a picture of isolation which still stalks our overpopulated times. No imagined planet was ever such a setting for the drama of Man Alone as is *Robinson Crusoe*. Though the emphasis on religion may have little appeal to modern tastes, a patient reading of the text reveals a book that lumbers to real greatness. As one critic has said of Defoe,* "He was never brilliant; but he employed dullness almost magically."

Defoe dropped religious orders; Swift took them.

Jonathan Swift (1667–1745) was born in Ireland of English parents. His father died before his birth; he was separated from his mother soon after birth. How far these facts, which find an echo in the life history of Edgar Allan Poe, influenced Swift's sense of separation from humanity, we cannot determine. He was brought to England as a baby, later returning to Ireland to complete his education at Trinity College, Dublin. Thereafter, his hopes, like his life, vacillated between the two countries. He was ordained in 1694.

Swift became a great pamphleteer, and was deeply involved in the politics of his time. Disappointed in his political ambitions in England, he returned to Ireland, where he eventually won great popularity as Dean of the Cathedral of St. Patrick. The last few years of his life were tormented by increasing madness, a fate that sometimes overcomes those otherwise most sane.

Swift's was a mysterious life, full of ironies. Romantics and psychiatrists have been attracted to the riddle of Swift's relationships with the two women in his life, his "Stella" and his "Vanessa." His remains lie now in the cathedral in Dublin, beneath the epitaph he composed for himself, *"Ubi saeva indignatio ulterius cor lacerare nequit":* "Where fierce indignation can no longer tear the heart."

Most of his many writings, like his women, appeared under guises, anonymously or pseudonymously. As if in retaliation, the public has always rejected the title of his most famous and living book, *Travels into*

---

* George Sampson, *The Concise Cambridge History of English Literature,* 1941.

*Several Remote Nations of the World: In Four Parts* (1726), and insists on calling it familiarly *Gulliver's Travels*.

It is fortunate that this masterly work does not count as science fiction, being satirical and/or moral in intention rather than speculative, for, if it did so count, then perfection would have been achieved straightaway, and the genre possibly concluded as soon as it had begun. But the book comes clawing its way out of any category into which critics try to place it.

Swift uses every wile known to Defoe, and more besides—the use of maps, for example—to persuade a reader that he holds yet another plodding volume of travel in his hand. Gulliver seems at first to resemble Crusoe, of York, Mariner—a solid man, a surgeon in this case, using a good plain prose, and as shipwreck-prone as his predecessor. But Gulliver proves to be one of the cleverest heroes a writer ever set up in a work of fiction, at once simple and sly, rash and cowardly, a man who likes to think himself unwaveringly honest and yet who is all too ready to trim his sail to whatever wind prevails. It is a mistake to identify Gulliver with Swift.

But Swift makes it difficult for readers not to identify with Gulliver. He spins so many layers of irony that we are bound to get caught somewhere.

The four voyages lead us ever deeper into Swift's web. We share Gulliver's amusement at the Lilliputians and their petty affairs, so that we are bound to share Gulliver's humiliation at the court of Brobdingnag. In these two first voyages, scale is considered in the worth of human affairs; in the third voyage, to the flying island of Laputa, we see what intellectual endowments are worth; while, in the last voyage, to the land in which Houyhnhnms and Yahoos are contrasted, we see what our animal nature is worth.

This splendid fourth part has acted like a lodestone on satirists since—on Holberg, as we have seen, and on Wells, Huxley, and Orwell. To the courteous race of horses, the Houyhnhnms, the filthy Yahoos are animals or, at best, peasants and servants. The Yahoos overwhelm Gulliver with disgust. Yet, when his clothes are off, he is almost indistinguishable from them; indeed, once while swimming, he is set on by a lust-mad female Yahoo. The Yahoos are humanity.

It is as if Swift, when drawing his portrait of the Yahoos, had a horror-comical vision of Stone Age hordes, long before theories of evolution had uncovered such an idea to human contemplation. Or he is setting up an image of the Id in contrast to the Super-ego of the Houyhnhnms. One of the book's strengths is its openness to differing readings.

Certainly Swift's mighty satire has gained power and meaning in the last century. It is indestructible, defying time and final exegesis.

*Gulliver's Travels* has had many interpreters. Thackeray, in mid-Victorian times, spoke for the opposition when (referring in particular to the fourth part) he called it "A monster, gibbering shrieks and gnashing imprecations against mankind—tearing down all shreds of modesty, past all sense of manliness and shame; filthy in word, filthy in thought, furious, raging, obscene." In another category entirely is the Irish bishop—or so Swift claimed in a letter to Pope—who read the book and declared he didn't believe a word of it.

Yet what book can compare with Swift's? It unshakeably has the vote of humanity, selling ten thousand copies in the first three weeks of its long life, and being translated and pirated at once all over Europe. So it has gone on ever since, bowdlerised, truncated, serialised, cartoonised, animated, plagiarised—and read over and over, like a dark obverse of *Pilgrim's Progress*.

The impulse which created this marvellous and mysterious book was complex. Swift intended to amuse a cultivated audience; readers have recognised a strong salting of truth in his view of humanity; and the fantasy of big and little people, of civilised horses, races of immortals, and the quizzing of the dead, all have a perennial appeal. And, one must add, this is some of the rarest wit delivered in some of the finest language.

Many of Swift's best effects are achieved through Gulliver's blind pride, which insists on appealing to something base or petty to bolster what he feels is a worthy claim.

Talking of trade in England ("the dear place of my nativity"), Gulliver tells his master, the Houyhnhnm, how European ships go out to all oceans and bring all sorts of provisions back. "I assured him, that this whole globe of earth must be at least three times gone round, before one of our better female Yahoos could get her breakfast, or a cup to put it in." This is the method of Pope's *Rape of the Lock*. Belinda opens her toilet box:

> Unnumbered Treasures ope at once, and here
> The various offerings of the World appear.

The question is one of reasonable scale.

Again, when "my master" is wondering at the Yahoos' disposition towards dirt and nastiness, compared with a natural love of cleanliness in other animals, "I could have easily vindicated human kind from the imputation of singularity upon the last article, if there had been any *swine* in that country (as unluckily for me there were not), which although it may be a *sweeter* quadruped than a Yahoo, cannot, I humbly conceive, in justice pretend to more cleanliness . . ."

Again, in Laputa, Gulliver's interpreter remarks that he has "observed long life to be the universal desire and wish for mankind. That whoever had one foot in the grave, was sure to hold back the other as strongly as he could."

These brief examples could be infinitely multiplied. They show a kind of *mistaken reasonableness* at work. If we accept *Gulliver* (among all the other things it is) as a great debate on Reason, many of the problems that have confronted commentators in the fourth part will vanish. At the end of his four-decker maze, we meet with Swift's creatures of pure reason, the Houyhnhnms. This is the climax of Gulliver's search, and he is converted to their outlook on life, lock, stock, and barrel—so much so that, when he returns to England, he cannot bear the proximity of his loving wife and children, regarding them as Yahoos.

We must always beware of Gulliver when he admires anything; his name does not begin with "Gull" for nothing. This is part of Swift's "fierce and insolent game," as F. R. Leavis calls it. These horse-shaped children of Reason are cold, uninteresting, and condescending—indifferent alike (as Gulliver becomes) to the lives of their children or the deaths of their spouses. They have limited vocabularies and limited imaginations, which is a fairly strong clue to Swift's real attitude to them. As George Orwell says, they are also racists;[*] yet Orwell, who numbers *Gulliver* among his six indispensable books, makes the mistake of confusing Swift with Gulliver and believing that it is Swift who admires the Houyhnhnms.

What Swift is showing us in the Houyhnhnm culture is a warning: this is what a utopia would be like if governed by pure reason: the nearest thing to death. Horrible though the Yahoos are, they are the oppressed, they have more life and vitality than their oppressors—and they probably have more of Swift's sympathy than is generally allowed.[†]

---

[*] George Orwell, "Politics vs. Literature," *Collected Essays*, 1961.

[†] Orwell should have got the message, since he appears to feel sympathy as well as distaste for his 1984 Proles—who are literary offspring of the Yahoos.

In *Gulliver's Travels*, black is never opposed to white: even in despicable Lilliput, wise laws are passed for rewarding virtue; Swift supposes us cultivated enough to be able to compare faulty states of living, and to understand (as we do when reading Aldous Huxley) that the civilised virtues may be represented only covertly in the text, for instance in a pure and urbane prose style. As his subject is Reason, so reason is needed to enjoy his entertainments to the full.

This is why *Gulliver's Travels* works so well over the centuries, why it continues to delight: paralleled by its pure vein of fantasy expressed in terms of naïve realism goes its intellectual paradox, for we have to be better than Yahoos to recognise that they are us, we they. So we are raised to the level of Swift's own ironical vision. Despite the subject matter that Thackeray disliked so much, the effect of this great book is to exalt us.

From the two masterpieces of Augustan prose, *Robinson Crusoe* and *Gulliver's Travels*, we move on over thirty years to glance at two other masterpieces which appeared at the same time—and a glance will have to be sufficient, for neither stand directly in the literary line developing towards science fiction, although, in their concern for the modern human predicament, they contain a great deal that is of interest to science fiction readers.

Voltaire's *Candide* was published in February 1759, to be followed less than two months later by Samuel Johnson's *Rasselas, Prince of Abyssinia*. Johnson was later heard to say that "if they had not been published so closely one after the other that there was no time for imitation, it would have been in vain to deny that the scheme of that which came latest was taken from the other." Coincidentally, Bulwer-Lytton's *The Coming Race* was published just before Butler's *Erewhon* in the following century, when Butler was at pains to deny that the scheme of his book was taken from the other.*

Like *Robinson Crusoe* and *Gulliver's Travels*, *Rasselas* and *Candide* were both immediate successes. Neither have been out of print since. Johnson's book was written in about a week, Voltaire's in three days: facts which should cause the modern denizens of Grub Street to take fresh heart.

* See the Preface to *Erewhon*, Enlarged Edition, 1901.

Both are cautionary tales against optimism. Voltaire's is much the more sprightly; but any reader susceptible to the cadences of prose will be attracted instantly by the noble melancholy with which Johnson embarks upon his narrative:

Ye who listen with credulity to the whispers of fancy, and pursue with eagerness the phantoms of hope; who expect that age will perform the promises of youth, and that the deficiencies of the present day will be supplied by the morrow: attend to the history of Rasselas, prince of Abyssinia.

In his attempts to escape from the happy valley in which he lives, Rasselas meets a man "eminent for his knowledge of the mechanic powers," who builds a flying machine. The machine absorbs a lot of work and time, and crashes in the end—not before the designer has made the perceptive remark, "What would be the security of the good, if the bad could at pleasure invade them from the sky?"

Whatever begins well, ends badly; the only consolation is the rueful moral to be drawn from it. In *Candide*, matters begin badly and get worse; the comedy is in the way Candide and his companions, Pangloss and Cunégonde, draw idiotically optimistic conclusions from each fresh disaster. Estrangement between hope and performance is complete; facts exist by the teeming multitude—they are interpreted according to individual temperament.

The nearest the utopian Candide gets to Utopia is in El Dorado, where the streets are paved with gold. There, pleasures are purely material, dinners always excellent. Courts of justice and parliament buildings do not exist; there are no prisons. But the Palace of Sciences has a gallery two thousand feet long, filled with mathematical and scientific instruments. Furthermore, the king's jokes are witty even in translation.

Voltaire, a French philosopher who wrote over ten million words, and produced a voluminous correspondence besides, had indulged his sense of surrealism before writing *Candide*, most notably in the two *contes Zadig, ou La Destinée* and *Micromégas* (1747 and 1752). In the former, Zadig's observation of clues which lead him to deduce that the queen's dog and the king's horse have passed qualify him as a predecessor of Poe's Auguste Dupin.

In *Micromégas*, a gigantic visitor from one of the planets of Sirius and his hardly less gigantic friend from Saturn arrive on Earth and fish a ship out of the Baltic. Holding it in the palm of one hand, the two giants examine it through a microscope and thus observe human beings aboard, with whom they talk. Rabelais was probably an influence here; Swift is also mentioned; but the inversion of having the space journey done *to* Earth rather than *from* it is characteristically Voltairean; so is the conversation. In the end, the two enormous visitors present the creatures of Earth with a volume in which, they promise, the explanation of the universe will be found.

When the secretary of the Academy of Sciences in Paris opens the volume, he finds it contains nothing but blank pages.

A reminder of this incident comes in *Candide*, in a passage of philosophical conversation between Candide and Martin which flows like Marx Brothers' dialogue:

"While we are on the subject, do you believe that the Earth was originally sea, as is stated in that great book which belongs to the captain?" asks Candide.

"I believe nothing of the sort, any more than I do all the other fancies that have been foisted upon us through the centuries."

"But to what end, think you, was the world formed?"

"To turn our brains."

"Were you not astonished by the story I told you, of the two girls in the country of the Oreillons, who had monkeys for lovers?"

"Not in the least. I see nothing strange in such an infatuation. I have seen so many extraordinary things that now nothing is extraordinary to me."

"Do you think that men always slaughtered one another, as they do nowadays? . . . "

"Do you think that hawks have always devoured pigeons at every opportunity?" (Chapter 21)

*Candide* was written soon after the Lisbon earthquake, an event which shook civilised Europe as severely as the sinking of the *Titanic* shook Edwardian society. Especially in *Candide* and *Gulliver*, we get a strong impression of the times, and of those weaknesses of the flesh eternally with us—then much complicated by the prevalent scourge of syphilis, to which both authors pay due tribute.

These two remarkable books, together with *Robinson Crusoe* and *Rasselas*, are not quite classifiable as novels by any strict accountancy, and in that many of today's science fiction "novels" resemble them. But they are, all four, examples of masculine intellect at work, sketching in character with economy, not concerned with ambivalences of human relationships, interested in telling a tale and, above all, looking outward and drawing conclusions about the world in which the authors find themselves. In this respect, this brilliant eighteenth-century quartet resembles some of today's science fiction—say Thomas Disch's *Camp Concentration* or Robert Sheckley's *Dimension of Miracles*—more closely than the somewhat wishy-washy Moon voyages immediately preceding them.

A more feminine sensibility was to rise and dominate the novel form, exemplified in the next century by the novels of Jane Austen in its early years and Henry James in its late—and by E. M. Forster and Ivy Compton-Burnett and many others in our century. These are the idols that literary critics have, on the whole, preferred; for they provide more scope for rival interpretations; and they have reduced the serious novel to a business of relationships. But, in science fiction, the tradition of looking outwards and measuring man against the world he has made or found, and the tradition linked with it of telling a bold tale (even if it happens to be no more prodigal of incident than Crusoe's long years on his island), have continued, on the whole, uninterrupted. Even the philosophical flavour has been preserved, as in George Stewart's *Earth Abides*, Pohl and Kornbluth's *Wolfbane*, and many other novels.

If it is easy to see how most of the tales and stories in this chapter point towards science fiction, it is equally easy to see how they are *not* science fiction or, at the closest, are ur-science fiction. They remain tall stories mixed with utopian ideas (like Lucian's writings), or extensions of travellers' tall stories (like Godwin's *Man in the Moone*), or parodies of previous stories (like de Bergerac's *L'Autre Monde*), or fake-travels (like *Robinson Crusoe*), or political satires (like *Gulliver's Travels*), or philosophical squibs (like *Candide*), or mixtures of everything (like *Niels Klim*). They are time-locked, unable to visualise change working in their own societies. Their view of man vis-à-vis nature is a modest one—it operates on him, or he on it, randomly. Although they acknowledge fantasy, it is never acknowledged as an internal force, but rather as an outside phenomenon, to be taken seriously or for its own sake—none of the quality of Inwardness, in other words. They operate in the present, without recourse to the wider canvas of past or, more particularly, future.

The greatest of these books would be the greatest of science fiction books if they were science fiction; but they are not, and it is only the growth of the genre since, stimulated by their vigorous example, which makes them seem to resemble it as much as they do.

Walpole's *Castle of Otranto*, already mentioned, was published five years after *Candide*. It inaugurates a new genre, closeted and introspective, in which "atmosphere" usurps the name of action. It lies closer to dreams than to the affairs of the busy world, as Gothic mists curtain the Age of Reason.

When we turn to the nineteenth and twentieth centuries, we find these two streams mingling. Sometimes the external world seems to predominate, sometimes the internal.

Both have their place in science fiction, as in life.

# SCIENCE FICTION BEFORE GERNSBACK

## H. Bruce Franklin

Because the nineteenth century was the first century in which science fiction became a common form of writing, the present century is the first in which it is possible to look back at a body of science fiction created in a different age. From the perspective of the present, this science fiction of the past shows just how much an age determines and displays itself through what it sees as remote possibilities. American science fiction of the nineteenth century can now provide insights into nineteenth-century America, into the history of science and its relations to society, into the predictions, expectations, and fantasies of the present, and into the nature of science fiction, and, thereby, of all fiction.

Science, a cumulative process which exists to be superseded, and fiction, a series of individual attempts to create matter which cannot be superseded, have vastly differing relations to time. Insofar as any work of science fiction is a form of science it partakes of the temporality and impermanence of science and surrenders the timelessness of fiction. The most brilliant prognostications of the past have, ironically, little immediate relevance to the present human situation; we in 1966 may admire their brilliance but only from our superior position in later time—to look back upon them, no matter how admiringly, is to look down upon them. . . .

Science fiction did not, as many still believe, begin either in the twentieth century or with Jules Verne and H. G. Wells. Half a dozen

FROM *Future Perfect*, Oxford, 1966

histories of science fiction now start with Lucian of Samosata and trace the development of the form through Ariosto, Kepler, Cyrano de Bergerac, Mary Shelley, and Poe to the present. But even these surveys barely hint of the extent and depth of nineteenth-century science fiction. To take its full measure it would be necessary to add up all the tales of strange psychic phenomena, utopian romances, wondrous discoveries, and extraordinary voyages in time and space to be found in all the books and periodicals of the century. But to get at least a glimpse of science fiction's importance in nineteenth-century American fiction, one has only to look directly at the works of the most important writers, something which, surprisingly enough, no one seems to have done from this angle.

There was no major nineteenth-century American writer of fiction, and indeed few in the second rank, who did not write some science fiction or at least one utopian romance. Charles Brockden Brown, often called the first professional American author, built his romances on the spontaneous combustion of a living man, almost superhuman ventriloquism, hallucinations, extraordinary plagues, and extreme somnambulism; Washington Irving's most famous story is a time-travel story; James Fenimore Cooper produced a society of monkeys who live in the polar regions in *The Monikins* (1835) and placed a utopian society on a group of islands that rises suddenly out of the ocean in *The Crater* (1848); William Gilmore Simms contributed to the lost-continent tradition in *Atalantis* (1832) and helped swell the tide of fiction about mesmerism with "Mesmerides in a Stagecoach; or Passes en Passant"; Melville's first major work of pure fiction was *Mardi*, a full-length philosophical voyage to all kinds of utopian and would-be utopian societies, and he later wrote one of the first robot stories in English; Oliver Wendell Holmes, insofar as he was a writer of fiction, was a writer of science fiction; Mark Twain's *A Connecticut Yankee in King Arthur's Court* is one of the greatest of time-travel books, and he experimented with a number of other forms of science fiction; William Dean Howells, in addition to writing two utopian romances (*A Traveler from Altruria* and *Through the Eye of the Needle*), was an editor, collector, sympathetic critic, and composer of fiction which explored the outer limits of telepathy, clairvoyance, and teleportation (see, for instance, his own *Between the Dark and the Daylight* and *Questionable Shapes* and one collection he edited and introduced, *Shapes That Haunt the Dusk*); Henry James wrote a number of ghostly stories based on strange psychic phenomena and left at his death in hundreds of pages of manuscript the unfinished *The Sense of the Past,* a tale of time travel; Stephen Crane's "The Monster" is a splendid variation on the *Frankenstein* theme; even Mary E. Wilkins Freeman left both realism and ghosts behind long enough to write "The Hall Bedroom," a story about a disappearance into "the fifth dimension"; and Hawthorne, Poe, Fitz-James O'Brien, Edward Bellamy, and Ambrose Bierce all play leading roles in the history of science fiction.

In fact, not until late in the nineteenth century did much American fiction operate in a strictly realistic mode, that is, by presenting counterfeits of common events in a society familiar to its readers. Born during the height of English gothicism and growing up during the full bloom of English romanticism, American fiction developed as its most characteristic form what its authors called the "Romance." And whenever that word Romance appears in a title or preface, the reader may expect to find something at least verging on science fiction. Slowly during the nineteenth century, writers and readers began to be aware that a new form had developed from the old Romance—something which began to be called the scientific romance. The term "science fiction" may have first been used in the twentieth century, but that may be simply because of the earlier taboo against using nouns to modify nouns; as early as 1876 (as pointed out by Thomas D. Clareson) an introduction to William Henry Rhodes's collection of fantasy and science fiction entitled *Caxton's Book* discussed "scientific fiction" as a distinct genre.

The same crowds that jammed the lecture halls when scientists spoke and that supported dozens of popularizing scientific journals insatiably yearned for any conceivable kind of fictional marvel. Specialized magazines of fantasy and science fiction did not appear until late in the century simply because a very high percentage of the fiction published in the leading periodicals (*United States Magazine and Democratic Review, The Southern Literary Messenger, Graham's, Godey's, Harper's Monthly, Putnam's, Scribner's, The Atlantic Monthly, Cosmopolitan*) was fantasy and science fiction. This fiction appeared often, just as it does in several of today's science-fiction magazines, alongside factual popularizations of scientific progress and theories. It was not until the last years of the century that the so-called rise of realism tended to make science fiction seem a lowbrow and puerile entertainment. The incredible career of the science-fiction "dime" novel helped solidify this abject position, a position from which science fiction, most people would think, has yet to emerge completely. But those who find science fiction "sub-literary" fail to see that:

1. Most twentieth-century science fiction, like most nineteenth-century science fiction, like most realistic fiction of the nineteenth and twentieth centuries, like most fiction of any variety of any human time and place, must of necessity be ordinary rather than extraordinary.

2. Much science fiction is based on ancient literary assumptions—such as the premise that literature teaches and delights by being delightful teaching, and the Platonic premise that the creative artist should imitate ideal forms rather than actualities—that happen today to be at the bottom of the wheel of fashion.

3. A different kind of literature from realistic fiction, science fiction demands a different kind of reading.

# THE SITUATION TODAY

## Kingsley Amis

The next part of the story, covering the early years of modern science
fiction, depends for documentation upon sources difficult of access, for
there cannot be many files of forty-year-old magazines outside private
hands. The canon at this point tends to resemble those name-dropping
catalogues, part acknowledgements, part bibliography, that I seem to
remember coming up with some frequency in works of Middle English
Literature. However, in April, 1911, a story called "Ralph 124C 41+: a
romance of the year 2660" began to appear serially in a magazine called
*Modern Electrics*. The author, a certain Hugo Gernsback, was also
founder-editor of the magazine. Gernsback occupies a position in science
fiction analogous to that of George Lewis in jazz, or perhaps, to be scholarly, that of Jelly Roll Morton, who likewise is no more than a name to
most people, though Gernsback's has been commemorated in the name of
the Oscar of the science-fiction world, the trophy known as the Hugo. At
any rate, "Ralph 124C 41+" concerns the technological marvels invented
or demonstrated by the ridiculously resourceful eponymous hero, whose
plus sign represents membership of a sort of scientific Order of Merit, and
who starts off by burning up from three thousand miles away an ava-
lanche that threatens the heroine in her native Switzerland. After some
trouble with a pair of rival suitors, one human, the other Martian, Ralph

FROM *New Maps of Hell*, Harcourt, Brace, 1960

restores the dead girl to life by a complicated deep-freeze and blood-transfusion technique. Other wonders include the hypnobioscope, a second anticipation of Huxley's hypnopaedia, and three-dimensional colour television, a term which Gernsback is credited, if that is the word, with having invented. Various successors to "Ralph 124" & so on began to appear, chiefly in magazines supposedly devoted to popular-science articles, but it was not until 1926 that Gernsback was able to found the first journal exclusively dedicated to science fiction, *Amazing Stories*, which is still with us. At this time and for some years afterwards, science fiction continued to be overshadowed, as regards bulk and circulation, by work in two adjacent fields.

The more important of these is fantasy, which I tried to differentiate in the previous section. *Weird Tales*, the first magazine of modern fantasy, was founded three years earlier than *Amazing Stories*, and I need do no more than allude to the existence—somewhere in the background—of Algernon Blackwood, Lord Dunsany, and Cabell's *Jurgen*. The most representative writer of the *Weird Tales* school was H. P. Lovecraft, much of whose work is horror fiction of the kind popular in England, at any rate, in the '20's and '30's. Some of Lovecraft's stories, "The Dunwich Horror," for instance, achieve a memorable nastiness; one or two, like "The Rats in the Walls," cross the boundary into the field of the ghost story, or are so anthologised, and a piece called "The Colour Out of Space" occasionally finds its way into science-fiction collections, chiefly I imagine on account of its title. Lovecraft's intrinsic importance is small, but he does give that impression of being much more than ripe for psychoanalysis which pervades much fantasy and early science fiction, and the difficulty of categorising some of his work faithfully reflects the confusion of a period when non-realistic writing was in the throes of internal fission.

The other adjacent field competing with science fiction is conveniently described as space-opera, justly recalling the horse opera which, under a skin of molecular thinness, it so much resembles. In space opera, Mars takes the place of Arizona with a few physical alterations, the hero totes a blaster instead of a six-gun, bad men are replaced by bad aliens looking just like bad men with green skins and perhaps a perfunctory sixth digit, and Indians turn up in the revised form of what are technically known as bug-eyed monsters, a phrase often abbreviated to BEMs under the psychobiological law that terms frequently used will undergo shortening. Some commentators are opposed to the BEM, and adopt a characteristic self-righteousness in rapping poor Wells over the knuckles for having started the fashion with his Martians.[13] This attitude seems justified if the BEM is a mere surrealist orangutan, rushing off into the Venusian swamp with the heroine in his tentacles, but menace is in itself a legitimate effect, and I have read many a good BEM story. A. E. van Vogt's *Voyage of the Space Beagle*, for instance, moves well for sixty thousand words simply by introducing a succession of BEMs, each nastier than the one before.

Actually, BEMs are not a *sine qua non* of space opera, and early examples often fill up with stuff lifted from the historical novel, or if you like the parry-and-thrust opera, things like princesses and palace guards and ancient codes of honour. Later space opera fills up from the 'tec yarn, with galactic hoodlums, alien dope-runners, etc. The kind of setup I have been describing is plainly an important ancestor and collateral of much contemporary fare as seen in comic books and strips aimed at those of immature age or inclination, and it even afflicts the occasional story in the serious science-fiction magazines. Moreover, space-opera with a full complement of BEMs and a small staff of mad scientists attended by scantily clad daughters constitutes, I should guess, the main brand-image of science fiction in the minds of the less *au-courant* trend-hounds, those who haven't yet caught on to how frightfully significant it all is. To go back in the other direction: the ancestral figure in the development of space-opera is clearly Rider Haggard, who in a book like *She* provided elements that needed only to be shifted to Mars and eked out with a BEM or two to get the whole new show on the road. Edgar Rice Burroughs performed this very feat in 1912 with *Under the Moons of Mars*, later republished as *A Princess of Mars*, and in the next quarter of a century or so more than a dozen successors flowed from his dreadfully fluent pen. The degree of scientific interest here can be gauged from the way Burroughs shows his contempt for all interplanetary devices, from waterspouts to gravity insulators: the hero, trapped in a cave by a band of Apaches, simply finds himself on Mars, and at once enough starts happening in the way of green men for the more technical questions to be quietly dropped. Burroughs' most celebrated and profitable creation, Tarzan, is, incidentally, a more complicated person than the continuing spate of films about him would suggest. Far from being a mere rescuer of lost wayfarers and converser with animals, he meets several adventures stemming even more directly from Rider Haggard, *Tarzan and the Lost Empire* or *Tarzan and the City of Gold*, for instance, which represent a kind of terrestrial space-opera,* and at least once, in *Tarzan at the Earth's Core*, we retrace the steps of Verne, though with a less dignified gait.

During the 1930's, science fiction established itself, separating with a slowly increasing decisiveness from fantasy and space opera, advancing in bulk and popularity (most of the time there were at least half a dozen pulps running), but remaining firmly at a humble level of literary endeavour. Some stories leaned heavily on the scientific element, echoing Verne in their reliance on technology, or gadgetry, occasionally far outdoing him both in degree of theoretical complication and in unreadability. For the most part, however, vulgarisations of the early Wells held the field, setting up a pseudo-scientific base for a tale of wonder and terror. I can remember one that fused Lucian with "The Flowering of the Strange Orchid," featuring a plant growth whose upper half was the upper half of a large and fierce young lady.[14] Another introduced a disguised alien leading a supposed mineralogical expedition to a remote underground chamber, where his friends awaited a hasty breakfast of human flesh before setting off to conquer the world. Although disposing of much lethal machinery, they never got their breakfast and expired in a shower of sparks. (I seem to recall that that one was rather well written, though I was only about twelve at the time.) Then there was the one about the scientist, not actually mad, but sternly denounced by his colleagues as irresponsible, who created life in the laboratory. The life was a sort of rubbery jellyfish that engulfed things, not at all unlike the Blob recently on view at our theatres—it was soon frozen into submission with dry-ice extinguishers. This early version was far tougher and at one stage successfully engulfed H.M.S. *Invincible*, on manoeuvres at the time in the North Atlantic. Finally, during its traditional task of attacking Manhattan Island, its creator managed to destroy it at the price of personal engulfment. As far as I know none of these pieces has ever been reprinted, but those of the same period which have shown a similar lack of subtlety and

---

* This is not a totally unfair label for a whole mode of writing located somewhere on the borders of science fiction: the tale of the lost race or undiscovered human tribe. Although most of the less accessible parts of the world have been ransacked to provide habitation for these isolates—from Atlantis and Mu to Tibet and the Grand Canyon, from the polar regions to the bowels of the earth—it is rare to find anything beyond an "adventure" interest emerging. Lord Lytton's *The Coming Race* (1891) and Joseph O'Neill's *Land Under England* (1935), which occur somewhere near the beginning and end of the period in which the theme was popular, are relatively isolated examples of its use for didactic and admonitory purposes—purposes recognisably characteristic of serious science fiction.

an almost incredible ignorance of, or indifference to, elementary literary pitfalls. Here is an extract from a story called "The Monster from Nowhere," published in 1935.[15] One of the characters is telling his friends about an unpleasant experience on the Maratan Plateau:

"We all looked then. And we saw . . . huge, amorphous blobs of jet black, which seemed to be of the earth, yet not quite of it. Sometimes these ever-changing fragments were suspended in air, with no visible support. At other times they seemed to rest naturally enough on solid ground. But ever and ever again—they changed!

"Afire with curiosity, we went to the open spot. It was a mistake."

"A mistake?" I said.

"Yes. Fletcher lost his life—killed by his own curiosity. I need not tell you how he died. It was, you must believe me, horrible. Out of nowhere, one of the jet blobs appeared before him . . . then around him . . . then—he was gone!"

"Gone!" exclaimed Ki. "You mean—dead?"

"I mean gone! One second he was there. The next, both he and the *thing* which had snatched him had disappeared into thin air.

"Toland and I fled, panic-stricken, back to camp. We told Gainelle what we had seen. Gainelle, a crack shot and a gallant sportsman, was incredulous; perhaps even dubious. . . ."

But whichever he was it did him no good, I'm afraid; a *thing* gets him as well. The point about this story, however (and there are plenty of others which prolong their flights of ineptitude nearly as far), is that it is not just a matter of *things*: their origin and the reason for their strange habits are explained quite conscientiously, though in the same repulsive style. "The Monster from Nowhere" is a good instance of the interesting idea badly set out, a very common phenomenon in science fiction even today, and I might remark here that nothing differentiates the addict from the inquirer more than the readiness of the former, and the understandable reluctance of the latter, to finish a story of this kind. Even I myself feel I should have read a little more really unreadable stuff in preparation for this investigation.

The present era in science fiction opened quite suddenly round about 1940; there were five magazines in 1938, thirteen in 1939, and twenty-two in 1941. (These of course were American; Britain had two publications of this sort at the time.) This expansion of outlet virtually coincided with the arrival of a large group of new writers in the field, among them many of the best-known names of today. Sensationalism began to diminish, some degree of literacy made its appearance, and the admonitory utopia, virtually the leading form of contemporary science fiction, came into being again after something like twenty years. The mode had not come of age—it has yet to do that—but at least its crawling days were over. Why this happened when it did, or at all, I am not sure. I cannot feel, for example, that World War II had much to do with it. The sudden increase in the number of magazines can perhaps be explained in part by the tendency of people who dislike the thought or the actuality of military service to grab at a gaudily covered pulp on a newsstand, but the stuff inside would be too full of conflict and unpleasantly possible weapons of war, I should have thought, to provide much of an escape: the funnies, true-life romances, or straight pornography would surely be better. As regards the emergence of the new and better writers, I can just suggest that while in 1930 you were quite likely to be a crank or a hack if you wrote science fiction, by 1940 you could be a normal young man with a career to start, you were a member of the first generation who had grown up with the medium already in existence. More simply, few things are much good to begin with, and the inferiority of early Elizabethan drama is not what makes Shakespeare's appearance remarkable.

Contemporary science fiction has not, I need hardly say, finally and everywhere turned its back on BEMs or stylistic imbecility. Let me tell you about a short work called "Legacy of Terror"[16] in the November, 1958, issue of *Amazing Stories*. Holly Kendall, a six-foot-tall siren in "abbreviated shorts and light cotton sweater," is driving through the Vermont wastes on her way to tidy up at the experimental laboratory of her recently deceased father, in life a "tall, gentle man" with "soft voice and distant eyes." Encountering en route an ant as tall as herself, Holly retreats in panic, more or less into the arms of a young man:

He wasn't handsome, but you couldn't help being attracted to his wide, boyish grin, or being respectful to the steady, penetrating gaze of his deep brown eyes. He was tanned, and the grin he gave her flashed white against his skin.

"I do believe you," he said. "My name's Bryce Cooper; I've been looking for these big bugs for the past month. This is about as close as I came."

"You—you're looking for them?"

"That's right. I'm an associate professor at the university; English Lit's my racket, but I got me a degree in entymology, too. So when I picked up reports of king-sized spiders and stuff in the vicinity . . ." etc.

Very little later in the same scene, Bryce proposes marriage to Holly, mentioning that he earns $5,120 a year. Access to her father's journal leads Holly to the conclusion that the old man had been working on how to get souls to transmigrate during life, that the ant had got to its present size through having the soul of a horse or something injected into it, and that Bryce, alongside his increasingly amorous behaviour, is actually her own father making free with Bryce's body. An "unholy glitter" rapidly comes into the eyes of the composite male ("Mad? An interesting conclusion, Hollyhocks"), he decides to kill the girl to ensure her silence and is stung to death in the nick of time by the king-sized bumblebee. Finally, when Holly tries to burn her father's journal, the parish priest prevents her, explaining "gently" that the professor's work must be carried on, for all understanding leads to God.

From this wealth of analysable material—only the detail about entymology perhaps banishes the suspicion that some fearsome cynic is responsible—very little needs to be singled out, not even the incest motif, the obtrusion of which bears witness rather to the author's naïveté, I feel, than to anything sinister in him or his readers or our culture. Before leaving this bumper number of *Amazing Stories*,* I will just mention that it also contains a story called "Mission: Murder!" of which the moral is that terrorism and summary execution are justified if the enemy is dangerous and unpleasant enough—evidence of a political attitude notably

---

* Its cover would delight any cultural diagnostician of pretension with its triad of horror (the king-sized ant, here blown up to emperor size), greed (Holly's Cadillac), and lust (Holly). The cover of a recent number of *Super-Science Fiction* simplifies matters further by depicting a space-girl, even more generously shaped than Holly, on the point of engulfment by a tentacled Thing, an event uncommemorated in any of the stories inside. In fairness to *Amazing Stories*, I might add here that it is a model of refinement compared with some of the stuff in this "Third Monster Issue!" of *Super-Science Fiction*. Passing over "Monsters That Once Were Men" and "Birth of a Monster," I draw attention to "The Horror in the Attic"—"it was a hideous, horrible THING on a gruesome errand." The errand consists of frightening to death the lover of a fifteen-year-old girl and then eating the girl alive:

*The creature held her tightly. With one massive paw it ripped away her clothing, tossing the tattered garments to the floor, exposing her firm white breasts, her soft woman's body. Close up, she could see the creature's teeth—hideous yellow fangs,* [etc. etc.].

Before giving way to panic at such a cultural manifestation, one would do well to remember that vampires, werewolves, and such were behaving exactly like that over a hundred years ago, fulfilling the same function of putting into acceptable form interests that realistic fiction could not accommodate: Sheridan Le Fanu's "Carmilla," with its blatantly lesbian theme, is the most famous example.

rare in contemporary science fiction. The same issue carries a new adventure of Johnny Mayhem, a slightly less incredible version of Superman, and a sensible, vigorously written, apparently well-informed article attacking some of the policies of the Atomic Energy Commission.

This co-presence of the adult with the stupidly or nastily adolescent is highly characteristic of the modern science-fiction magazines, of which we might now make a general inspection. Their number and circulation continues to fluctuate with surprising sharpness—there was a notable drop, I am told, immediately after the launching of the first Russian sputnik—but the present tendency° is clearly one of expansion, with twenty or more titles coming out monthly or, occasionally, bi-monthly. In the current year we can expect something between one hundred and fifty and two hundred complete novels and collections of short stories, of which only about half will be paperbacks. A tendency for established publishers to open a science-fiction list can also be detected, and there are two paperback houses turning out nothing else. It seems that, despite regular jeremiads from editors and authors, the medium is not yet in disrepair. If I now go on to concentrate for a moment on the magazines, it is because they afford a far more catholic view of the field, and far more clues to the nature of its readership, than do anthologies or individual volumes. These, in any case, regularly derive something like sixty per cent of their material from the magazines. The physical aspect of the latter is uniformly repellent, far more so than could be excused by any talk of the technical exigencies of pulp publication. Crude sensationalism vies with crude whimsy on the covers, and although wit occasionally makes an appearance—a recent one had a pirate boarding a space-craft with a slide rule between his teeth—many a potential recruit to the medium must have been lost without having to stretch out a hand. It is hard to believe that anything likely to interest a grown man could lie under a cover picture of a multi-armed alien Santa Claus, or within a journal called *Fantastic Universe* or *Astounding Science Fiction,* but I hope to establish that these natural suspicions are often unjustified. They would not be much lulled, admittedly, by a quick look through the interior of any given issue, which offers advertisements of the Rosicrucians and of Royal Jelly

---

° Since this was written there has been another drop, viewed in the relevant circles with wonderfully spontaneous concern. Voluble anxiety about its own commercial future has always been a demerit of the science-fiction industry, one which may be expected to disappear if the medium attains respectability.

("it's the secret of prolonged life"), of firms offering computer construction kits—125 computers with Geniac, only $19.95, or 150 small ones with Brainiac for only $17.95;* more appalling art-work; and silly editorial epigraphs: "Hunted by the living and haunted by the dead . . . Blaine had to do a lot better than merely look alive to stay alive in this grim world!" —this prefixed to an exceptionally able and original story. If the stage of actually beginning to read is attained, the material will be found to include a novella of perhaps fifteen thousand words, three or four short stories of between three and eight thousand words each, sometimes an instalment of a three- or four-part serial running up to fifteen thousand (failing that, another novella or a couple of shorts), editorial matter often marked by a hectoring, opinionated tone, readers' letters covering a staggering range of IQs, a book-review section conducted with intelligence and a much greater readiness to be nasty than one finds, say, in the Sunday *Times*, in some cases a popular-science article on atomic physics, sea serpents, telepathy, or the evaporation of the Caspian Sea, and an interesting department in which are tabulated the results of the readers' voting on the stories in the previous issue—these are arranged in order of popularity and, in at least one case, the author receiving the most votes regularly gets a cash bonus from the publisher. While there is a lot of reason for calling the devotees of science fiction uncritical, there is no doubt that in what must often be an ill-instructed way they are far more concerned about the merit of the stories they read than, for instance, the

---

* The cheaper and nastier magazines offer material that is more sinister (or more absurd). Here, though presumably not only here, you are given the chance of mail-ordering for $1.00 the Exploding Army Hand Grenade (Exact Replica):

*Here's real battle authenticity. This menacing hand grenade looks and works just like a real one. All you do is pull the pin, wait 4 seconds, throw the grenade, and watch the fun as it explodes automatically. It's completely harmless, but the explosion it makes can be heard for a block. Really scatters the gang when you throw this baby in their midst. It sure looks and sounds real, [etc. etc.].*

If your interests differ slightly, what about a "Stuffed" Girl's Head for only $2.98?

*Blondes, redheads and brunettes for every man to boast of his conquests . . . the first realistic likeness of the exciting women who play an important part in every man's life . . . and one of the nicest qualities is that they don't talk back! Accurately modelled to three-quarters life-size and molded of skin-textured pliable plastic, these heads are so life-like they almost breathe. Saucy, glittering eyes, full sensuous mouth and liquid satin complexion, combined with radiant hair colors give astonishing realism to these rare and unique Trophies. Blonds [sic], redhead or brunette mounted on a genuine mahogany plaque is complete and ready to hang on the wall for excitement and conversation.*

people who buy women's magazines. I shall return to this point in a moment.

To offer a full-dress division of contemporary science fiction into thematic categories would be laborious and out of proportion to its critical usefulness; here instead is a brief gallop through the fiction contents of a representative recent magazine. The October, 1958, *Astounding Science Fiction*, then, kicks off with a story[17] by Clifford D. Simak, who has been writing the stuff for twenty-five years. In the present instance, a small country trader discovers a shortcut from his house into another world and sets up a bartering arrangement with its inhabitants. The main cruxes are (a) that the arrangement will not work without the intervention of the trader's dull-witted and despised neighbour, who turns out to be telepathic; and (b) that out of sympathy for the neighbour, and feeling that his own house ought to remain his, the trader insists that no outsiders, from the local Chamber of Commerce to the United Nations, shall be allowed to interfere. Thus the rights of the individual are—perhaps rather dully—upheld against the forces of convention and authority. The next story, "The Yellow Pill," by another established writer,[18] presumptively introduces a psychiatrist in New York trying to cure a patient of the delusion that both of them are actually aboard a space-ship in flight. After some exchanges, in which each party systematically explains the other's world in terms of his own, the supposed psychiatrist swallows the yellow pill, an anti-delusion compound which works by amplifying sense-data, and finds himself on board a space-ship. Meanwhile, the other man has acquired the psychiatrical delusion, imagines himself cured of the space-ship delusion, and walks out of the door, which unfortunately leads into empty space instead of the outer office. This is mainly an ingenious little puzzle-thriller, but it also grapples—perhaps rather dully—with an aspect of solipsism. "Big Sword," by a newer author,[19] shows us a distant planet harbouring an intelligent telepathic race of minute size but with some powers of self-defence. When the human expedition is about to destroy a colony of these creatures, out of inadvertence rather than malice, it is left to a small boy to strike up communication with the aliens and persuade his elders to offer them assistance instead of casual harm. Outwardly, the story falls into a familiar category, the biological puzzle (the aliens have a partly vegetable life-cycle that defeats understanding for some time), but again something is clearly being said—not so dully this time—about the rights of the insignificant and the outlandish. There is some sexual interest here, but minor and highly respectable. There is some too in the next story, ". . . And Check the Oil,"[20] even more minor and hardly less respectable; the rest of it is an inconclusive but not illiterate space-filler about some amiable visiting aliens who run out of food. Finally, "False Image"[21] shows alien and man agreeing to overlook the differences of appearance and habit that repel or frighten each of them and so coming to an understanding.

You will have to take my word for it that none of these five stories is offensive in style, since extracts demonstrating inoffensiveness make for wearisome reading. Anyway, there are no degrees in entymology or wide, boyish grins here. Nor, you will have noticed, are there any king-sized spiders or BEMs of any sort. All four of the alien races introduced are friendly creatures, raising difficulties in communication only. In three out of five cases—a representative proportion, probably—there is recognisable moral concern of a sort: I am not interested for the moment in just what sort, merely in noting its presence. I could, of course, go on to note other shared characteristics, such as the comparatively minor role played by science, pseudo-science, technology, gadgetry, sex, but I think I have said enough about the October *Astounding* and the November *Amazing* to have evoked the experience of reading a science-fiction magazine in all its multifariousness and majesty. I have only to add the practical tip that, in addition to *Astounding,* the other periodicals of pretension are *Galaxy Science Fiction* and *The Magazine of Fantasy and Science Fiction,* before rounding off this section with a brief note on other outlets.

Anthologies of short stories, virtually all reprinted from magazines, form a strikingly high proportion, something like a quarter, of total publication in volume form, another quarter being formed by individual collections of shorts or novellas, most of which will also have appeared earlier in magazines. Of the remaining half, the novels, a large minority will be originals, but probably the bulk can again be traced back to the magazines, either in serial or in rudimentary form. It will be seen firstly that science fiction is to a great extent a short-story form, another point for later consideration, secondly that the magazines are a decisive source. A third deduction might be that people like reading stories twice over, or are unaware of doing so, but in fact the number of magazines makes it impossible to catch more than a few of the good stories as they come out, unless one is doing so full-time. A footnote on distribution is that science-fiction stories are spreading into general magazines, including *Playboy,*

*Harper's, Esquire, McCall's, Good Housekeeping, The Reporter,* and *The Saturday Evening Post.* Science fiction has also appeared in *Ellery Queen's Mystery Magazine, Cats,* and *PEN* (The Public Employees' News).

A survey of readership can start with a figure or two: *Galaxy* sells about 125,000 an issue in the United States, plus editions in England, France, Belgium, Switzerland, Germany, Italy, Finland, and Sweden, in the appropriate languages. The Swedes are reported to be particularly keen, which recalls the fact that they are also the most jazz-conscious nation in Europe. *Astounding* has its foreign editions and sells something like 100,000 an issue in America, 35,000 in England, with subscribers in Africa, the Near East, Russia, and China. *Amazing,* which seems to circulate only in English, has an American sale of 50,000. Taking into account the tendency whereby those who read science fiction at all will read *Astounding,* and presupposing a good deal of swapping between enthusiasts, one comes up with a total science-fiction readership in the United States of something approaching half a million. Numbering about three-tenths of one percent of the population, this is far from being a mass audience, a conclusion supported by the qualities of the material. Without making extravagant claims, one can suggest that the characteristics attributable to a mass medium—expensiveness, avoidance of the obscure or heterodox, reassuringness, anonymity—do not appear in a considerable quantity of contemporary science fiction, and I remind you that *Galaxy,* which rarely utilises BEMs or salacity, sells two and a half times as well as *Amazing,* in which they appear less rarely. I might just momentarily expand the point about anonymity by asserting that the best-known science-fiction writers are the reverse of anonymous or interchangeable: they are more likely to be annoyingly idiosyncratic. Moreover, readers' letters in the magazines often show a genuinely critical attitude, however crude its bases and arguments, and acquaintance with the whole body of a given author's work is commonly appealed to, implying some sort of power to make distinctions. Science-fiction readers are addicts, but they are active addicts, positive enthusiasts who are conscious, often all too conscious, of being a specialised minority, highly vocal, and given to banding together in fan clubs.

These clubs are a fascinating feature of American—and British—society, and a full account of them would demand an article to itself. A compressed account would have to start with the foundation of the first clubs in the early '30's and go straight on to the situation today, with groups in a score of major cities and dozens of others: the regional breakdown seems to show that interest is strong in the Midwest and on the West Coast, not so strong in New England and Texas. Many clubs will meet weekly, have a hierarchy of officials, hold organized discussions, and mimeograph or even print a magazine. These fan magazines, or fanzines, appear and disappear at a great rate, but there are pretty sure to be forty or fifty different titles in the current year, with critical, fictional, and gossipy contents. The nomenclature of the field is not reassuring—one fan club is called "The Elves', Gnomes' and Little Men's Science Fiction, Chowder and Marching Society," one of the national federations is "The Little Monsters of America"—but the evidence of energy and serious interest is overwhelming. Every year there are regional conferences and a three-day world convention. There are perhaps twenty fan clubs in Great Britain; I don't know about the Continent. Politically, the clubs are inclined to be progressive, especially on racial questions, and thus reflect a feature of the medium itself: many stories allegorise the theme of discrimination, some treat it directly. At one stage, an immoderate degree of radicalism was attained when a Communist group from Brooklyn, baulked in their attempt to win over the national convention, formed an association for the Political Advancement of Science Fiction—a short-lived organization, I imagine. I will add as a footnote that apparently fantasy fans are content to march under the banner of their science-fiction friends, who far exceed them in number. However, there must be many who make no distinction between the two forms, and there is evidence that the name "fantasy" carries some kind of unwelcome connotation. Anthony Boucher, when acting as co-editor of *The Magazine of Fantasy and Science Fiction*, reported that "our readers do not prefer science fiction to fantasy, but they think they do," adding that the magazine sold more copies when it carried a science-fiction cover (men in space suits) than when it had a fantasy cover (leprechauns). These facts would strengthen the hand of those who claim that, without being essentially escapist itself, science fiction is often used as a means of escape by its addicts.

Apart from being likely to belong to a fan club, what sort of person reads science fiction? Information about this is profuse, both in bulk and in self-contradiction. A gingerly attempt to reconcile a number of sources gives something like this. Males greatly predominate over females—the

proportions given vary between fifteen to one and five to one. The dispar-
ity is probably on the decrease. As regards age, the average would come
somewhere in the later twenties, with a sprinkling of schoolchildren and a
number of veteran fans like the present writer. As for occupation, not
unnaturally there is a pronounced technological or scientific bias, with
engineers, chemists, research workers, and so on accounting for perhaps
forty percent of readers, though the editor of *Astounding* says that "nearly
all" of his readers are "technically trained and employed." Other groups
mentioned as numerically important are the non-scientific professions,
college students, and the armed forces. As a counterillustration of occupa-
tional diversity, I will just mention an anecdote of de Camp's which tells
how a science-fiction writer,[22] happening to visit a New Orleans bordello,
found his works so popular with the staff that he was asked to consider
himself their guest for the evening. To speculate about the motives and
attitudes of readers is precarious, but for what it may be worth I will
quote what a number of leading writers have to say about this. Science-
fiction readers are "the curious who are looking for stimulation or sensation"; "people with technical training who want fictionalised shop-talk
and teen-agers who find glamour and excitement in science"; "ten percent
mental juveniles who still like fairy stories, ninety percent chronic nosey-
parkers who like having their imaginations stimulated"; "misfits in society,
often subversive misfits"; "idealistic, forward-looking, well-read, interested in the arts." Except for the last of these, I detect a welcome lack of
reverence here, but on the whole the writers and editors would, I think,
echo the boast of the editor of *Astounding* that the medium reaches a
large minority of a highly creative and influential section of the nation—
the younger technologists. However one regards technologists, there is no
doubt that they are important, and since I regard science fiction as a
humanising rather than a brutalising force, its circulation among these
people strikes me as a hopeful sign.

What sort of person writes science fiction? He—it is "she" once in
about fifty times—very seldom depends wholly on the writing of science
fiction for his living. The financial rewards are such as to demand either a
fantastic output or resignation to modest living standards. Secondary occupations adopted are often concerned with science—teaching and
research—or with fiction—sometimes detective stories and/or Westerns,
sometimes "general," as they say. A scrutiny of their work and of their
own utterances suggests that most of the writers and editors treat their

calling with great, sometimes excessive, seriousness. Their claims for the medium often strike a missionary note: science fiction is "the last refuge of iconoclasm in American literature"; it exists "to afford objectivity to the reader, for better consideration of himself and his species"; its function is "to modify the natural conservatism of the creature"; "it helps mankind to be humble." Occasionally, a legitimate pride in a specialised calling unites with an equally understandable desire to see science fiction treated respectfully and produces wild hyperbole. Thus, Reginald Bretnor, an established author and critic, seems to think that science fiction is a much broader field than the whole of the rest of literature; Robert A. Heinlein, an excellent writer, says the stuff "is much more realistic than is most historical and contemporary-scene fiction and is superior to them both," it is "the most difficult of all prose forms," it is "the only form of fiction which stands even a chance of interpreting the spirit of our times." Here one is reminded of the modernist jazz musician claiming that what he plays is superior in subtlety to serious music as well as being more difficult to perform. But to feel that what one is doing is the most important thing in the world is not necessarily undignified, and indeed is perhaps more rather than less likely to lead to good work being done. I have no objection if the science-fiction writer is sometimes a serious and dedicated kind of person.

He would certainly unloose a disapproving frown at my next topic, science fiction on film, television, and radio. The obstacles to successful translation are formidable enough, perhaps resembling, as one commentator sees it, those of converting into the terms of *Life* the values and interests of a class periodical like *The Saturday Review*. In the visual media the effects have got to be lavish: it is no use trying to produce a convincing BEM by fiddling around with slow-motion process shots of newts, and I remember a fearful effort called *The Man from Planet X* in which they made do with just one alien, whose frequent reminders that a lot of his friends from Planet X should be turning up any moment produced only very moderate consternation. Lavishness is costly, and cost must be certain of being recovered; with few exceptions only the most blatant menaces have got on to the screen. With a sad lack of inventiveness, most of the animal kingdom has been successively blown up to giantism and launched against the world: we have had king-sized wasps, ants, spiders, squids, sea-snails, lizards, beetles, birds, and pterodactyls, all doing their best to bring mankind to its knees. *The War of the Worlds*,

with excellent Martians and some attempt to set up a logical alien technology, was probably the best of the menace series, if only because it
provided a really formidable menace, one that couldn't be polished off
with a few rounds of rifle fire. Nowadays, it appears that the boom in
science-fiction films has passed—I couldn't find a single one to go to in
New York the other day—and without having explored more than a fraction of the possibilities.* The same applies to television: my own survey,
which took a long time and was very horrible to do, shows that of five
hundred programme-hours studied, only six and one-half, or one and
three-tenths percent, could possibly be classed as science fiction, compared with four and three-tenths percent of mystery and detective and
nearly six percent of Westerns. Radio is often spoken of as the most
promising of the three media for science fiction, but, for my own part,
that promise has yet to be honoured: I was spoilt, perhaps, by sitting
through *Journey into Space*, an interminable saga on the B.B.C., and by
having made rather a mess of a play of my own which was done on the
Third Programme, the first science fiction they ever attempted and doubtless the last as well. Noises are good fun all right, but I do not much care
for having things "left to my imagination," and the most blood-curdling
roars will curdle a good deal less blood, I take it, than the jerkiest king-
sized spider on the screen.

From the foregoing hasty and subjective sketch one could at any rate
deduce, I think, that on the whole, attempts to present science fiction
through mass outlets have failed, though not irretrievably so. It remains
only to sum up by considering what use the written medium serves or
might serve. I cannot see much justice in the commentators' repeated
claim that it sugars the pill of a scientific education: most of the science is
wrong anyway, and its amount is such that one might as well be reading
Westerns in the hope of finding out about ranching methods. Nor is the
medium valuable simply as prophecy: science fiction must in its very
profusion seem occasionally to have guessed right, and to have guessed
wrong invalidates nothing. Its most important use, I submit, is a means of
dramatising social inquiry, as providing a fictional mode in which cultural
tendencies can be isolated and judged. To be sure, it does this only at its

---

* The reported sale to the movies of Christopher's *No Blade of Grass* and Arthur
C. Clarke's *Childhood's End*, both of them serious and non-sensationalist efforts, perhaps
portends a return to the charge in a less frivolous frame of mind.

most ambitious, and then it is often vulgarly presumptuous; but many a trend-hound would be surprised and perhaps mortified to discover how many of his cherished insights are common ground in science fiction. Any Martian survey team would be well advised to read a sample of the stuff before reporting on Terran civilisation.

# III.
# CRITICISM, DESTRUCTIVE AND OTHERWISE

# ON SCIENCE FICTION

## C. S. Lewis

Sometimes a village or small town which we have known all our lives becomes the scene of a murder, a novel, or a centenary, and then for a few months everyone knows its name and crowds go to visit it. A like thing happens to one's private recreations. I had been walking, and reading Trollope, for years when I found myself suddenly overtaken, as if by a wave from behind, by a boom in Trollope and a short-lived craze for what was called hiking. And lately I have had the same sort of experience again. I had read fantastic fiction of all sorts ever since I could read, including, of course, the particular kind which Wells practised in his *Time Machine, First Men in the Moon* and others. Then, some fifteen or twenty years ago, I became aware of a bulge in the production of such stories. In America whole magazines began to be exclusively devoted to them. The execution was usually detestable; the conceptions, sometimes worthy of better treatment. About this time the name *scientifiction*, soon altered to *science fiction*, began to be common. Then, perhaps five or six years ago, the bulge still continuing and even increasing, there was an improvement: not that very bad stories ceased to be the majority, but that the good ones became better and more numerous. It was after this that the *genre* began to attract the attention (always, I think, contemptuous) of the literary weeklies. There seems, in fact, to be a double paradox in its history: it

From *Of Other Worlds*, Harcourt, Brace, 1967

began to be popular when it least deserved popularity, and to excite critical contempt as soon as it ceased to be wholly contemptible.

Of the articles I have read on the subject (and I expect I have missed many) I do not find that I can make any use. For one thing, most were not very well informed. For another, many were by people who clearly hated the kind they wrote about. It is very dangerous to write about a kind you hate. Hatred obscures all distinctions. I don't like detective stories and therefore all detective stories look much alike to me: if I wrote about them I should therefore infallibly write drivel. Criticism of kinds, as distinct from criticism of works, cannot of course be avoided: I shall be driven to criticize one sub-species of science fiction myself. But it is, I think, the most subjective and least reliable type of criticism. Above all, it should not masquerade as criticism of individual works. Many reviews are useless because, while purporting to condemn the book, they only reveal the reviewer's dislike of the kind to which it belongs. Let bad tragedies be censured by those who love tragedy, and bad detective stories by those who love the detective story. Then we shall learn their real faults. Otherwise we shall find epics blamed for not being novels, farces for not being high comedies, novels by James for lacking the swift action of Smollett. Who wants to hear a particular claret abused by a fanatical teetotaller, or a particular woman by a confirmed misogynist?

Moreover, most of these articles were chiefly concerned to account for the bulge in the output and consumption of science fiction on sociological and psychological grounds. This is of course a perfectly legitimate attempt. But here as elsewhere those who hate the thing they are trying to explain are not perhaps those most likely to explain it. If you have never enjoyed a thing and do not know what it feels like to enjoy it, you will hardly know what sort of people go to it, in what moods, seeking what sort of gratification. And if you do not know what sort of people they are, you will be ill-equipped to find out what conditions have made them so. In this way, one may say of a kind not only (as Wordsworth says of the poet) that "you must love it ere to you it will seem worthy of your love," but that you must at least have loved it once if you are even to warn others against it. Even if it is a vice to read science fiction, those who cannot understand the very temptation to that vice will not be likely to tell us anything of value about it. Just as I, for instance, who have no taste for cards, could not find anything very useful to say by way of warning against deep play. They will be like the frigid preaching chastity, misers

warning us against prodigality, cowards denouncing rashness. And because, as I have said, hatred assimilates all the hated objects, it will make
you assume that all the things lumped together as science fiction are of
the same sort, and that the psychology of all those who like to read any of
them is the same. That is likely to make the problem of explaining the
bulge seem simpler than it really is.

I myself shall not attempt to explain it at all. I am not interested in the
bulge. It is nothing to me whether a given work makes part of it or was
written long before it occurred. The existence of the bulge cannot make
the kind (or kinds) intrinsically better or worse; though of course bad
specimens will occur most often within it.

I will now try to divide this species of narrative into its sub-species. I
shall begin with that sub-species which I think radically bad, in order to
get it out of our way.

In this sub-species the author leaps forward into an imagined future
when planetary, sidereal, or even galactic travel has become common.
Against this huge backcloth he then proceeds to develop an ordinary love-
story, spy-story, wreck-story, or crime-story. This seems to me tasteless.
Whatever in a work of art is not used, is doing harm. The faintly imagined, and sometimes strictly unimaginable, scene and properties, only
blur the real theme and distract us from any interest it might have had. I
presume that the authors of such stories are, so to speak, Displaced
Persons—commercial authors who did not really want to write science
fiction at all, but who availed themselves of its popularity by giving a
veneer of science fiction to their normal kind of work. But we must
distinguish. A leap into the future, a rapid assumption of all the changes
which are feigned to have occurred, is a legitimate "machine" if it enables
the author to develop a story of real value which could not have been told
(or not so economically) in any other way. Thus John Collier in *Tom's
A-Cold* (1933) wants to write a story of heroic action among people themselves semi-barbarous but supported by the surviving tradition of a literate culture recently overthrown. He could, of course, find an historical
situation suitable to his purpose, somewhere in the early Dark Ages. But
that would involve all manner of archaeological details which would spoil
his book if they were done perfunctorily and perhaps distract our interest
if they were done well. He is therefore, in my view, fully justified in
positing such a state of affairs in England after the destruction of our
present civilization. That enables him (and us) to assume a familiar

climate, flora, and fauna. He is not interested in the process whereby the change came about. That is all over before the curtain rises. This supposition is equivalent to the rules of his game: criticism applies only to the quality of his play. A much more frequent use of the leap into the future, in our time, is satiric or prophetic: the author criticizes tendencies in the present by imagining them carried out ("produced," as Euclid would say) to their logical limit. *Brave New World* and *Nineteen Eighty-Four* leap to our minds. I can see no objection to such a "machine." Nor do I see much use in discussing, as someone did, whether books that use it can be called "novels" or not. That is merely a question of definition. You may define the novel either so as to exclude or so as to include them. The best definition is that which proves itself most convenient. And of course to devise a definition for the purpose of excluding either *The Waves* in one direction or *Brave New World* in another, and then blame them for being excluded, is foolery.

I am, then, condemning not all books which suppose a future widely different from the present, but those which do so without a good reason, which leap a thousand years to find plots and passions which they could have found at home.

Having condemned that sub-species, I am glad to turn to another which I believe to be legitimate, though I have not the slightest taste for it myself. If the former is the fiction of the Displaced Persons, this might be called the fiction of Engineers. It is written by people who are primarily interested in space-travel, or in other undiscovered techniques, as real possibilities in the actual universe. They give us in imaginative form their guesses as to how the thing might be done. Jules Verne's *Twenty Thousand Leagues Under the Sea* and Wells's *Land Ironclads* were once specimens of this kind, though the coming of the real submarine and the real tank has altered their original interest. Arthur Clarke's *Prelude to Space* is another. I am too uneducated scientifically to criticize such stories on the mechanical side; and I am so completely out of sympathy with the projects they anticipate that I am incapable of criticizing them as stories. I am as blind to their appeal as a pacifist is to *Maldon* and *Lepanto*, or an aristocratophobe (if I may coin the word) to the *Arcadia*. But heaven forbid that I should regard the limitations of my sympathy as anything save a red light which warns me not to criticize at all. For all I know, these may be very good stories in their own kind.

I think it useful to distinguish from these Engineers' Stories a third sub-species where the interest is, in a sense, scientific, but speculative. When we learn from the sciences the probable nature of places or conditions which no human being has experienced, there is, in normal men, an impulse to attempt to imagine them. Is any man such a dull clod that he can look at the moon through a good telescope without asking himself what it would be like to walk among those mountains under that black, crowded sky? The scientists themselves, the moment they go beyond purely mathematical statements, can hardly avoid describing the facts in terms of their probable effect on the senses of a human observer. Prolong this, and give, along with that observer's sense experience, his probable emotions and thoughts, and you at once have a rudimentary science fiction. And of course men have been doing this for centuries. What would Hades be like if you could go there alive? Homer sends Odysseus there and gives his answer. Or again, what would it be like at the Antipodes? (For this was a question of the same sort so long as men believed that the torrid zone rendered them forever inaccessible.) Dante takes you there: he describes with all the gusto of the later scientifictionist how surprising it was to see the sun in such an unusual position. Better still, what would it be like if you could get to the centre of the earth? Dante tells you at the end of the *Inferno* where he and Virgil, after climbing down from the shoulders to the waist of Lucifer, find that they have to climb up from his waist to his feet, because of course they have passed the centre of gravitation. It is a perfect science fiction effect. Thus again Athanasius Kircher in his *Iter Extaticum Celeste* (1656) will take you to all the planets and most of the stars, presenting as vividly as he can what you would see and feel if this were possible. He, like Dante, uses supernatural means of transport. In Wells's *First Men in the Moon* we have means which are feigned to be natural. What keeps his story within this sub-species, and distinguishes it from those of the Engineers, is his choice of a quite impossible composition called cavorite. This impossibility is of course a merit, not a defect. A man of his ingenuity could easily have thought up something more plausible. But the more plausible, the worse. That would merely invite interest in actual possibilities of reaching the Moon, an interest foreign to his story. Never mind how they got there; we are imagining what it would be like. The first glimpse of the unveiled airless sky, the lunar landscape, the lunar levity, the incomparable solitude, then the growing terror, finally the overwhelming approach of the lunar night

—it is for these things that the story (especially in its original and shorter form) exists.

How anyone can think this form illegitimate or contemptible passes my understanding. It may very well be convenient not to call such things novels. If you prefer, call them a very special form of novels. Either way, the conclusion will be much the same: they are to be tried by their own rules. It is absurd to condemn them because they do not often display any deep or sensitive characterization. They oughtn't to. It is a fault if they do. Wells's Cavor and Bedford have rather too much than too little character. Every good writer knows that the more unusual the scenes and events of his story are, the slighter, the more ordinary, the more typical his persons should be. Hence Gulliver is a commonplace little man and Alice a commonplace little girl. If they had been more remarkable they would have wrecked their books. The Ancient Mariner himself is a very ordinary man. To tell how odd things struck odd people is to have an oddity too much: he who is to see strange sights must not himself be strange. He ought to be as nearly as possible Everyman or Anyman. Of course, we must not confuse slight or typical characterization with impossible or unconvincing characterization. Falsification of character will always spoil a story. But character can apparently be reduced, simplified, to almost any extent with wholly satisfactory results. The greater ballads are an instance.

Of course, a given reader may be (some readers seem to be) interested in nothing else in the world except detailed studies of complex human personalities. If so, he has a good reason for not reading those kinds of work which neither demand nor admit it. He has no reason for condemning them, and indeed no qualification for speaking of them at all. We must not allow the novel of manners to give laws to all literature: let it rule its own domain. We must not listen to Pope's maxim about the proper study of mankind. The proper study of man is everything. The proper study of man as artist is everything which gives a foothold to the imagination and the passions.

But while I think this sort of science fiction legitimate, and capable of great virtues, it is not a kind which can endure copious production. It is only the first visit to the Moon or to Mars that is, for this purpose, any good. After each has been discovered in one or two stories (and turned out to be different in each) it becomes difficult to suspend our disbelief in

favour of subsequent stories. However good they were they would kill
each other by becoming numerous.

My next sub-species is what I would call the Eschatological. It is
about the future, but not in the same way as *Brave New World* or *The
Sleeper Awakes*. They were political or social. This kind gives an imaginative vehicle to speculations about the ultimate destiny of our species.
Examples are Wells's *Time Machine*, Olaf Stapledon's *Last and First
Men*, or Arthur Clarke's *Childhood's End*. It is here that a definition of
science fiction which separates it entirely from the novel becomes impera-
tive. The form of *Last and First Men* is not novelistic at all. It is indeed in
a new form—the pseudo history. The pace, the concern with broad, general movements, the tone, are all those of the historiographer, not the
novelist. It was the right form for the theme. And since we are here
diverging so widely from the novel, I myself would gladly include in this
sub-species a work which is not even narrative, Geoffrey Dennis's *The
End of the World* (1930). And I would certainly include, from J. B. S.
Haldane's *Possible Worlds* (1927), the brilliant, though to my mind de-
praved, paper called "The Last Judgement."

Work of this kind gives expression to thoughts and emotions which I
think it good that we should sometimes entertain. It is sobering and
cathartic to remember, now and then, our collective smallness, our apparent isolation, the apparent indifference of nature, the slow biological,
geological, and astronomical processes which may, in the long run, make
many of our hopes (possibly some of our fears) ridiculous. If *memento
mori* is sauce for the individual, I do not know why the species should be
spared the taste of it. Stories of this kind may explain the hardly disguised
political rancour which I thought I detected in one article on science
fiction. The insinuation was that those who read or wrote it were probably Fascists. What lurks behind such a hint is, I suppose, something like
this. If we were all on board ship and there was trouble among the
stewards, I can just conceive their chief spokesman looking with disfavour
on anyone who stole away from the fierce debates in the saloon or pantry
to take a breather on deck. For up there, he would taste the salt, he would
see the vastness of the water, he would remember that the ship had a
whither and a whence. He would remember things like fog, storms, and
ice. What had seemed, in the hot, lighted rooms down below to be merely
the scene for a political crisis, would appear once more as a tiny eggshell

moving rapidly through an immense darkness over an element in which man cannot live. It would not necessarily change his convictions about the rights and wrongs of the dispute down below, but it would probably show them in a new light. It could hardly fail to remind him that the stewards were taking for granted hopes more momentous than that of a rise in pay, and the passengers forgetting dangers more serious than that of having to cook and serve their own meals. Stories of the sort I am describing are like that visit to the deck. They cool us. They are as refreshing as that passage in E. M. Forster where the man, looking at the monkeys, realizes that most of the inhabitants of India do not care how India is governed. Hence the uneasiness which they arouse in those who, for whatever reason, wish to keep us wholly imprisoned in the immediate conflict. That perhaps is why people are so ready with the charge of "escape." I never fully understood it till my friend Professor Tolkien asked me the very simple question, "What class of men would you expect to be most preoccupied with, and most hostile to, the idea of escape?" and gave the obvious answer: jailers. The charge of Fascism is, to be sure, mere mud-flinging. Fascists, as well as Communists, are jailers; both would assure us that the proper study of prisoners is prison. But there is perhaps this truth behind it: that those who brood much on the remote past or future, or stare long at the night sky, are less likely than others to be ardent or orthodox partisans.

I turn at last to that sub-species in which alone I myself am greatly interested. It is best approached by reminding ourselves of a fact which every writer on the subject whom I have read completely ignores. Far the best of the American magazines bears the significant title *Fantasy and Science Fiction*. In it (as also in many other publications of the same type) you will find not only stories about space-travel but stories about gods, ghosts, ghouls, demons, fairies, monsters, etc. This gives us our clue. The last sub-species of science fiction represents simply an imaginative impulse as old as the human race working under the special conditions of our own time. It is not difficult to see why those who wish to visit strange regions in search of such beauty, awe, or terror as the actual world does not supply have increasingly been driven to other planets or other stars. It is the result of increasing geographical knowledge. The less known the real world is, the more plausibly your marvels can be located near at hand. As the area of knowledge spreads, you need to go further afield: like a man moving his house further and further out into the country as the new building estates catch him up. Thus in Grimm's *Märchen*, stories told by peasants in wooded country, you need only walk an hour's journey into the next forest to find a home for your witch or ogre. The author of *Beowulf* can put Grendel's lair in a place of which he himself says *Nis þaet feor heonon Mil-gemearces*. Homer, writing for a maritime people, has to take Odysseus several days' journey by sea before he meets Circe, Calypso, the Cyclops, or the Sirens. Old Irish has a form called the *immram*, a voyage among islands. Arthurian romance, oddly at first sight, seems usually content with the old *Märchen* machine of a neighbouring forest. Chrétien and his successors knew a great deal of real geography. Perhaps the explanation is that these romances are chiefly written by Frenchmen about Britain, and Britain in the past. *Huon of Bordeaux* places Oberon in the East. Spenser invents a country not in our universe at all; Sidney goes to an imaginary past in Greece. By the eighteenth century we have to move well out into the country. Paltock and Swift take us to remote seas, Voltaire to America. Rider Haggard had to go to unexplored Africa or Tibet; Bulwer-Lytton, to the depths of the Earth. It might have been predicted that stories of this kind would, sooner or later, have to leave Tellus altogether. We know now that where Haggard put She and Kôr we should really find groundnut schemes or Mau Mau.

In this kind of story the pseudo-scientific apparatus is to be taken simply as a "machine" in the sense which that word bore for the Neo-Classical critics. The most superficial appearance of plausibility—the merest sop to our critical intellect—will do. I am inclined to think that frankly supernatural methods are best. I took a hero once to Mars in a space-ship, but when I knew better I had angels convey him to Venus. Nor need the strange worlds, when we get there, be at all strictly tied to scientific probabilities. It is their wonder, or beauty, or suggestiveness that matter. When I myself put canals on Mars I believe I already knew that better telescopes had dissipated that old optical delusion. The point was that they were part of the Martian myth as it already existed in the common mind.

The defence and analysis of this kind are, accordingly, no different from those of fantastic or mythopoeic literature in general. But here sub-species and sub-sub-species break out in baffling multitude. The impossible—or things so immensely improbable that they have, imaginatively, the same status as the impossible—can be used in literature for many different purposes. I cannot hope to do more than suggest a few main types: the subject still awaits its Aristotle.

It may represent the intellect, almost completely free from emotion, at play. The purest specimen would be Abbott's *Flatland*, though even here some emotion arises from the sense (which it inculcates) of our own limitations—the consciousness that our own human awareness of the world is arbitrary and contingent. Sometimes such play gives a pleasure analogous to that of the conceit. I have unluckily forgotten both the name and author of my best example: the story of a man who is enabled to travel into the future, because himself, in that future when he shall have discovered a method of time travel, comes back to himself in the present (then, of course, the past) and fetches him.[23] Less comic, but a more strenuous game, is the very fine working out of the logical consequences of time-travel in Charles Williams's *Many Dimensions*: where, however, this element is combined with many others.

Secondly, the impossible may be simply a postulate to liberate farcical consequences, as in "F. Anstey's" *Brass Bottle*. The garunda-stone in his *Vice Versa* is not so pure an example; a serious moral and, indeed, something not far from pathos, come in—perhaps against the author's wish.

Sometimes it is a postulate which liberates consequences very far from comic, and, when this is so, if the story is good it will usually point a moral: of itself, without any didactic manipulation by the author on the conscious level. Stevenson's *Dr Jekyll and Mr Hyde* would be an example. Another is Marc Brandel's *Cast the First Shadow*, where a man, long solitary, despised, and oppressed, because he had no shadow, at last meets a woman who shares his innocent defect, but later turns from her in disgust and indignation on finding that she has, in addition, the loathsome and unnatural property of having no reflection. Readers who do not write themselves often describe such stories as allegories, but I doubt if it is as allegories that they arise in the author's mind.

In all these the impossibility is, as I have said, a postulate, something to be granted before the story gets going. Within that frame we inhabit the known world and are as realistic as anyone else. But in the next type (and the last I shall deal with) the marvellous is in the grain of the whole work. We are, throughout, in another world. What makes that world valuable is not, of course, mere multiplication of the marvellous either for comic effect (as in *Baron Munchausen* and sometimes in Ariosto and Boiardo) or for mere astonishment (as, I think, in the worst of the *Arabian Nights* or in some children's stories), but its quality, its flavour. If good novels are comments on life, good stories of this sort (which are very much rarer) are actual additions to life; they give, like certain rare dreams, sensations we never had before, and enlarge our conception of the range of possible experience. Hence the difficulty of discussing them at all with those who refuse to be taken out of what they call "real life"—which means, perhaps, the groove through some far wider area of possible experience to which our senses and our biological, social, or economic interests usually confine us—or, if taken, can see nothing outside it but aching boredom or sickening monstrosity. They shudder and ask to go home. Specimens of this kind, at its best, will never be common. I would include parts of the *Odyssey,* the *Hymn to Aphrodite,* much of the *Kalevala* and *The Faerie Queene,* some of Malory (but none of Malory's best work) and more of *Huon,* parts of Novalis's *Heinrich von Ofterdingen, The Ancient Mariner* and *Christabel,* Beckford's *Vathek,* Morris's *Jason* and the *Prologue* (little else) of the *Earthly Paradise,* MacDonald's *Phantastes, Lilith,* and *The Golden Key,* Eddison's *Worm Ouroboros,* Tolkien's *Lord of the Rings,* and that shattering, intolerable, and irresistible work, David Lindsay's *Voyage to Arcturus.* Also Mervyn Peake's *Titus Groan.* Some of Ray Bradbury's stories perhaps make the grade. W. H. Hodgson's *The Night Land* would have made it in eminence from the unforgettable sombre splendour of the images it presents, if it were not disfigured by a sentimental and irrelevant erotic interest and by a foolish, and flat archaism of style. (I do not mean that all archaism is foolish, and have never seen the modern hatred of it cogently defended. If archaism succeeds in giving us the sense of having entered a remote world, it justifies itself. Whether it is correct by philological standards does not then matter a rap.)

I am not sure that anyone has satisfactorily explained the keen, lasting, and solemn pleasure which such stories can give. Jung, who went furthest, seems to me to produce as his explanation one more myth which affects us in the same way as the rest. Surely the analysis of water should not itself be wet? I shall not attempt to do what Jung failed to do. But I would like to draw attention to a neglected fact: the astonishing intensity of the dislike which some readers feel for the mythopoeic. I first found it out by accident. A lady (and, what makes the story more piquant, she herself was a Jungian psychologist by profession) had been talking about a dreariness which seemed to be creeping over her life, the drying up in her of the power to feel pleasure, the aridity of her mental landscape. Drawing a bow at a venture, I asked, "Have you any taste for fantasies and fairy tales?" I shall never forget how her muscles tightened, her hands clenched themselves, her eyes started as if with horror, and her voice changed, as she hissed out, "I *loathe* them." Clearly we here have to do not with a critical opinion but with something like a phobia. And I have seen traces of it elsewhere, though never quite so violent. On the other side, I know from my own experience, that those who like the mythopoeic like it with almost equal intensity. The two phenomena, taken together, should at least dispose of the theory that it is something trivial. It would seem from the reactions it produces, that the mythopoeic is rather, for good or ill, a mode of imagination which does something to us at a deep level. If some seem to go to it in almost compulsive need, others seem to be in terror of what they may meet there. But that is of course only suspicion. What I feel far more sure of is the critical *caveat* which I propounded a while ago. Do not criticize what you have no taste for without great caution. And above all, do not ever criticize what you simply can't stand. I will lay all the cards on the table. I have long since discovered my own private phobia, the thing I can't bear in literature, the thing which makes me profoundly uncomfortable, is the representation of anything like a quasi love affair between two children. It embarrasses and nauseates me. But of course I regard this not as a charter to write slashing reviews of books in which the hated theme occurs, but as a warning not to pass judgement on them at all. For my reaction is unreasonable: such child-loves quite certainly occur in real life and I can give no reason why they should not be represented in art. If they touch the scar of some early trauma in me, that is my misfortune. And I would venture to advise all who are attempting to become critics to adopt the same principle. A violent and actually resentful reaction to all books of a certain kind, or to situations of a certain kind, is a danger signal. For I am convinced that good adverse criticism is the most difficult thing we have to do. I would advise everyone to begin it under the most favourable conditions: this is, where you thoroughly know and heartily like the thing the author is trying to do, and have enjoyed many books where it was done well. Then you will have some chance of really showing that he has failed and perhaps even of showing why. But if our real reaction to a book is "Ugh! I just can't bear this sort of thing," then I think we shall not be able to diagnose whatever real faults it has. We may labour to conceal our emotion, but we shall end in a welter of emotion, unanalysed, vogue-words— "arch," "facetious," "bogus," "adolescent," "immature" and the rest. When we really know what is wrong we need none of these.

# ALIEN MONSTERS

## Joanna Russ

Good morning—or rather, good afternoon, everybody. I'm very glad to be here and very glad to be speaking to you. In asking me here to speak, you know, Tom Purdom really paid me a tremendous compliment. After all sorts of things about how intelligent I was, and how he was sure I'd be so interesting and give such an interesting talk on a fascinating subject, he paid the ultimate compliment: He said, "And most of all we want you to be first on the program because you're a teacher." (I thought he was going to say, you know how to talk, you'll be fascinating, fluent and so on, but this wasn't it.) No, he said, "You're a teacher and you have a regular job and you're the only one we can depend on to get up early enough in the morning." Little does he know!

I am glad to see, looking around, that this is not true. I'm not the only one. Thank you all. It was heroic. It was heroic for me, anyway.

Now I'm going to try, today, to talk about something that people will disagree with—some people, anyway—and some of you may get pretty mad at me before I'm finished. But I think it's worth it, anyway. I'm trying to operate on the old Leninist principle of presenting a united front to outsiders but being perfectly free to quarrel among ourselves. I think this is something science fiction ought to do—I mean the quarreling among ourselves. And if we're going to indulge in it, we had better do so

SPEECH delivered at the Philadelphia Science Fiction Conference, November 9, 1968 pretty quickly; there isn't much time left. The days of our privacy are numbered. Really, the academicians are after us, and there is going to be an invasion of outside people into this field of the kind none of us has ever seen before—all sorts of goggle-eyed, clump-footed types' who will be bringing in all sorts of outside standards (good or bad), outside experience, outside contexts, outside remarks, naïveté in some things, great sophistication in other things, all sorts of oddities, all sorts of irrelevancies —well, heaven only knows what. I don't even know if it'll be good or bad or how good or how bad. But it is going to happen. The academicians are after us.

Now, if you don't already know it, literary academicians—and, by the way, I want to include what you might call semi-professional types, like the sort of writers and critics who write for magazines like the *Atlantic*, even though they may not be actually connected with universities— anyway, literary academicians are always looking for something new to criticize or some new way to criticize something old, and they are just beginning to realize that right under their noses is a whole new, absolutely virgin field of literature that nobody has even had a go at yet. What's going to happen when they realize this fully will be a sort of literary California gold rush with what we have always considered our own private property trampled under mobs and mobs of people who haven't the slightest respect for our uniqueness, or the things we like about ourselves, or the pet grievances we've been nursing for years, and so on. Some of these people are fools, but some of them—and I know some of them—are a lot more sophisticated than anybody in this room. I know that they are certainly much more sophisticated than I am. I think when they get into the field of science fiction, as critics of course, that they will find s.f. is an antidote for a lot of nonsense that *they* are subject to, but I'm afraid it's going to work the other way round, too.

Actually, I want to get my own licks in before the crowd arrives.

All this was brought home to me in a very personal way a couple of weeks ago. I teach at Cornell, and when Cornell University people find out that I write science fiction, there's this sort of wary and cautious couple of steps back—"Oh, you write science fiction?"—and then, with a kind of glaze over the eyes, they say, "Ah—that's H. G. Wells and all that, isn't it?" and I say, "Right!" And then they run away. This is how it happens. Well, this is no longer so. Just two weeks ago today I found in my office mailbox a note asking me to teach a course in Science Fiction this summer: ENGLISH 305; SCIENCE FICTION—*Open to Graduate Students.*

And that started me thinking about all the things I've just been saying here this afternoon. And it made me feel very strongly that instead of trying to please both other people and myself, I had better be as nasty as possible. After all, *we* know we're good. *We* know we're on to something. I knew it ever since I was fourteen, when I found out that science fiction was more exciting than vampire stories. And it is, too. I've been reading the stuff for about sixteen years now—I'm addicted to it, like everyone else here—but lately what you might call the Long-Term Fan Syndrome has been happening to me. This is the disease that everybody gets sooner or later and the symptoms are always the same. "Oh, they used to write it better. Oh, it was better in the old days." Of course, when you talk to people, you find out that they never have quite the same old days in mind—some will pick the thirties, some the early fifties, some the late fifties, etc., etc. Then there is this student of mine—"Oh, they used to write it better. Oh, it was better in the old days." I asked him how old he was—seventeen—and what the old days were. It turned out that by the old days he meant *last year.* When people start differing like that, it's obvious that what they mean is the days of their own youth, that is, the days when they first started reading s.f.

Now, I don't like this. I want to keep on reading the stuff. I want to enjoy it. So I started thinking, and out of all the things I could complain about, all the things I could kvetch about and criticize, *one* story and *one* picture somehow stuck in my mind.

I'm not going to tell you what magazine the story was in, or who wrote it, or who did the picture, because those things really aren't important. You can find many, many other stories like it, and quite a few other pictures like it. And I want to make clear at the very beginning that I am *not* talking about the individual defects of individual writers or individual editors—this is not the point at all. What I am trying to do is get at something that is in the air, and that affects science fiction as a whole. It's not a question of there being a multitude of coincidental decisions as to what to write, just by happenstance. Because a lot of these writers are very different from each other personally. I know many of them. But something in the field is affecting all of them and making people who are not alike write alike.

Anyway, the story itself was a very clear, simple little story—very delicately and carefully told. It was about homosexuality on Mars. Why

Mars I don't know, except that wherever you are as a reader, you're not *there* at any rate. The point of the story was that men who are isolated for a long time without women will attempt to get their sexual satisfaction from each other—and this is quite true; this is the sort of thing that any warden of any prison in the United States can tell you, not to mention the people who know perfectly well that such things happen—although not, of course, to everyone—in places like the Army. Anyway, the story was perfectly unsensational and even decent to the point of reticence. There wasn't even any sex in it. Instead—and this is typically American—one man killed another. It was really an all-right story, very rational, very reasonable, and not in the least shocking. I read it. I had to sort of prop my eyes open, you know, because actually it was pretty dull, but I read it.

Then I came to that picture.

It was a picture of the murderer—this one guy who had killed the man who had made advances to him. Out of horror and disgust, you see. And the story made the point that such exaggerated horror was a product of unconscious, latent homosexuality. Well, apparently the artist had taken alarm even at *latent, unconscious* homosexuality, and had decided that by God, he was going to show you that this character was no effeminate sissy—he was a *man*—so what he did was put layer on layer of muscles on this character, and give him beetling eyebrows and a snarl—I simply cannot describe the effect. He would've made an adult male gorilla look fragile. It was absolutely wild.

I was reading my magazine in the student cafeteria and as I reached this picture, I think I made some sort of extraordinary noise, like "Eeyah," which attracted the attention of a student who was nearby.

"What are you reading?" "Science fiction." "Can I see?"—he was very interested—"Oh, that's an alien."

Well, he was right, of course. He was absolutely right. In the anxiety to show you a real he-man, the artist who did the picture had created a megalith, a monster, an armored tank, something that had only the faintest resemblance to a human being. I loved that picture. It was so awful that it was wonderful. I wanted to keep it but it fell in my orange juice and got sort of messed up. Still, every once in a while I think of that picture—and then I think of one of those megaliths trying to rape another megalith—and it makes me feel good. In its own way, it's perfectly inimitable.

Of course, the trouble is that the science fiction illustrator who did the picture was *not* trying to be funny. And therein lies the whole point of my speech today.

It is a scandal, a real scandal, that in a field like ours, which is supposed to be so unconventional, so free, free to extrapolate into the future, free of prejudice, of popular nonsense, so rational and so daring, it is an especial scandal that in *our* field so many readers and so many writers—or so many stories, anyhow—cling to this Paleolithic illusion, this freak, this myth of what a real man is. And it's a scandal that he ruins so many stories. Because he does, you know, he ruins everything he touches. He has only to make one appearance and at once the story he is in coughs, kicks up its heels and dies dead. He has only to look at a woman to turn her into pure cardboard.

Let me put it more generally, and I hope more clearly.

Science fiction is still—very strangely and very unfortunately—subject to a whole constellation or group of values which do not have any really necessary connection with science fiction. I would call them conventional or traditional masculine values except that they are really more than that; they are a kind of wild exaggeration of such values. Of course, everything becomes exaggerated in s.f. because we don't show things in the here-and-now, but as they might be. It's a kind of fantasy and dramatic high relief. By the way, I think what I'm talking about is particularly American; I don't think American s.f. has in the past owed very much to British s.f. or that they spring from the same roots at all. American science fiction began in the pulps—I'm not downgrading this, I think it's a very good thing, although I can't go into the reasons why—now—because I don't have time. But this origin in trash—real, popular trash—may have something to do with the persistence of this really strange kind of image. If I wanted to put it in one sentence, it would be something like this:

The only real He-Man is the Master of the Universe.

Which, of course, leaves out a great many people.

If you believe this but are a little less extreme about stating it, it comes out something like this:

The real He-Man is invulnerable. He has no weaknesses. Sexually, he is super-potent. He does exactly what he pleases, everywhere and at all times. He is absolutely self-sufficient. He depends on nobody, for this would be a weakness. Toward women he is possessive, protective and patronizing; to men he gives orders. He is never frightened by anything or for any reason; he is never indecisive; and he always wins.

In short, he is an alien monster, just as I said.

The trouble with this creature—the megalith with the beetling eyebrows—is the trouble with all mythologies. It's not that he doesn't exist, because everybody *knows* that he doesn't exist. I don't think there's a single sane man on earth who could seriously and honestly say: Yes, I am all that. I am like that. I am never frightened of anything. I have no weaknesses whatsoever. I am a sexual dynamo. I always have my own way. Everybody obeys me—and so forth. We all know that such a person is impossible. We don't really believe that he exists.

But we do believe that somehow—despite what we actually know about other people and ourselves—that he *ought* to exist, or that he's in some sense ideal, or that there's something wrong with people who are *not* like that. Or, at the very least, that it would be a hell of a lot of fun pretending you really are like that, even though you know you aren't and you couldn't possibly be.

Now I don't like this—part of the reason is obvious. This is an ideal that is *by definition* absolutely closed to me. I can pretend to be Cleopatra but I can't very well pretend to be Antony. And for various reasons, Cleopatra doesn't appear in science fiction much. I like to think that because I'm a woman I can stand outside this whole business and be somewhat more objective than if I were caught up in it, as I think a man has to be, to some degree.

I also don't like this strange myth that is set up as a person, because he kills every story he touches, or almost every story—they're usually stone dead before the first word comes out of the typewriter. If the stories are alive, they live through the other characters, or through the alien characters, or through incidental comedy or through other interesting things that come in as sort of sidelines. But this turns the story into a grab bag, with no center. The story cannot live through its central character, its central conflict, or its central system of values.

The third reason I don't like this kind of thing—and this is the most important of all—is that this ultramasculine scheme of values messes up one of the most important and fascinating subjects science fiction is dealing with today. Also, *was* dealing with, by the way, although I will stand corrected about this—but I think it's been a preoccupation of s.f. from way back.

I am talking about the subject of power. Now this is a serious business. What you and I think about power, and what we expect powerful people to do, what we are willing to let them do, the kinds of people we give power to, whether *we* have any power, and how much—these are really important. And for some reason, s.f. seems to have gone right to questions like this from the beginning. How should power be used? What does power justify? How can power be overcome? All this sort of thing. For a contemporary novel—only one among many—*Bug Jack Barron.* It's practically about nothing else.

I think again that this may be a particularly American thing, the flavor(?), well, the quality, the particular kind of concern we have with power. Europeans tend to concentrate on the ethical side, and you get things like Albert Camus writing about suicide being the supremely moral act, things that tend to seem pretty bizarre to an American. Europeans— would you believe European movies? after all, I haven't read *everything* —seem to take it for granted that people are pretty powerless, pretty helpless, everybody has weaknesses, everybody is limited by society—and that's just the way it is. For us, power seems to be a problem *per se*, just because it exists. And vulnerability, too—the opposite side of power— this, too, is a problem just because it exists. We aren't just concerned with power; we're downright obsessed with it. And we tend to link up the idea of power with that old, beetling-browed he-man I was talking about. We insist that power—mind you, *absolute* power, too, power of all kinds—is equivalent to masculinity.

This leads to trouble. The trouble with making masculinity equal to power—especially the sort of absolute, ultimate power that s.f. writers like to write about—is that you can't look at either power or masculinity clearly. This is bad enough when you can't think clearly about masculinity, but when you can't think clearly about power, it's godawful. In politics, for instance, power is simply real—it exists—it's like the electricity in the lights of this room; and if you look at a real political situation or a real moral situation, and instead of seeing what's really there, you see Virility—Manhood at Stake—goodness knows what—everything gets all mucked up. Of course, this sort of problem isn't confined to science fiction; you can see it happening all over the place. But science fiction has a unique chance to deal with these things in the chemically pure form, so to speak, to really speculate about them. But so often we don't.

One of the strangest things in s.f., when you meet this concern with power, is that s.f. writers seem pretty much to insist on an either-or situation. That is, people in stories tend to be either all-powerful (this is the Ruler of the Universe again) or absolutely powerless. Either the hero is conquering the world or the world is returning the compliment by conquering *him*. In any case, it's a completely black-and-white situation with nothing in between. Alexei Panshin once complained about characters who are strangled by their vacuum cleaners. Well, I think this idea of megalithic, absolute power has a lot to do with being strangled by your vacuum cleaner. If the real man is absolutely invulnerable, then if you're not absolutely invulnerable, you're not a real man, and if you're not a real man, you're absolutely weak and absolutely vulnerable, so even a vacuum cleaner can get you. You even sometimes get this weird hybrid, who is at the same time a superman (utterly powerful) and is being persecuted by the whole world (i.e., he is utterly powerless). In fact, he's being persecuted *because* he's a superman, that is, because he's powerful. But if he's persecuted, he's powerless. That is, he's powerless because he's powerful. Or vice versa. Sometimes the brain just reels.

Also, you get something else very bad in science fiction from this confusion of maleness—masculinity—with power. You get what's been called pornoviolence, that is, violence for the sake of violence. ("Pornography of violence"—pornoviolence. An elegant word.) I certainly think that science fiction is less of an offender here, if you want to call it an offense, than what's called "mainstream" writing. But we do get a lot of this. I am also getting tired of characters who are tortured or flayed or impaled alive in various ways, or who have to drag themselves along corridors "in a blaze of pain" (it's always a *blaze of pain* in these stories, nobody ever feels just *bleh*) or they climb mountains while their lungs are bursting just so the author can enjoy himself masochistically by showing what strong stuff his heroes are made of. "Every nerve screamed with the pain that was coursing through him." We've all read this dozens of times. Sometimes it's pain and sometimes it's rapture, but it's always bullshit. Bullshit is nice for fun and games, but when you adopt the attitude behind the bullshit and try somehow to apply it or believe in it in real life, that's not good. What I mean is, power is a real thing. It exists. To have power over other people, to control other people, is a real thing which produces real emotions, real problems, real anxieties, real pleasures. A writer can depict these. But if he is all hung up on the masculinity-equals-power bit or the heroes-must-be-all-powerful-or-they're-not-heroes bit, then he is going to thrash around in a sort of void. At the worst, he will simply produce stuff that is too dull to read. At best, he will produce a kind of pornography. But he won't get beyond that. I wish I could bring in here a book by Stephen Marcus called *The Other Victorians*. It has one of the best definitions of pornography that I've ever seen. Mr. Marcus's point is that what makes something pornographic is not simply that it excites you sexually. After all, even a book like *Madame Bovary*, which we consider very reticent, should excite you sexually, among all the other things it does. What pornography does is exclude everything else, and—in the process, ironically enough—it ends up excluding real sex, too. Porno-violence is pornographic because it excludes real violence, and the real experience of what violence is and means and feels like. It excludes real power, and the real experience of what power is and means and feels like. In their place, it puts myths, fantasies—in a word, nonsense.

Let me return now to my beetle-browed, lumpy-muscled friend. I've complained about the bad effects of a system of values that makes being Ruler of the Universe the only decent position in life for a red-blooded American boy. But there is another objection to this system of values besides the way it messes up people's heads when it comes to thinking about power. I mentioned before, that although nobody actually sets up as the Invulnerable Superman, still there's this kind of omnipresent, vague feeling that it would be pretty nice if you *could* be an invulnerable superman, though, alas, one can't be in real life. Let me run down the list again: No weaknesses. Super-potent. Absolutely uncontrolled by others. Absolutely self-sufficient. Depends on nobody. Gives everybody orders. Never afraid. Never indecisive. He always wins.

Ah! if only one could be like this.

But is it so attractive, really?

It seems to me that for the one quality—being invulnerable—every other quality has been given up. The super He-man is super-potent (he has to be, this is an expression of strength) but does he have super-pleasure? Not in the stories I've read. Pleasure involves a kind of letting-go, a kind of loss of self, and he can't afford this. This would be weakness. Is he super-happy? Usually not. He does exactly what he wants—that is, nobody controls him—but is he therefore super-spontaneous? Super-impulsive? No. Being spontaneous would be dangerous; it would expose him to weakness, and he must not be weak. He can be fond of other people, in a sort of parental or protective way, and he can behave tenderly toward them—although he doesn't usually—but no one can be tender to *him* because that would mean he depended on someone, and depending on someone would mean he was weak. People admire him but they can't love him, and if you think for a minute, you'll see that he can't love anyone else, because love is possible only between equals and by definition he has no equals. He is a very lonely man. There is a kind of sadness that runs through stories about the superman, and the rugged he-man hero, too—sometimes the author is aware of it and sometimes he is not—but there is often (underground, sometimes) this profound, despairing sadness. I'm thinking now of Gordon Dickson's Dorsai, the warrior people, where the sadness is quite explicit. You see, the price you have to pay for absolute mastery of every situation is awful. It's the whole rest of life.

Well, if you don't have traditional masculine values, then what? Traditional feminine values? I can't answer this vehemently enough. No, no, a thousand times no. There *are* stories like that in s.f. and I hate them. If I opened *Analog* tomorrow and found that by divine fiat it had suddenly turned into *The Ladies' Home Journal*, I think I would drop dead. And not just from shock, either.

If anything gets me madder than the strong, laconic individualist who defeats Ming the Merciless by killing sixteen million billion aliens with his bare hands in four pages, it's the sweet, gentle, compassionate *intuitive* little woman who solves some international crisis by mending her slip or something, when her big, strong, brilliant husband has failed to do so for twenty-three chapters.

I find conventional masculine heroics funny, but conventional feminine heroics are nauseating without being funny. To me, anyway.

Well, what I want—I can't describe it really, because it would be different for every writer, but maybe I can give a sort of general impression.

I would like to see science fiction keep the daring, the wildness, the extravagant imagination that we got from starting out in the pulps—but I would like to see us shed the kind of oversimplified values and attitudes it got from the same place—this business about the He-Man is only one of them. So many science fiction stories operate on assumptions about people and assumptions about values that would hardly be adequate to describe the social relations of a bunch of flatworms. There are science fiction novels—whole big fat novels—built around moral problems that would be instantly solvable by a year-old chimpanzee. I have also, by the way, seen first-rate adventure stories ruined by people who insisted on reading them as if they contained profound moral problems, though the story itself clearly had no such intentions. There is no reason on earth why a story *has* to be didactic, *has* to teach an explicit moral. But if you are going to moralize, you had better make sure it's above the kindergarten level.

Anyway, as I said, the barbarian hordes are knocking at the gate. And these people are *sharp*. I think we're going to open their eyes to an awful lot, but I think the converse is going to happen, too, and sometimes I don't like the idea at all. They're very sneaky and they're very erudite. Unfortunately, the academic critics are going to bring along their own brand of nonsense, but not all these people are bad critics, or academics, or even critics at all. There are writers, too, people from other fields— movie-makers and painters and all sorts of people. And what is important is not what they will like or dislike about science fiction. After all, nobody has to be bound by what *any* critic says, inside the field or outside it— what matters is that once you've let an outsider into your private preserve, your own personal backyard, the place never looks the same to *you* again. It's like letting a stranger into your house—it's not what the stranger thinks, but that suddenly you find yourself looking at your own domain with a difference. You turn into a stranger yourself. You know, "Oh, lovely rug. Oh, beautiful chairs. Nice picture. . . . What, no storm windows?" Things are never quite the same again. This is what's been happening to me, ever since I learned I was going to have to teach science fiction this summer. Everybody knows that you don't *teach* science fiction; you just do it. But you do teach it.

So, I picked on one thing for today. There are dozens of others. There are good things, wonderful things, too, of course. And I'm not complaining about things I don't like *just* because there are going to be outsiders analyzing s.f. and watching what we do and criticizing what we do and so forth. It's the kind of thing I would complain about anyway. I want the stuff to be better. I enjoy reading it even more than I enjoy writing it. I want it to be thrilling, and real, and alive, and about real people. I want it to be complicated and various and difficult like life—not smooth and predigested and simpleminded, the way nothing is but bad stories. I want my sense of wonder back again.

And I have it all figured out for the summer, what I'm going to do in

the class, I mean. When this keen, studious, frighteningly brilliant graduate student comes up to me and says, "You know—I've been reading
*Savage Orbit*. Now of course I understand the peripety in the last chapter, but I can't quite place the mythic resonance of the objective correla-
tive." Then I will look at him—and smile, just a little, knowingly—a sort
of Ellisonian smile—and say, "Read it again. Page seventy-eight. *Lithium
hydroxide?*" And he will be flattened for life!

# CATHEDRALS IN SPACE

*Autumn, 1953*

## William Atheling, Jr. [James Blish]

About three decades ago—more or less coinciding with the first of the great theism-vs.-atheism arguments to rage in the letter columns of the professional magazines—H. P. Lovecraft remarked (in *Supernatural Horror in Literature*, Abramson, 1945) that it was futile to attempt to describe possible peoples of other planets simply by exporting to them wholesale the folk customs of Earth. One of the folk customs listed by HPL in the course of his comment was royalty; another was religion.

It is perfectly obvious, of course, that the "alien princess" of *Planet Stories* and Edgar Rice Burroughs is nothing more than a trope, and a long-dead one at that (though reviewers for such journals as *Time* and *The Saturday Review of Nothing* have yet to notice the fact). It is not quite so self-evident that we will not find gods, or the belief in them, on other planets. We find them everywhere on Earth, which cannot be said of royalty or the other folk customs mentioned by Lovecraft; and even where we do not find specific deities, we find religion's immediate precursor, magic.

A case could be made, I think, for the proposition that any humanly conceivable thinking creature will arrive at magic, and hence eventually at religion in some form, before he can arrive at scientific method, since the basic proposition of the one is, in essence, a less precise form of the other. The root assumption of sympathetic magic, as any reader of Pratt/de Camp (or Frazer) already knows, is "Similar actions produce

---

From *The Issue at Hand*, Advent, 1964

similar results." The root assumption of scientific method might be stated in the same form: "Identical actions produce identical results." The difference between the two assumptions, aside from the fact that the first does not work and the second does, is a matter of refinement of observation—and it is difficult to accept that any thinking creature, no matter how bug-eyed or many-tentacled, could so evolve as to arrive at the more precise formulation first. He may, of course, have since outgrown the earlier faith, as we have not, but nevertheless traces of it would almost surely remain buried in his culture.

Whether or not you accept this proposition, however—and there are doubtless many anthropocentric assumptions in it—we can at least be sure that man will export his own gods into space, as surely as he exports his languages, his nationalisms, and his belief in his own rationality. Science fiction has already dealt at some length with the problems of interplanetary man's allegiance to a home country, to a government, to the family he left behind, and even to the home sexual code. Lately there have been several science-fictional inquiries into his relationship with the home god—as distinguished from the local gods, such as the one Heinlein's "Methuselah's Children" (*Astounding*, July/September, 1941) ran afoul of.

This is of peculiar interest to the practising writer or critic, be he theist or mechanistic materialist himself, because it represents an enormous potential extension of the subject matter of science fiction in the direction of real human problems—which is the direction in which the medium must be extended if it is to remain viable. You may feel, for instance, as Arthur C. Clarke does, that to carry national boundaries into space would be to export a primitive superstition which it would be criminal to continue on other worlds than ours—yet the chances are good that we will export this folk custom, along with our penchant for killing each other and many similar quaint, unidealistic practices. By the same token, like it or not, a real human being sitting in a real lunar crater is more than likely to be spending a certain proportion of his time wondering whether or not the god of his fathers is with him yet—and using his decisions on this subject as bases for action. The science fiction writer can no more ignore this than he can the probable extension of nationalism into space. It is one of the ways that human beings think, a way so basic that it involves their emotions as well. As such, it is not only a proper but a fertile subject for fiction of any kind, and science fiction in particular.

These remarks arise primarily out of several rereadings of "A Case of

Conscience," by James Blish (*If*, September, 1953), an exhaustive and occasionally exhausting study of a Roman Catholic priest thrown into an ethical and theological dilemma by what he finds on a new planet. Almost the whole text of the story, which runs to about 25,000 words, is devoted to the problem, its background, its implications, the lines of reasoning involved in making a decision, and the nature of the decision itself. Though several things "happen," there is no action as such in the yarn, and most of the drama is dialectical. Part of the length of the story is contributed by sheer physical description of the planet, in which the author indulges so extensively as to delay telling the reader the story's central problem until he is nearly two thirds of the way through it—and probably losing two thirds of his readers in the process; but the detail, as it turns out, is valuable, first because it establishes a slow and discursive tone *before* the reader is plunged into the elaborate four-way argument which is the essence of the piece, and second because most of the details (though not all) are integral to the argument itself.

What the general reader of science fiction will make of this story is still an unanswered question,* and in my judgment an important one— not only because of the subject matter, which is not as novel as editor Shaw's promotional smokescreen would lead you to believe, but also because of its narrative technique, which is unique in my experience. My initial impression was that readers who enjoy what Poe called "ratiocination" for its own sake, and who in addition could suspend their own prejudices about the subject matter long enough to feel Father Ruiz' dilemma as acutely as he himself felt it, would find the story intensely exciting, while everyone else would yawn and look baffled. Then I remembered G. K. Chesterton's Father Brown stories, where there is also considerable display of straight reasoning, plus a uniformly religious point of view brought to bear upon the problems of a specialized idiom (in this case, the detective story). Conceivably, "A Case of Conscience" is well enough told as a story to carry a similar general appeal; although intricate, it is anything but incoherent, and it is so paced—as I've noted above—as to make the final argument seem highly dramatic, in the face of the obvious obstacles to such an impression. Furthermore, several other attitudes toward the religious problem are represented by other characters in the story, so that, although the author obviously intended the

* See the Afterword to this essay.

reader to identify himself with Father Ruiz' point of view, he has provided handles for dissidents to grasp if they will.

This took considerable doing. I have made no secret of the fact that I mistrust the average reader's ability to weigh technical competence, or even to recognize it, so that I can make no present assessment of the effectiveness of what Blish has done here; theoretically he should have captured his audience, even though most of it will not know why it is captured or how the trick was turned. On the other hand, he may have captured nobody but a cross-section of other writers who are in a position to appreciate how much work this kind of story takes, without being any better able to weigh its effectiveness with a non-technical reader than I am. (In any group of experts, the incidence of a disease called "expertitis," the major symptom of which is a perverse delight in talking over the heads of the rabble, is invariably high. In our field, even Damon Knight shows touches of it now and then, and Atheling was permanently put to bed of it long ago.) The question is somewhat clouded, furthermore, by several direct failures of technique in the Blish story, so that if the yarn as a whole fails to communicate, it will be hard to tell whether (a) it failed because the techniques we think most effective are really of little value, (b) it failed because these techniques, though valuable enough, were not well enough realized in this story, or (c) it failed because no conceivable attention to technique could prevail against the novelty and the touchiness of the story's subject matter. If it succeeds, of course, the same questions remain to be answered.

Insofar as evidence exists on point (c), it seems safe to say that novelty and touchiness of subject matter probably will not seriously affect the verdict. The subject matter of "A Case of Conscience" is still unusual in our field, but it is no longer strange. As I noted at the beginning of this essay, the extension of science fiction story problems into this realm has now become quite marked, so that Blish's story is not a freak but part of a trend. It is perhaps not quite an accident that one of the earliest and best of such science fiction stories, Hugh Benson's *Lord of the World* (Dodd, Mead, 1908), was called to fandom's attention by Virginia Kidd, then Blish's wife—and that Benson, like Blish's Father Ruiz, was a Jesuit. (Father Benson also wrote a sequel to the novel, of which Miss Kidd was apparently unaware.) The wildly, floridly spooky M. P. Shiel charged into the arena, exclamation points shooting in all directions, with his 1901 novel *Lord of the Sea* (and it is ridiculous but characteristic of Sam

Moskowitz to call the book anti-Semitic; the book's subject is the politics of Zionism, and its climax the advent of the Messiah; but of course style-deaf people who think books about Jews should contain no Jewish villains had better be restricted to Peter Rabbit anyhow). The interplanetary novels of C. S. Lewis (*Out of the Silent Planet, Perelandra,* and *That Hideous Strength*) offer more recent examples; they set out to impose upon the solar system a strange Anglican-cum-Babylonian theology and cosmogony, with amazingly convincing results despite Lewis' decidedly foggy view of astronomy and most of the other sciences he seeks to diabolize.

The first notable stirrings of religious interest in the magazines during the 1950 science fiction boom probably can be traced back to Ray Bradbury's "The Man" (*Thrilling Wonder Stories,* February, 1949), a parable of the Second Coming of Christ. I have mentioned this before, because it has been the subject of considerable imitation; but it is also interesting because it proposes that Christ is traveling from planet to planet with his Message, a project which will take Him forever and hence reduces Bradbury's intended devoutness to a numerical absurdity by proposing that an omnipotent God can arrange a multiple Advent only seriatim, by turning His Son into the Wandering Salesman. (The Messiah of the Jews, be it noted, is under no such limitation; he can turn up everywhere at once, like Santa Claus, and indeed this doctrine is specifically celebrated in Judaism's children's festival.) A much more sensitive short story by one of *Planet's* former editors, Paul L. Payne ("Fool's Errand," *Thrilling Wonder Stories,* October, 1952), dealt with an attempt to hoax a devout Jewish member of the first spaceship crew to Mars, by planting a phony cross on the planet; it fails because the hoaxer's boot also sheds a nail on the site of the plant, a coincidence which the Jewish spaceman is too hard-headed to accept, though it would have thrown most Sunday Christians into paroxysms of easy superstition. (And not just Protestants, either; think what the Fatima-worshippers would have made of such a juncture, despite all that the Devil's Advocates could possibly try to discourage them.)

The pattern that begins to emerge here—and I have selected only a few of many possible examples—is a startling one. Before I put a name to it, let me call to your attention what these writers are talking about, underneath the science-fictional trappings, the easy gestures and the Sunday sentimentality. Putting "A Case of Conscience" aside for the moment because we have thus far considered only half of it, we find Father

Benson talking about the coming of the Anti-Christ; Shiel about the coming of the Messiah; Lewis about the coming of the Next Sacrifice (Ransom), the magical Messiah (Merlin), and the Anti-Christ (his scientist-villain who turns into Satan in *Perelandra*, and anticlimactically into H. G. Wells in *That Hideous Strength*); Bradbury and his imitators about Christ the Wandering Salesman, scorned by His audiences (thus combining the Anti-Christ legend and the Flying Dutchman); and Payne about the human agent of a false Messiah, who is seen through easily by a Jew to whom "Messias ist *nicht* gekommen" has been an article of faith since 2 A.D.

Now, I think, we know more exactly what it is that we are considering here. These science fiction stories are not fundamentally theological at all. Every one of them, including "Case" and some others I am about to cite, are instead instruments of a chiliastic crisis, of a magnitude we have not seen since the world-wide chiliastic panic of 999 A.D., when everyone expected the Second Coming and the Last Judgment on the next New Year's morning, and nobody in his heart of hearts could bring himself to believe in the forgiveness of Christ. We no more believe in it now than we did then, and small wonder; and our modern Apocalyptic literature, overlaid though it is with the mythologies of scientific humanism and heroic technology, takes just as dim a view of it.

One science fiction story about religion which at first glance does not seem to fit this definition is Anthony Boucher's "The Quest for Saint Aquin," which was written for Raymond J. Healy's 1951 anthology, *New Tales of Space and Time* (Holt). This piece dealt with the soul-struggles of a post-atom-war Catholic priest against a robot tempter, while in search of a saint who also turned out to be a robot. But the story about atomic Armageddon and the post-bomb world is almost by definition apocalyptic—and to reinforce the tie, Mr. Boucher has it that Aquin, being a perfectly logical machine, is *therefore* a Roman Catholic, thus providing a Second Coming complete with the presently fashionable Neo-Thomism. (One wonders what St. Thomas would have thought of this; after all, the legend tells us that he smashed Albertus Magnus' magical brass head for getting the better of him in an argument.)

Incidentally, Boucher remarked of his story, in the preface to the book, that it "could almost certainly never have appeared in any magazine in the field" because of its theme. If this was so at the time—and it probably was—the appearance of Blish's story in *If* affords a rough measurement of the progress of the trend in two years. ("Case" did not get into print initially without some resistance, however—Horace Gold of *Galaxy* offered to take it only if "there's some way we can get rid of this religious jazz—I run a family magazine." Happily, both Shaw of *If* and Lester del Rey of *Space Science Fiction* wanted it, Shaw without conditions, del Rey on the promise of a sequel.)

All the elements of the Boucher story appear writ large in Walter M. Miller, Jr.'s deservedly admired novel *A Canticle for Leibowitz* (Lippincott, 1960), which was foreshadowed by a moving Miller short story, "Crucifixus Etiam" (*Astounding*, February, 1953), and which itself originally appeared as a series of magazine short stories. Several commentators, Boucher in particular, have called attention to the fact that almost all science fiction stories dealing with religion assume a Roman Catholic frame, and that this cannot entirely be explained by assuming that the authors are Catholics (Blish is a professed agnostic; Bradbury and Payne are not on record, but their texts show no doctrinal commitments). This observation ceases to be puzzling, however, the moment one realizes that the stories all seek to express, or perhaps sometimes exploit, a common chiliastic panic, so that the choice of the most complex, best organized and oldest body of Christian dogma as an intellectual background seems only natural. Only the always sportive Shiel made another choice, which emerged naturally from the fact that he was writing about a *First* Coming (though he rather clouds the issue in the last few pages of the novel with a sort of Christian psalm). He was, of course, pre-Bomb; so was Benson, but he was a priest.*

So much for precedents. The major difference between all these stories and "A Case of Conscience" is simply technical, not philosophical. It lies in the deliberate avoidance of anything which could wear the name of action, or, to put it positively, in an intensive concentration upon dialectic as the major storytelling device. For the most part, I think it successful; but such single-mindedness often runs to excess, and this story is no exception. It is necessarily a talky story, but it probably did not need to

---

* I find that Jungian analysts share my view that fear of the Bomb is the modern version of the 999 riots, and that Jung himself notes that the religious character of the flying saucer cults is based specifically on a hope that the Saucerites are going to Save us; one such cult even maintains that Christ was born on Venus, which makes the Earth just another of Bradbury's way-stations for the Wandering Salesman. I quite agree, but I wish I could rid myself of the suspicion that Jung himself thinks the saucers to be real.

be so damned talky; the long conversation between Ruiz and Chtexa which falls immediately after the yarn's best cliffhanger, for instance, drags on beyond the merely suspenseful into the maddening, and could have been cut nearly in half to the story's profit. The huge mass of detail and local color is also overdone: when it deals with such integral features of the local landscape as the Message Tree, it justifies itself, and the detailed discussion of the local method of reproduction is essential to the main argument—but the descriptions also include long catalogues of the local raw materials, discussions of the weather, and similar dead or at least indifferent matter which would overbalance any story of this length, even one as slow-paced as this one obviously needed to be. (Expertitis again?)

Finally—and this may well be the oddest complaint I ever have to make about a story—the ending of "A Case of Conscience" fails to be ambiguous enough. It is intended to leave the whole question posed by the story up in the air, for the reader to answer as best he can, but instead Blish traps himself in a piece of elementary symbolism which can easily be taken to imply a ready-made answer. I refer to the business of Cleaver's crates, which so dominates Ruiz' final dialogue with Chtexa as to suggest that Cleaver may be preparing to blow up the ship in mid-space, or otherwise tamper with the evidence. The falling of Cleaver's shadow over Ruiz' in the airlock, and the slamming of the airlock door ("Cleaver's trademark") reinforces the impression that it is Cleaver's point of view which will win in the long run, an impression which is totally false to the story as I read it.

In the meantime, religion, like science, is certainly doing its best to catch up with science fiction. "A Case of Conscience" includes a speculation that the creatures of other planets may never die, because, never having been in the Garden of Eden in the first place, they may not be considered by God as subject to the Curse of Adam. The identical speculation was making the rounds of the Vatican at the time the story was published (only a revival, of course; the problem of "the plurality of worlds" was not precisely new when Galileo inconveniently made it seem acute). The feeling is shared, furthermore, by many people with no sectarian axe to grind; I quote the July, 1953 issue of *The Journal of the British Interplanetary Society* (p. 178): "One day a landing on the moon will be made. . . . One would like to think that amid all the technical jubilation somebody will get up and say: 'Remember! For the first time since Adam the slate is clean.'"

AFTERWORD 1964

Looking at a story of one's own in this fashion is a difficult and perhaps a foredoomed exercise, and one impossible to free from suspicions of disingenuousness or outright dishonesty (of which I was duly accused at least once). Nevertheless, I'm glad I tried it; and in retrospect, it affords me the chance to check my critical performance in several ways that I couldn't have predicted and hence couldn't have attempted to set up for myself even had I wanted to.

That I did indeed capture some sort of audience is now established. The story brought me many letters, some from Catholics pointing out minor errors of ritual and dogma, some from militant atheists accusing me of being a Jesuit proselytizer, and all shades of opinion in between. It was anthologized only once, in England, but so dominated the other stories with which it appeared that reviews of the book barely mentioned most of them. The novel version (Ballantine, 1958)—not an expansion of the story, but a continuation of it, long after Lester del Rey had requested one—took the "Hugo" award for the best science fiction novel of 1958; in addition to its first American publication, it has seen three British editions, plus one each in France, Italy, Brazil, and Japan; has been dramatized at Hardin-Simmons University, made the subject of a half-hour lecture on the BBC's Third Programme, and discussed almost endlessly almost everywhere. All this is doubly gratifying when I remember that the night I finished the story, I predicted to my then wife that nobody would ever buy it (except Fletcher Pratt, who, having commissioned it for a Twayne anthology, was stuck with it).

The trend in subject matter which I predicted arrived and accelerated on schedule; so I have not hesitated to expand my 1953 remarks on that subject with a few more words I added nearly ten years later in Dick and Pat Lupoff's fan magazine *Xero*. As noted earlier, no credit is due me for this prediction anyhow, since the question of the plurality of worlds is an old one, and it was bound to arise once more as soon as spaceflight began to seem imminent to laymen as well as to science fiction readers. The distinction between the Apocalyptic and the chiliastic types emerged during the course of a recent all-night discussion with del Rey, and I don't think either of us could have arrived at it back in 1953, when there were still too few examples of religious science fiction to make the division evident. (Even del Rey's magnificently blasphemous Apocalyptic story, "For I Am a Jealous People," in *Star Short Novels*, Ballantine, 1954, was unwritten then, though he had been brooding about it earlier.)

The technical criticisms of the 1952 story still seem to me to be sound, if what we are talking about is still that story only. This must indeed be borne in mind, because at the time I wrote the criticism, I had no intention of writing a sequel, and had none in mind; the piece was supposed to be complete as it stood—and as such, I still think, it had the flaws I pointed out. When I was later afforded the chance to go on into novel length, I had the benefit of my own second thoughts, and I believe I used most of them.

For example, Atheling complains of the "catalogues of the local raw materials"; but eventually it becomes important to the story that one of these raw materials is amazingly abundant, whereas certain other more likely ones are very rare—and both these facts are buried in the catalogues, detective-story fashion, for the reader of the novel. Neither Atheling nor the author of the story were in a position to appreciate this a decade ago. Similarly, the heavy weighting of the end of the magazine story toward Cleaver still seems inexcusable if the story is to stop there—but if the story is to go on, then it becomes a fine multiple cliffhanger, making Ruiz' situation seem quite hopeless when the feel of the book in the reader's hands says plainly that there is more to come—indeed, more than half.

In fact, a curious effect of the novelization of the story is that it is now too short, although section one—the magazine story—was further expanded, and the new section is still longer than the first. Even at this length, there is just too much material there to escape an effect of breathlessness as the novel draws toward a close, and there was nothing I could do about it; at the time of writing, I was held by contract to 75,000 words, that being the largest book that Ballantine could then bind in the paperback format. Hence I am afraid that even today Atheling would find the completed work somewhat out of balance, though for reasons neither he nor I had anticipated.

If Robert A. Heinlein's *Stranger in a Strange Land* (Putnam, 1961) is not the longest single science fiction novel of the last three decades, at least it has very few peers. Yet despite its length, it seems crowded, and for good reason: it is about everything. In the course of unfolding the plot—which is itself very rich in incident—Heinlein explores politics, aesthetics, ethics, morals, theology, the occult, history, economics, a double handful of sciences, and a whole hatful of subsidiary matters. The result is not only impossible to do justice to in a review, but almost impossible to describe or characterize; I hardly know where to begin.

In such circumstances it is the part of wisdom to follow the author's lead and begin at the beginning. The book is science fiction, as the opening sentence establishes firmly: "Once upon a time there was a Martian named Valentine Michael Smith." Smith is the bastard of an adultery which occurred on the first manned expedition to Mars, and the sole survivor. (It is quickly established that the book is not for children, also.) He has been raised from infancy by the Martians, and thinks of himself as one of them. He is the stranger of the title, and the Earth, to which he is brought back at about the age of twenty-five, is the strange land.

Ostensibly, the novel tells the story of his education, career, and fate on Earth, a standard gambit for a satirical novel with a long and distinguished lineage. Heinlein, however, does not follow the usual procedure of showing how ridiculous our Earth customs are to Smith's Martian eyes, except in very small part. This role is allotted to an Earthman, one more in Heinlein's huge gallery of marvellously crusty eccentrics, "Jubal E. Harshaw, LL.B., M.D., Sc.D., bon vivant, gourmet, sybarite, popular author extraordinary, and neo-pessimist philosopher," who takes Smith in when the heat becomes too great for the fledgling, and rapidly takes on the role of Smith's foster father. As a popular author, Jubal sits beside a swimming pool in the Poconos dictating amazingly soppy confessions, love stories, and anything else he can turn into money, to three beautiful secretaries who also help to run his household; as a "neo-pessimist philosopher," he is charged with interpreting everything on Earth to Smith, to everybody else in the plot, and to the reader. He is livelier as a philosopher, but much more expert at soppy copy; of this, more later.

As for Smith, he is often amazed at Earth customs but tends to be uncritical, largely because it is Martian to *grok* every experience (the word means to drink, to drink in, to understand, and a host of related concepts, like a Chinese root) in the hope of embracing it, rather than rejecting it. Thus he is enabled to accept many Earth customs for which Jubal has nothing but scorn, and sometimes seems to Jubal to be in danger of being swallowed up in one or another of them. And in fact one does swallow him; sex, which on Mars is completely sensationless, accidental, and uninteresting (but at which Smith proves expert "by first intention," as a surgeon might put it).

From this point on, *Stranger in a Strange Land* becomes so heated on this subject that it may well inspire twice as many would-be book-burners as Heinlein's *Starship Troopers* (Putnam, 1959) did.* Heinlein supplies no on-stage orgies, no anatomical details, and no washroom graffiti, nor does he ever adopt the pornographer's device of treating a woman solely as a sexual object; indeed, his attitude is about as far toward the opposite pole as it is possible to go, short of *Barchester Towers*. I choose my example carefully, for Heinlein's treatment of sex is confessedly, designedly, specifically reverent—and this very reverence has produced the most forthright and far-out treatment in the whole history of science fiction, guaranteed to turn bluenoses positively white.

At this point I am going to abandon the plot, which has already developed as many knots as a gill-net, and which in any event can be depended upon to take care of itself. It goes, as good Heinlein plots always do, and this is a good one. Now, however, I think I have reached a position from which to characterize the novel: It is religious.

No communicant to a currently established religion is likely to think it anything but blasphemous, but its dominant subject is religion, and its intellectual offerings and innovations are primarily religious too. The sex, the politics, the sciences, the action, all are essentially contributory; the religious material is central. The religion is a synthetic one, of which Smith is the Messiah (or perhaps only the prophet), and the main task of the novel is to show it as sane, desirable and exalting—in contrast to both the systems of large established orders such as Islam and traditional Christianity (toward all of which Heinlein is sympathetic and apparently well informed) and those of highly commercial enterprises like the California nut-cults (some features of which, with Smith's Martian assistance, he also manages to view with at least moderate tolerance).

* It did; but also like its predecessor, it won the Hugo for its year.

Heinlein-Smith's eclectic religion is a fascinating potpourri, amazingly complicated to have come from a single brain rather than from centuries of accumulated haggling and hagiography; it contains something for everybody, or bravely gives that appearance, though by the same token it contains something repulsive for everybody too. I am not going to say which parts I like and which I don't, this being a purely private act of value judgment which must be reserved by each individual reader to himself, but the solely intellectual parts of the structure are well worth some analysis, particularly since they are as often in conflict with each other as are those of all other Scriptures I have ever encountered.

Heinlein-Smith's system is pluralistic: it admits of no single God, but instead says "*Thou* art God"; and if you are capable of understanding this sentence, then you *are* God whether you agree with the sentence or not. In other words, every being capable of thinking, understanding, embracing, is God, and that is all the God there is. Since a proper God cannot really die, survival after death is granted by the system (dead Martians continue to hang around the planet composing art-works and giving advice, but dead Earthlings go somewhere else, location not given); Heinlein shows directly (that is, without the intervention of Smith) that the dead are busy running the universe, as befits gods, and suggests in at least two places—though not explicitly—that they are at least occasionally reincarnated as "field agents." Because all who grok are God, there is no punishment in the hereafter; even the worst villain in this life graduates directly after death into being an assistant Archangel, though he may find himself not in a position to give orders to someone who was less villainous than he.*

Thus far, then, the system resembles that of the *Perelandra* trilogy in its special emphasis on intelligence and empathy (you will remember that C. S. Lewis says that any *hnau* or reasoning being is a special child of God regardless of its shape or demesne); it also includes much of

---

* My flippancy of tone is not intended to denigrate the subject matter, but to reflect the treatment. Like George O. Smith, G. Harry Stine and other engineers-turned-writers, Heinlein sometimes tries to prove his characters wits and sophisticates by transcribing page after page of the painful traveling-salesman banter which passes back and forth over real drawing boards and spec sheets. There is not an intolerable amount of this in *Stranger in a Strange Land*, considering the length of the whole, but unfortunately the conversations of the dead in heaven are conducted *entirely* in this style. Though I value the Laughing Buddha for his laughter, I don't want him to sound like he is about to sell me a set of vacuum cleaner fixtures as soon as I'm suitably off guard.

Schweitzer's "reverence for life," whether thinking or not, as is demonstrated early in the book when Smith is reluctant to walk on grass until he groks that it grows to be walked on; but there is no overall deity. The suggestion of reincarnation, if I am not misreading Heinlein in raising this question at all, is a common feature of Eastern religions, and I think it would naturally appeal to a writer trained in the sciences because it is conservative of souls, thus preventing the afterlife from becoming overcrowded beyond the limits of infinity and eternity. The implied dubiety about what really happens to the soul after death is Judaic, though without Judaism's 600-fold intellectual modesty on the subject; and the absence of any sort of punishment in the hereafter might be traced to many sects, a number of them Christian (see for example the heresy of Origen, who maintained that such was the mercy of God that if there is a Hell it must be empty).

Now, what are the implications of all this for the living? That is to say, how should we behave if all this should be true? Here the Heinlein-Smith religion, asked to supply its ethical imperatives, becomes a little murky, but at least a few doctrines can be fished up. Since there is no death— only "discorporation," a MaryBakerEddyism if ever I saw one—murder is not necessarily a crime. Under some circumstances it is wrong to push a soul on into the afterlife if it doesn't want to go yet, but if the adept "groks wrongness" (for instance, if the offender is threatening someone else's life and no easy alternatives present themselves) then he may kill without compunction. Smith frequently does this; he's the bloodsheddingest holy man since Mohamet, though he is delicate enough not to leave behind any actual bloodstains. The system implies that the true adept will always make the right decision in this matter; and besides, even if he's wrong he won't be punished. Not even the gas chamber can punish him, since for the true adept discorporation can be no more than an inconvenient or inartistic exit.

In many other ways the system is ethically even more permissive, and it has no visible use at all for custom or morality. Because all experiences must be grokked to the fullest and embraced, and because the act of every grokking being is an act of a God, it would be very difficult to predict under what circumstances an adept would "grok wrongness," other than in circumstances where his own will or desire is about to be thwarted. Heinlein-Smith short-circuit this objection to some extent by making the sharing of experience (which equals the sharing of Godhead) superior to solo grokking. From this value judgment emerges the novel's emphasis upon promiscuity, communal mating, orgy and voyeurism; there is an extended defense of the joys of strip-teasing and feelthy pictures which is both extremely funny (Heinlein's wit is surer here than it is almost anywhere else in the book) and rather touching (because it emerges from the completely unclouded naivete of Smith, who does not yet recognize, and indeed never wholly recognizes, how much heartbreak can be bound up even on the peripheries of sex). But the same value judgment also allows Heinlein-Smith to read many people out of the Party as people it is not possible to grok with, and who therefore can be rejected and discorporated ("murdered" is a word *I* am fond of in this context) because they are boobs. (And besides, boob, "thou art God" and it doesn't really hurt.)

One of the more curious acceptances of the system is cannibalism. In part this emerges out of the givens of the plot: the Martians conserve food as they conserve water, and after an adult Martian discorporates, his friends eat him before he spoils, praising as they do so both his accomplishments and his flavor. This Martian custom is explicitly, if delicately, carried over into the Heinlein-Smith religion on Earth: In very nearly the last scene of the novel, Smith deliberately cuts off a finger, and his father-surrogate and his closest friend make soup of it. (It turns out to need a little seasoning; one suspects that so critical a remark would have been blasphemy on Mars, but the pun for once is pungent.) This scene has been prepared by a long analysis, by Jubal Harshaw, of the role ritual cannibalism has played in almost all the great Western and near-Western religions, in which the well-known present-day facts are buttressed at length from Frazer.* Heinlein, also a thoroughgoing Freudian—as has been evident ever since "Gulf" (*Astounding*, November, 1949)—does not

---

* A minor puzzle is why the author has made Jubal so tentative on this point, especially in view of the enthusiastic way the novel tramples on toes considerably more sensitive. I do not see that it would have offended anybody—and it would have strengthened Jubal's case considerably—to have pointed out that in most major communions of the Christian faith, "Take My body and eat; take My blood and drink" is not only a symbolic command, but also and most explicitly a literal one, since the wafer and wine of the Eucharist not only represent but *become* the body and blood of Christ through the miracle of transsubstantiation (a point perfectly clear to every medieval Englishman through the much more vigorous, if more homely verb, "to housle"). However the character Jubal is speaking to presumably belongs to a Middle-Western Protestant sect which retains the ceremony but does not espouse transsubstantiation; a poor excuse, all the same, for dodging this point in favor of Frazer, whose doctrines are preached in no church whatsoever.

mean this equating of love, death, and high tea to pass unnoticed, but it is more interesting for its unorthodoxy than for its patness; Freud, a reductionist on the subject of religion, is here made to serve as the theorist for a ceremony of reverence. It's also interesting that in this scene the father eats the child, an act unsanctified in any society less primitive than that of guppies, and ruled out on Mars by the givens of Martian society; this is to my eyes the most extreme example of Heinlein's permissiveness, and he may have inserted it to suggest (as Smith himself has earlier suggested) that the Martianizing of Earth has gotten more than a little out of hand.

Almost all of the other ethical questions in the novel are subsumed under the head of bilking the mark, from the world of the carnival to the world of high politics—a subject on which Heinlein is as expert and amusing as always (and as infuriating to readers who believe that all grokkers are created equal). Their exploration takes up a substantial part of the novel, that part devoted mostly to Smith's education, but they pose few ethical problems unique to the system. Most of the crises are brought off by Jubal, not by Smith, without reference to the system, which is still in a state of very imperfect revelation while these machinations are going on. Most of the interesting minor characters, however, get in their licks in this earlier part of the book, and tend to fade back into the tapestry as the theology emerges—which is a shame, for they're a wonderful crew while they last. Thereafter, only Jubal and Smith continue to appear in the round. The others are ghostly and disconsolate, their promise not so much unfulfilled as pushed off onto a spur-line while the Powers and Propositions thunder by.

Nor does it seem to me that Jubal Harshaw's rather extended remarks on the arts constitute a true system of aesthetics referrable back to the central vision. Mostly, they are made in defense of representational or story-telling art, and this is what might be expected from a glorified, curmudgeonly and rich hackwriter, which is how Jubal is defined; so perhaps they are only characterizations. The only other hint we are offered in this area is an account of a work of art which was being composed by a gifted Martian when he inattentively discorporated. Though Heinlein says that the nature (that is, the medium) of the artwork cannot be described, he makes it plain that this too is a story-telling work, and that the Martians are prepared to spend centuries thinking about its value. On this showing, if the Martians ever do turn out to be a menace we can ship them the score of Liszt's "Mazeppa" or a *Post* cover and immobilize them to the end of time. Heinlein-Jubal reads a fine story, instinct with the courage the author has admired and which is vaguely integrated into the religion of *Stranger in a Strange Land*, into Rodin's Fallen Caryatid, but except for a few such insights his aesthetics have always been those of an engineer and continue to be so here, neither contributing to nor detracting from his present subject.*

The final question I would like to raise—not the final one raised by the novel, not by a thousand—is that of the metaphysics of Heinlein-Smith's system. Ordinarily this is a very late inquiry to bring to bear upon a religion, because it is usually accepted that God is only acting sensibly in not trying to make His early prophets explain quantum theory to a pack of goat-herders; better to stick to the ethical imperatives which the goat-herders should be able to understand with no difficulty, especially if the orders involved are accompanied by a rain of fire or some other practical use of physics. Later on, medieval scholars may presume that the God wrote two works, one being the universe conceived complete and perfect,

---

* This raises once more the perennially interesting question of what Heinlein actually thinks, a form of mind-reading I would prefer to eschew if it were not that so much of this novel is specifically author-omniscient—that is, presented without the intervention of any character's point of view. The passage about the Martian work of art is one such; but again, it could be dismissed as only the groundwork for a plot point (though not a plot point of which the novel stands in any need, or of which any important use is made) rather than an illustration of the author's biases. This view would have the advantage of allowing Jubal's aesthetics to remain strictly Jubal's, and never mind that he is obviously the wise man of the novel—the only one who can grok without reading minds—whose opinions are more to be respected than anyone else's, even Smith's ninety per cent of the time.

It would also leave unposed the question of why, if storytelling is the essence of the best art, Heinlein is on record with an expression of contempt for opera. Under Jubal's aesthetics, the opera, the tone-poem and the song should be the supreme forms of music, while "absolute" music such as string quartets without accompanying literary programs should be as beneath notice as non-representational painting (presumably the work of composers who can't read music, as abstract painting is said to be the work of painters who can't draw). This is clearly one of the few questions about which Heinlein has not had the opportunity to think very much, and hence has formed convictions in the absence of data. He has never, for example, shown any interest in or knowledge of music. In *Stranger in a Strange Land* he invents a "Nine Planets Symphony" from which he can extract a "Mars movement" for a minor plot purpose, rather than invoking the famous work of Gustav Holst which, being real, would have served his purpose much better, and would have spared him the embarrassment of being caught with the notion that nine movements is a reasonable, let alone a likely number for a symphony.

The consequences for the novel in question are vanishingly small, of course; but it's interesting, if fruitless, to think of how much larger they might have been. Suppose that Jubal, during his tippy-toe discussion of the Eucharist, had happened to think of *Parsifal?*

and the other the Scriptures ditto; and still later, somebody (who will be burned for it) will ask why the metaphysics of the first work are so badly out of true with the metaphysics of the second. In the first or prophetic stage, however, this question is generally deemed unfair.

But it can hardly be deemed unfair to ask of a science fiction writer, who *starts* from assumptions about the nature of the real world which are as sophisticated as modern knowledge allows (this is not true of most of us, but it is true of Heinlein, at least by pure and consistent intention). In *Stranger in a Strange Land* he enforces the current acceptances of modern (scientific) metaphysics by beginning every major section with an author-omniscient review of how these events look in the eye$_{1961}$ of eternity; furthermore, he is scornful throughout of anybody (read, boobs) who does not accept this specific body of metaphysics.

So it is fair to ask him about the metaphysics of his proposed system; and it is, to say the best of it, a shambles. Smith appears on the scene able to work miracles, as is fitting for a prophet; in fact, he can work every major miracle, and most of the minor ones, which are currently orthodox in Campbellian science fiction. He can control his metabolism to the point where any outside observer would judge him dead; he can read minds; he is a telekinetic; he can throw objects (or people) permanently away into the fourth dimension by a pure effort of will, so easily that he uses the stunt often simply to undress; he practices astral projection as easily as he undresses, on one occasion leaving his body on the bottom of a swimming pool while he disposes of about thirty-five cops and almost as many heavily armored helicopters; he can heal his own wounds almost instantly; he can mentally analyze inanimate matter, well enough to know instantly that a corpse he has just encountered died by poisoning years ago; levitation, crepitation, intermittent claudication, you name it, he's got it—and besides, he's awfully good in bed. My point is not that this catalogue is ridiculous—though it surely is—but that Heinlein the science fiction writer does not anywhere offer so much as a word of rational explanation for any one of these powers. They are all given, and that's that. Many of them, the story says, turn out to be communicable to Smith's disciples, but the teaching, unlike the lovemaking, never takes place onstage and again is never grounded in so much as a square pood of rationale.

The more general features of the system fare equally badly. In what kind of continuum or metrical frame do the Martian Old Ones and the

Earthly sub-Archangels live on—and in what sense do they live on? How is an intricate relational system like a personality conserved without a physical system to supply energy to it? What role in the vast energetics of the known universe can be played by the scurrying sub-managerial dead souls, and how are the pushes applied? What currently warrantable metaphysical system *requires* this illimitable ant hill of ghosts; or, what possibly warrantable system *might* require it, and if so, how would you test the system? I think it more than likely that a brain as complicated as Heinlein's might have produced a highly provocative schema of metaphysics in support of the rest of the system; I don't propose these questions because I think them unanswerable, but only to call attention to the fact that Heinlein didn't even try.

Or perhaps he did, and the results got cut out of the manuscript. (Which was longer than the book; Heinlein did his own cutting.) If that is the case, had I been the author I would have cut the aesthetics instead, since they have nothing to do with the system; but I'm not the author, to the satisfaction of us both; so all that remains is that there's no accounting for tastes, as the master said as he kissed his Sears-Roebuck catalogue.* Certainly the version left us, for all its unknowable and/or visible omissions, is as provocative, difficult and outré a science fiction novel as Heinlein has ever given us. At the very least it will entertain you for months —or perhaps, if it does what it sets out to do, for the rest of your afterlife.

---

* Heinlein once remarked, in an autobiographical note, that he considered a Sears-Roebuck catalogue to be a greater cultural achievement than any opera.

# CONTACT

## Pierre Versins

### Translated by Damon Knight

The theme of Space divides itself logically into a number of sub-themes: **Interplanetary Communications** which put us in touch with astonishing creatures, the creatures themselves (the theme of **Extraterrestrials**, who may be humanoid or non-humanoid); **Astronautics** properly so-called (the machines and techniques by means of which we leave our globe); **Contact** with extraterrestrials; and finally the establishment of relations with them (**Interplanetary Colonization, Imperialism,** or pure and simple cohabitation).

Sometimes the contact cannot be established (see under **Antimatter** Theodore Sturgeon's story, "Minority Report"), often it poses few problems (the classic voyages to the Moon and the planets). Only in modern times has the question really been raised.

An anthology of Soviet science fiction contains an interesting story for our purposes. And when in the course of his narrative the author criticizes another story, by an American, on the same subject, the confrontation may be one of some importance. In "Cor Serpentis," by Ivan Yefremov (1961 in French translation),[24] the subject is an encounter in deep space with another "humanity." And the same theme is treated in "First Contact," by Murray Leinster (1945).

FROM *L'Encyclopédie de l'Utopie et de la Science Fiction*, Éditions L'age d'Homme, 1972

Let us take "Cor Serpentis" first. This long story is written in the same context as *The Andromeda Nebula*, an admirable novel by the same author: the world has been communized, indeed has attained a classless society, and our fortunate descendants no longer have any of our present problems. What is envisaged here is that they have other problems. The astronauts have departed in a pulse-ship, that is, a spaceship that leaps through subspace (or some other "extratemporal" realm) and so eats up the parsecs. And it is on the return leg of this voyage toward the constellation "Cor Serpentis" that the radar picks up a brief flash: an interstellar vessel, where no Earth spaceship could be. Therefore it must be a machine belonging to a race as advanced as the Terran, with which contact must be made. Here we find a clever detail which did not occur to Murray Leinster, that the spaceships' mass must be multiplied enormously by their speed. Whereas in Leinster's story the two strange ships come to a halt relative to each other almost instantaneously, in Yefremov's the probable reality is given its due, and it is only after long and delicate maneuvers that the two cosmic vessels come to rest in close proximity. Moreover, Yefremov himself, in criticizing "First Contact" through the mouth of one of his heroes, mentions this rather important oversight.[25]

All the same, this is not the essential point. For it is at the moment when the contact becomes inevitable (it is desirable, in any event, and is seen as such by the two crews in the two stories) that the divergence between the views of the Soviet and American authors becomes clear. Yefremov makes one of his characters say to another, "Any thinking being from some other world that has been able to reach the Cosmos must be just as perfect and universal as the humans of our Earth, and hence just as beautiful. There can be no thinking monsters, no mushroom-men, no octopus-men!" Let us hope that the thinking monsters, mushroom-men and octopus-men of space don't share this opinion, otherwise they would kill us on sight, because we would not be "beautiful" to them. . . . At any rate, Leinster maintains a similar view, at least in this story, for his "strangers" are not particularly frightful either.

But the divergence between the two conceptions becomes nakedly apparent when it is a question of judging these "strangers," of anticipating their behavior, their reactions—in fine, of knowing whether we can trust them or not. Yefremov says yes. Leinster says no. The Soviet commander says simply, ". . . and I realized that at the highest stage of development all thinking beings must reach a state of perfect mutual understanding," while the American commander, with reluctance, it must be emphasized, says: "We're going to make contact and try to find out all we can about them—especially where they came from. I suppose we'll try to make friends—but we haven't a chance. We can't trust them a fraction of an inch. . . . They've locators. . . . Maybe they could trace us all the way home without our knowing it! We can't risk a nonhuman race knowing where Earth is unless we're sure of them! And how can we be sure? They could come to trade, of course—or they could swoop down on overdrive with a battle fleet that could wipe us out before we knew what happened."[26]

Just so.

But now it is time to listen to the words of Ivan Yefremov, or more exactly those of his spokesman, the spaceship commander who, in the Soviet version, establishes the first contact. These two pages are a resumé of Murray Leinster's story, and already it is a critical resumé:

"The First Contact," as it was called, was a dramatic story of the meeting between a space ship from Earth and one from another world in the nebula of Cancer at a distance of more than a thousand parsecs from the Sun.

The commander of the Earth ship ordered the crew to prepare all the astronomical charts, records of observations and calculations of the course for immediate destruction and to train all their anti-meteorite guns at the approaching ship. The Earthlings then proceeded to wrestle with the momentous problem: should they attempt to enter into negotiations with the other ship or were they in duty bound to attack and destroy it without warning? They feared that the men from another world might be able to trace back the course of their ship and use their knowledge to try to conquer the Earth.

These ridiculous apprehensions aroused no opposition on the part of the entire crew. It was taken for granted that the meeting of two civilizations that had sprung up in different parts of the Universe was bound to lead to the subordination of one by the other, to the victory of the one possessing the strongest weapons. A meeting in space could only mean one of the two things—trade or war. They could not conceive of anything else. It soon turned out that the men from the other world closely resembled the Earthlings except that they could see only in infra-red light and communicated with one another by radio waves. Yet the Earthlings at once deciphered the strangers' language and intercepted their thoughts. It turned out that the commander of the space ship from the other world entertained just as primitive views on social development and relations as the Earthmen and was primarily concerned with how to get out of the situation in which he found himself without jeopardizing his own life or destroying the Earth ship.

. . . Both captains gave each other assurances of their peaceable intentions and at the same time declared their distrust of the other. The situation might indeed have been hopeless had it not been for the ingenuity of the hero of the story—a young astrophysicist. Concealing bombs of terrific destructive power in their clothing, he and his commander boarded the strange ship ostensibly to continue the negotiations. Once there, however, they presented an ultimatum to the strangers: to exchange ships, with part of the strange ship's crew going over to the Earth ship, and part of the Earthmen boarding the unknown craft, first putting all meteorite guns out of commission; the boarding parties were then to learn to run the ships and all the supplies were to be transferred from each of the ships to the other. In the meantime the two heroes with the bombs would remain on board the strangers' ship, ready to blow it up at the first sign of treachery. The captain from the other world accepted the ultimatum, and the exchange of ships proceeded smoothly. Finally the black space ship with the Earthlings on board and the Earth ship now manned by the strangers hastily drew apart, vanishing into the feeble luminosity of the nebula.

Thus Yefremov's resumé of his American colleague's story. No fault can be found in it, except for a few omissions: 1) The whole crew did not share the "absurd" ideas of the commander; on the contrary, the young astrophysicist of whom mention is later made did all he could to present the problem in a less pessimistic light. 2) It was not only the Earthlings who concealed a bomb in their clothing; the strangers, at the same time, since it was a "fair exchange," did exactly the same and with the same intention.

But there is worse to come. The playful anticommunism of most occidentals is not in our line, but we severely criticize Yefremov, more severely than he himself criticized Leinster, because his fault is more serious, particularly in a communist. In the Soviet story, in fact, the specter of war on a galactic scale does not so much as brush the Earth commander with its pallid wing. That's most commendable, and there would have been nothing to reproach him with, quite to the contrary, if his thesis had appeared even a little bit "realistic"—speaking of Marxist realism, if you like, but at least realism. The Earth ship and the strangers' ship have no possibility of direct contact, since the Earthlings and strangers do not breathe the same atmosphere (in fact, it's even worse than that). Nevertheless they all conduct themselves like Victorian gentlemen. They are so good, so considerate, that it's embarrassing. It occurs to us inevitably that the slaves of the Assyrians, who had their limbs cut off, would necessarily think of us, their distant descendants, as kindly and gentle beings, without insoluble problems; and we blush.

But what is science fiction? Among other things it is really the only possibility we have of examining our future without knowing what it will be. It concerns itself therefore with foreseeing the worst and studying means of evading it. Murray Leinster, in "First Contact," has played the game and written accordingly. Not so Ivan Yefremov. On one hand, a conjecture; on the other, a pious wish. We leave to our descendants the final criticism.

# IV.
# S.F. AND SCIENCE

# NO COPYING ALLOWED

## John W. Campbell

The proposition involving the science-fiction hero who captures the enemy device, brings it home, copies it and puts it into production is being abandoned in modern stories. But the actual difficulty of such a problem is always interesting and worthy of consideration. Only recently has Earth's own technology reached the point where such copying is not possible; today it is definitely impossible in a large field of devices.

Let's first consider this situation: Time: About 1920. Place: An American Army Air Base. Action: High overhead a small airplane tears across the sky with a high, thin whistle. Ground observers, after tracking it for a minute or so—during which time it has passed out of sight—report incredulously that it was doing between nine hundred fifty and one thousand miles per hour. It circles back, slows abruptly as the whistle dies out, and makes a hot, deadstick landing. Investigators reach the cornfield where it landed, and find it ninety percent intact—and one hundred percent impossible. Swept-back wings, no tail, automatic control equipment of incredibly advanced design, are all understandable insofar as function intended goes. But the metal alloys used make no sense to the metallurgists when they go to work on them. The "engine," moreover, is simply, starkly insane. The only indication of anything that might remotely be considered an engine is a single, open tube—really open; open at both ends. But the empty fuel tank had tubes leading into some sort of

From *Collected Editorials from* Analog, Doubleday, 1966

small jets in that pipe. The athodyd being unheard of in 1920, the thing is senseless. Filling the fuel tanks simply causes a hot fire that must be extinguished quickly to prevent burning out the tube. The fact that this is a guided missile intended for launching from a four-hundred-mile-an-hour bomber makes the situation a little difficult for the 1920 technologists; the athodyd won't start functioning below two hundred fifty m.p.h., and nothing on Earth could reach that speed in 1920.

Meanwhile, the Signal Corps experts are going equally chittery trying to figure out the controls. First off, the plane's markings were clearly an advanced United States Army design. Many equipment parts bore United States Army Signal Corps markings and serial numbers. But the equipment inside is not only of advanced design, it's of meaningless design. The idea of printed circuits is fascinating, but understandable if not reproducible. Pentode amplifiers the size of a peanut are fascinating, not reproducible, and only vaguely understandable. For one thing, the filament isn't used at all; an indirectly heated cathode is a new item to them. However, the items that really stop them are several varieties of gadgets, all about the same size, but of violently different characteristics. There are units one eighth inch in diameter by about three fourths long which have resistance varying from one hundred to ten million ohms. Incredible, but true. Others have infinite resistance, and are condensers of capacity so high for their tiny size as to be unbelievable. Still others have three leads, and, opened, seem to be crystal detectors—understandable—but are amplifiers, which doesn't make sense. They also turn out to be nonreproducible. They are simple mechanical structures, using the very unusual element germanium, in the crystals. But the chemical expert's best purified germanium won't work when a reproduction is tried. (You've got to have the right amount of the right impurity introduced in the right way. Techniques in the twenties weren't up to it.)

Furthermore, there's a tube that's obviously a triode oscillator, but the frequency involved is so high as to be detectable only when using crystal detectors from the plane's own equipment. The circuit, too, doesn't make sense to the radio engineers, though the physicists from the Bureau of Standards finally figured it out. (It's a tuned-line oscillator operating at about four hundred megacycles. The physicists had to go back to Hertz's original work with tuned-rod oscillators to get a glimpse of what went on.) They can't reproduce the tube, and no tube they can make will oscillate in the circuit used.

Finally, there's another group of equipments they've simply agreed to forget. It seems to center around a permanent magnet of fantastic power which embraces a copper block drilled with holes of odd sizes, having a central electron-emitting rod through it. The magnetron is bad enough—obviously beyond reproduction, since the cathode can't be duplicated, the magnet can't be duplicated, and the metal-to-glass seals are beyond any available technique. But the associated equipment is worse. There is a collection of rectangular pipes made of heavy silver-plated copper. The pipes contain nothing, carry nothing, and appear totally meaningless. This time the physicists are completely stumped. (Wave-guide theory is a recent development; without some basic leads, and understanding of the order of frequencies involved, they'd never get there.) And worst of all, the physicists find that several bits of the equipment contain radioactive material. They know about radium, uranium, thorium, et cetera. But—this is highly radioactive, and it's *cobalt*. But cobalt isn't radioactive! But this is, and it is cobalt. (It's the transmit-receive tube; the radio-cobalt is used to keep it ready to ionize easily and instantly.) They also find radioactive emanations from much of the plane's material, with faint indications that half the elements in the chemical table are radioactive—which is arrant nonsense! (The guided missile had been flown through the fringes of an atomic bomb test gathering report data.)

In summary, the aerodynamicists report that the tailless monstrosity is interesting, but the principles of its design are confusing. The engine group report the engine, so-called, can't be the engine. It was thought for a while that it might be a rocket, but since both ends are, and always were, wide open, it can't possibly be a rocket. The radio experts of the Signal Corps agree that some of the equipment is an immeasurably advanced type of radio apparatus, but the design is so advanced that it is futile to study it. It can't be reproduced, and involves principles evidently several centuries ahead of the knowledge of 1920—so advanced that the missing, intermediate steps are too many to be bridged. The mystery electronic equipment, called Equipment Group X, remains simply mysterious, save that, in some way, it involves a receiver operating on an unknown, but very high frequency. (By which they meant not the ten thousand megacycle input but the "low" frequency intermediate frequency amplifier, operating at only thirty megacycles. Having no means of generating thirty megacycles at that time, they could only say it was higher than the highest available. And they didn't, of course, recognize the ten kilomegacycle RF head as a receiver at all.)

The physicists would be inclined to ascribe it to Mars, Venus or any other non-terrestrial planet, if it weren't for the obvious Signal Corp⸱ markings. Since terrestrial cobalt isn't radioactive, and the cobalt in this ship is—

But anyway, the reports can only be tucked in the "File And Forget" division. About the only thing they can lift out of that piece of marvelous equipment is the secret of making good, small, high-resistance electronic resistors. The chemists and physicists did crack that one, and it's the answer to an electronicist's prayers; the tiny resistors are not wound with sub-microscopic resistance wire, as was at first believed—they're little ceramic tubes filled with a composition of clay and graphite which is such an extremely bad conductor that it does the job beautifully. By varying the composition, resistors of a standard size can range from one ohm to one hundred million.

At that, our 1920 group was really lucky. Suppose the item that fell through a time-fault had carried an atomic warhead. If it didn't go off, it would have presented the physicists with two of the most dangerous, utterly inexplicable lumps of matter imaginable. Pure U-235 or pure plutonium—that would have driven the chemists mad!—before they'd even discovered synthetic radioactivity. They would have been certain to kill themselves by bringing those two masses too close to each other, though, out of the bomb mechanism, they wouldn't have exploded.

But—write your own ticket, in your own special field. Let 1920, or 1910, or 1890 try to understand the functioning of any one of your modern gadgets. Even though, in those years, first-rate scientists with a full understanding of scientific methodology, and with fairly complete laboratory equipments, were available!

# SCIENTISTS IN S.F.: A DEBATE

## Philip R. Geffe, Milton A. Rothman, John W. Campbell, James V. McConnell

Lance Leatherhide, boy graduate, stood in dismay before his angry thesis advisor, Prof. MacBlast. Stern in his frock coat and pince-nez, MacBlast thundered his disapproval, "Of all the idiotic fantasies I have ever seen, *this* one takes the cake for sloppy experiments, moronic calculations, sophomoric ideas, and sheer imbecility! No scientist worthy of the name would give serious consideration to any childish theories that ignore every law of physics in the book." He paused to take a deep breath, while waving the offending sheaf of papers under Lance's nose. "And don't imagine," he continued, "that I am going to permit my daughter to marry an imitation scientist like *you*. There hasn't been any insanity in my family so far, and I intend to keep it that way."

Sadly, Lance took the manuscript, with all its revolutionary discoveries, under his arm and left the professor's office. "But it still moves," he muttered under his breath, "and someday I'm going to prove it to you, and to all the other mossbacks of the scientific 'establishment!' "

What is wrong with this cliché? It is based on the stereotype of the nineteenth-century scientist who declined to extinction about the time

From *SFWA Bulletin*, August 1966–January 1967

that the Theory of Relativity became universally accepted, after World War I.

Before the Michelson-Morely experiment (1887), scientists nearly all adhered to a world view in which the outlines of the Grand Design were completely drawn. In the way of general principles, everything of importance was known, and all that remained for research to do was to fill in the details. This attitude persisted for decades, and led to widespread dogmatism. If either the Michelson-Morley experiment or the Theory of Relativity had been offered by a graduate student in those days, it very possibly would not have been given a fair hearing.

Today, scientists are a different breed of cat altogether. Nearly all take the view that science is advancing on a day-to-day basis, and that today's crazy speculation may be tomorrow's sensation. *All* laws of nature may have to be modified; perhaps *none* are exactly correct as they are understood today. Newton's law of gravitation has been modified by Einstein. It may have to undergo further changes to account for discrepancies observed in nuclear interactions, or to describe the recession of distant galaxies. Similar reservations apply to every physical law you can name.

The reactionaries are scarce. To become a senior professor at a great university, one has to have built a reputation for creative and original thinking, and these qualities militate against conservatism—at least, in the line of one's own special field of competence.

Today, a crazy new idea is often received by senior professors with more interest than it deserves. As he reads the revolutionary thesis, the old guy's imagination is dancing with rock-'n-rolling Nobel Prizes, department chairmanships, and huge federal grants. Heresy is becoming a way of life, because it pays off.

The scientists of my acquaintance usually greet a new idea with the following in mind: 1. Can it be tested? 2. If any known facts appear to contradict the theory, how does the theory account for them? 3. If the difficulty appears to be fundamental, can the theory be modified to get around this? 4. If it looks OK on a provisional basis, let's generalize it, work out any alternatives that will preserve the basic idea, and make sure that the tests to come will provide the maximum information, and discriminate between the alternative formulations.

In short, then, the advisor does not offer an oracular acceptance or rejection of a new idea: he collaborates in developing and testing it. He is equally ready to discuss new wrinkles in flying saucers, telepathy, little green men from Mars, or meromorphic functions.*

These facts lead to some advice for s.f. authors. If you want the hero's crazy theory to be disapproved by his seniors (circa 1966), let it be done for professional jealousy, mental aberration, or ulterior motives. But, please, don't ascribe the fault to a reactionary "establishment" unless you can justify it by the history of science which preceded the action in the story. When the wheel of history turns again, we may see another such establishment a century or so from now—hardly sooner.

Scientists are mostly to be found in their natural habitat: academia. They can generally be described as intellectuals whose attitudes are not dissimilar to those of s.f. authors. They are usually theoreticians, and few are competent with gadgetry. They are deeply involved in research and teaching, and will not often be found piloting spaceships, engaging in political conspiracies (how many scientists tried to assassinate Hitler?), or writing revolutionary papers in more than one branch of knowledge.

On this last point, it is true that Oppenheimer can read Sanskrit, and that Einstein was fluent in higher mathematics. Nevertheless, neither made creative contributions in these fields. Einstein regarded mathematics as a tool, not as an object of investigation. There *are* a few very brilliant men who have Ph.D.'s in two or three different fields. So far as I know, none of these can be called great scientists. The great ones are so fascinated by their own field that they have little patience, or time, for anything outside it.

Naturally, there are some exceptions to these rules, and authors like to write about exceptional men, because readers like to read about them. OK. But let's not populate the entire story with them. Make it clear that your man is a phenomenon. He was a child prodigy, has the highest IQ on record, works like a steam engine, and his colleagues view him with awe because he is unique.

Great scientists make great discoveries. But, individually, they make few per lifetime, and they do not make them on demand. "Necessity is the mother of invention" applies mostly to ingenious applications, not to fun-

---

* See the recent discussions in *Science* regarding dermo-optical perception, and extrasensory communication between identical twins as revealed by electroencephalographs. Incidentally, when I attended Cal Tech, in the late 1940s, s.f. magazines were lying all over the place, and not only in the student houses. E. T. Bell, one of my math professors, wrote s.f. novels under the name of John Taine.

damental discoveries. Doc Smith had the formula right in *The Skylark of Space*: Richard Seaton discovered a metal, X, with remarkable properties. Then all the gadgets arose logically out of this one discovery. Furthermore, most of the original set of gadgets were actually reduced to practice in collaboration with Crane, the engineer, not solely by Seaton, the pure scientist. This is the way it is in life. Seaton made no more basic discoveries either in that story or in *Skylark Three*. Instead, his knowledge was advanced by dissecting a Fenachrone battleship, and by technical aid from Norlamin. These matters could not have been arranged more plausibly, and it is no accident that they were written by a man who was a Ph.D. himself.

Authors should be advised that a scientist seldom refers to himself as a "scientist," any more than you would call yourself a "white-collar worker," or a "litterateur." "I am a physicist," he will say, or "I am an organic chemist."

There is a related point here. Scientists and engineers are not "technicians," they are technologists. A technician is a laboratory worker of lower rank. A few have (at most) one college degree, but most are high-school graduates who went to a trade school for a few months to better themselves. Many of them, in today's shortage of technical people, are in the warm-body class.

Incidentally, it is my opinion that the shortage of trained people should be extrapolated indefinitely into the future, unless you can display definite future-historical reasons why a surplus might exist. Science cannot become a mass profession because the measured IQ-distribution of the human race shows that only a certain fraction of the population is genetically equipped to absorb a technical education.

The present trend toward specialization must inevitably continue. New fields will arise at the interfaces between disciplines, but these, too, will be narrow fields. Thus, a specialist on the analogy between computer-thinking and animal-thinking will probably not be competent to design computer hardware, and he will probably not be able to tell you that *Lycosa rabida* and *Dugesiella hentzi* are both members of the class Arachnida. (Neither would I, if I hadn't looked it up.)

Several years ago I was walking down a street in Santa Monica. Ahead of me a few paces were two tweedy individuals discussing current events. Immediately I said to myself, "Aha, I'll bet this is a pair of mathematicians on a summer job at the Rand Corporation." Sure enough, in a few moments, their conversation switched to the technicalities of game theory. How did I know? Easy. Most scientists (especially mathematicians) have a tendency to speak with extraordinary precision, using qualifiers that most people would regard as redundant. Despite these occasional redundancies, they find ways of being remarkably concise. This habit is forced onto writers of research papers, because the referees (who decide whether the paper will be published) ruthlessly return manuscripts to have review-material cut, discussions reduced, and prolix sentences slashed. Beginners' pages are reduced to sentences. Technical journals suffer printing setup charges of over $65 a page, and their circulation is often less than 5,000 copies. I have often spent many hard-working hours on a fifty-word abstract, so that it will be a "truly informative" summary of my paper.

Here is another example:

"But if what you are beginning to suspect is really true, it means that Boskonia is intergalactic in scope—widerspread even than the patrol!"

"Probably, but not necessarily—it may mean only that they have bases farther outside . . . I got just part of a thought, here and there. However, the thought was 'that' galaxy; not just 'galaxy'—and why think that way if the guy was already in this galaxy?"

The speaker's reasoning would be fallacious if he were referring to housewives, taxi drivers, storekeepers, or other laymen. He was implicitly assuming that his enemy would express himself with scientific precision even when discussing administrative detail. Given the story background, he had to be right.

And now it is both appropriate and pleasing for me to air one of my pet peeves. Old friends who see me kicking and screaming on the floor know that the conversation must have just turned to the subject of scientists vs. engineers. Pause a moment and consider the most spectacular achievements of the twentieth century: space rockets, atom bombs, supersonic aircraft, martini-olive microphones, the San Francisco Bay Bridge, and antibiotics, fiberglass, etc., etc. These things were done by *engineers*, not by scientists. True, they were based, as all engineering things are, on scientific principles. But scientists drop these things with a thump as soon as they have published their paper. Reducing the principles to practice is not trivial work. It requires the ability to understand and develop the basic principle, and a lot of other things as well. This work is done by engineers.

Is von Braun a rocket "scientist"? Nonsense, there is no such thing as a rocket scientist. And don't tell me that von Braun got his degree in chemistry or physics. I don't know what his degree was in, but anyone can see that he has been working as an engineer for many years, and is an ornament to the profession.

In World War II, penicillin was a new thing. The scientists who did the first work on the stuff were given the job of mass-producing it in sufficient quantities to meet the military demand overseas. They grew it in one-ounce batches in little bottles—thousands of them. Stock in bottle companies went up. Finally, in desperation, the government went where they should have gone in the first place: to the engineers. Within months, the chemical engineers were making penicillin in batches of a ton each, and all the bottles were melted down for packaging beer, which helped to relieve another overseas shortage.

It is important to understand here that, generally speaking, scientists cannot do what engineers do, and vice versa. If your scientist hero has to do a hasty job of rewiring a control panel, have him fumble a bit, and make deprecatory comments on his ineptitude with a soldering iron, or on the complicated and illogical wiring diagrams of "those dumb engineers." If, on the other hand, he is an engineer, you might let him get a little exasperated over the way a scientific paper ignores the practical side of things, and assumes that the reader could make working hardware from a bare theory, and no practical hints at all.

That is the way it is, and that is the way it is going to be! Forever and ever.


### Milton A. Rothman

In the August issue of the *Bulletin*, Philip R. Geffe brings out the point that scientists nowadays are not as conservative as they used to be, and that they are more receptive to new ideas and to changes in their old ideas. This is true: scientists in general have a better understanding of philosophy of science, and they have seen how many cherished ideas have been overturned in the past. So they are now cautious about saying: "This is impossible."

However, I do think that Mr. Geffe oversimplifies the response of the scientist to a new idea. If somebody were to come to me with a new idea, and if this new idea went counter to some of my old ideas, my response would depend on the circumstances.

For example: if a student comes to me with an idea for a device which violates certain basic laws of nature (conservation of energy, conservation of momentum, Maxwell's equations, etc.) then I will say to him, "Don't waste my time until you bring me a working model." Because you cannot overthrow an experimentally verified law with a theory. You can only overthrow it with another experiment. That's why I have no patience with people who argue verbally about the Dean space drive.[27]

On the other hand, if a student comes to me with a device or experiment which violates a previously held law, then we have to find out why we believed the old law, whether it had been properly tested, and under what conditions the law must be changed. For example, when Lee and Yang showed that the law of conservation of parity did not hold under certain circumstances, they recognized the fact that this law had never been tested under these particular circumstances (weak nuclear interactions). People had simply assumed that if the law was good for strong interactions it was also good for weak interactions. Also, some people had fallen for the notion that "nature likes symmetries," so that certain laws of symmetry were "intuitively obvious." But now we know that it is really people who like symmetry. Nature doesn't care.

This brings me to the point I wish to make. Now that conservation of parity has been altered, time reversal is shaky, and even matter-antimatter symmetry is being challenged, there results a commonly held feeling that our knowledge of science is somehow temporary, that the known laws of nature may have to be modified in the future, and that, as Mr. Geffe says, "perhaps none (of the laws of nature) are exactly correct as they are understood today."

I think that this statement leads to great misunderstandings, because it sometimes makes the unwary reader feel that nothing we know is definite, and that all of our laws of nature are subject to change in the future.

But just the opposite is true: we do know certain things with a great amount of precision, and these things are not going to change. Those things that we know "for sure" are experimental results. As a result of many, many measurements, we know that (within certain limits of accuracy) the energy and momentum of the objects in a closed system do not change during the course of a reaction. We also know that to a high degree of accuracy the strength of the gravitational force between two objects varies inversely as the square of the distance between them, with certain very small corrections necessary to take care of nonlinear effects which are part of the theory of relativity. These observations are not going to change.

Therefore we say that within the domain in which these laws have been experimentally tested, the laws of conservation of energy, conservation of momentum, the law of gravity as modified by relativity, Maxwell's equations, and many other laws of a fundamental nature are NOT going to change in the future. Because these laws are simply descriptions of things that have been observed. They don't try to explain anything.

Now if we go to domains where we have not tested these laws and where conditions are radically different from normal conditions (like inside a nucleus or at the center of a star), then we are not so sure about the laws, and possible changes may be expected.

So you see, in order to predict whether a new idea is likely to be valid, you have to ask yourself whether it violates any of the basic laws, whether these laws have been tested within the domain covered by your new idea, how accurately the laws are known, what are the experimental bases of the laws, etc., etc., etc. In other words, you have to know a hell of a lot of physics.

The point I am making is that we do know more physics now than we did a hundred years ago, and so I think we are better equipped to judge the validity of new ideas. This is a good thing, especially when it costs several million dollars to try out a new idea experimentally. And even then you run into situations such as the thermonuclear power program in which I work, where there are no laws that say it is impossible, but nobody is able to show how to make it work, and nobody is able to show why it won't work. (At least for the time being.)

One of the reasons it is so hard to write good science fiction nowadays is that we are more sure of the foundations of science, and as a result many of the pet devices of science fiction become very hard to swallow when analyzed in terms of our contemporary knowledge. My son, having just turned 13, recently discovered the works of E. E. Smith, and both of us proceeded to plow our way through all the Skylark and Lensman stories. Reading all of E. E. Smith in one fell swoop brought very forcefully to me the realization that Smith paid no attention whatsoever to modern science. He didn't understand it, he ignored everything learned since 1895, and he simply used the jargon of science as a kind of magic wand to produce the magic chariots, potions, emanations and other necessary paraphernalia of his fairyland. (Don't misunderstand me; I loved and still love the stories of E. E. Smith, but now I know they are fantasies, not science fiction.) Right at the beginning, in *Skylark of Space*, he talks about the ship attaining an acceleration of one hundred thousand miles per second *per second* (sic) (that is, nearly one light-speed per second) and expects us to believe that putting a spring under the floor will soften the effects of such an acceleration. In later stories he became more sophisticated and used the words "inertialess drive" instead of a spring under the floor. But it's the same magic wand.

However, Smith is no worse than many another science fiction writer, and if we eliminated all the science fiction plots which are probably scientifically impossible, there would be very little science fiction left to read.

To return to "Scientists in S. F.," I am surprised to see that Mr. Geffe thinks the Theory of Relativity would not have been given a fair hearing had it been offered by a graduate student. As a matter of fact, Einstein was not even a graduate student during the early years when he first worked on relativity and quanta. He had finished his course at the Zurich Polytechnic Institute and was working at the Swiss Patent Office in order to spend the evenings doing his research. He was without a doctorate and absolutely unknown when at the age of twenty-five he published his first paper on relativity. Recognition at the highest levels came immediately.

So you really can't generalize about the response of scientists to new ideas. It has always depended on individual psychology. Some have been more liberal than others, as in any field. But if you think for one minute that scientists in general have abandoned their faith in the basic laws of nature, you just try asking them about the Dean space drive. Or about perpetual motion. Or about traveling faster than light. Or about time travel.

There's just one more thing in Mr. Geffe's article I want to quarrel with, and that is the oversimplification of the physicist–engineer polarization. In real life there is a continuous gradation of skills from the most abstract mathematical physicist through the experimental physicist, the applied physicist, the theoretical engineer, the developmental engineer, and the cook-book industrial designer. It's really quite silly to argue about labels because nowadays you have physicists acting like engineers and engineers acting like physicists. You come to the Princeton Plasma Physics

Laboratory and I'll show you engineers doing theoretical calculations on magnetic fields, and physicists drawing blueprints for hardware.

As an experimental physicist I have wired up circuits, built cloud chambers, overhauled betatrons and Van de Graaff generators, and dirtied my hands tightening nuts and bolts on vacuum equipment. In the old days, the distinction between the physicist and engineer was that the physicist knew the basic laws, and so was better equipped to develop new principles and radical new devices using these new principles. The engineer was supposed to be good at applying the principles to build a marketable product. Nowadays this distinction is blurred because many of the engineering schools are turning out essentially applied physicists.

This is partly a result of the experiences during World War II, when it was found that to develop entirely new technologies such as atomic energy and radar, it was easier to turn physicists into engineers than vice versa. This same thing is happening now as we see NASA training Ph.D.'s to pilot space laboratories.

Rather than make artificial semantic distinctions between scientists and engineers, we might make a more meaningful classification by noting that some people are better at manipulating abstract concepts, some like to manipulate solid materials, and others prefer to manipulate human beings. They are all useful.

## John W. Campbell

I'd like to comment on one part of Philip R. Geffe's "Scientists in S. F."

His discussion of the difference between engineers and scientists I agree with one hundred percent; I've been trying to make that same distinction for years. An engineer, fundamentally, doesn't care *why* something works—but is acutely concerned with making it *work*. Typical example: Edison hadn't the foggiest notion of what electricity was—but practically single-handed he invented electrical engineering, because his light bulb wasn't useful if there wasn't a way to supply it with electricity.

Burb, the pre-caveman, didn't know that fire was simply a self-sustaining, rapid chain reaction of oxidation of carbonaceous material—but he found a way of starting one, and keeping it going.

The scientist insists on knowing *why*, and isn't at all concerned about making anything work practically.

And this leads to my quarrel with Geffe.

Because the scientist cares only about the why—the explanation—and not about the practice, he will not pay much attention to the fact that something works, if his theory says it can't exist.

That is true of scientists, Mark 1966. It will also be true of anyone having the true scientist type orientation as of Mark 2066 and also 6066. It's the orientation that does it, and until that's changed, they will continue to react against contrary-to-their-theories ideas, precisely as Pope, Urban and Co. rejected Galileo's observational facts.

And please—*don't* tell me human beings have changed their character fundamentally in a mere three centuries!

Modern examples: Nicholas Christofilos proposed the "strong focusing principle" for synchrotrons; the scientists rejected the idea sent in by a Greek elevator technician from Athens, because he didn't use their form of math—no calculus, just algebra. Christofilos patented it—the Patent Office is an engineering-based outfit, and accepted it. The scientists were blackmailed into accepting Christofilos when they finally got around to inventing the idea themselves, and found he had the basic patent. Christofilos is now recognized as one of the most brilliant scientist-engineers in the world.

Again: ball lightning was "superstition," "folklore," "scientifically impossible" despite thousands of accurate eye-witness accounts by people ranging from farmers and woodsmen to physics professors.

It's recently become acceptable—now called "kugelblitz," however, to distinguish it from the superstitious stuff "ball lightning"—because some Westinghouse engineers, using electronic computers, showed the scientists *why* it could happen.

Scientists won't admit a thing happens at all until they first are shown *why* it happens; no amount of evidence that it *does* happen suffices.

Prof. MacBlast would sound off with full-throated fury, for instance, if his grad student wanted to make an analytical study of UFO phenomena, dowsing, or the "green thumb" phenomena.

Only when Student Leatherhide comes up with a *theory*—not mere observational data—would MacBlast calm down.

## Philip R. Geffe

I seem to be caught in a crossfire: Editor Campbell says I'm wrong because scientists will accept only theories; physicist Rothman says I'm wrong because they will accept only facts. Campbell says the difference between engineers and scientists is fundamental—Rothman says it is superficial.

Well. I may not agree to what they say, but I will defend to the death my right to refute it.

*On Dogmatism*   Let me put it this way: *Anyone* is liable to give a negative reaction to something new if he thinks it is an example of crass ignorance, which is an insult to his intelligence (myself included). Like Rothman, I don't listen very hard to descriptions of crude perpetual motion machines.

I admit that there is a little dogmatism in this, and I suspect that its inner principle is not widely understood, even by those who practice it. A technologist's first question, in response to a new idea, is usually an unconscious one, and he answers it himself: "Is it sophisticated?" A negative answer leads to loss of interest. The discrimination here is really against laymen, not against newness. It is usually justified, because all science is sophisticated nowadays, and laymen have little possibility of making a worthwhile contribution.

This is a corollary of the Fundamental Theorem of Beatnik Geometry, "A square on the hypotenuse is the same as any other damn square."

*On the Mutability of Physical Laws*   There are two statements involved here:

(1) "Perhaps none of the laws of nature are exactly correct as they are understood today."

(2) "Perhaps all of the laws of nature are grossly wrong as they are understood today."

Rothman quotes me as saying (1), and then objects that (2) is false. He is correct, but which of us is being misleading?

I was not writing for "unwary" readers. Instead, I was addressing a strictly limited audience of intelligent people who are difficult to mislead. I would express myself differently if I were speaking to an audience of girls down at the Junior High School.

Some of the general laws which Dr. Rothman insists on are less reverently regarded in equally respectable quarters. Are conservation laws gospel? We all know what happened to the laws of conservation of matter and conservation of energy. They were exploded with truly remarkable violence. What about their successor, conservation of matter-energy?

Well, cosmologists consider that the "steady-state" theory of the universe is a violation of this law. Since no one has yet described a sensible model which creates matter in a steady-state universe, this attitude seems justified. Do they get overheated about conservation? Certainly not.* After all, the only visible alternative is an absurd picture of a proto-cosmic egg exploding $n$ million years ago. Plausibility here is nothing to get excited about either. Conservation (of anything except bank capital) is definitely less sacred than it used to be.

*On Traveling Faster than Light*   Rothman was not explicit here, but let me try putting these words in his mouth: "No material object can have a velocity greater than $c$. This is a general law, which is merely a description of many observed facts. Unless Nature changes its mind, the law will continue to hold in the future."

OK, I'll grant one point. When something has been shown to go faster than light, an account of it will be published in *Nature*.

While I am not a physicist, I am in possession of essentially the same facts as Dr. Rothman. I will say that it is a plausible theory. It describes many observations made under rather limited conditions. But does it apply to an electron moving in a field of $10^{10}$ gauss? Does it apply to neutrinos? Does it apply in the core of a super-nova, or a quasar? Well . . . maybe.

My point here is not that I have good reason to disagree about physics with Dr. Rothman, but that I received this skepticism at the hands of some of his more heretical colleagues. They are not so sure of these things as he is.

*A Saving Fact*   Once again putting words in my opponent's mouth (a sneaky trick which gives me great pleasure), I suggest that Dr. Rothman could have expressed himself with more rigorous logic as follows:

"Geffe claims that scientists are not dogmatic, but I am a scientist, and

---

* Albert Wilson, "Physical Views on the Origin of the Universe," October, 1965, The Rand Corporation, Santa Monica, Calif., p. 14.

I am dogmatic. My friends are dogmatic. We all love it. Therefore Geffe is wrong."

While this weakens my position, I call attention to the saving fact that I did admit to some exceptions.

*Concerning Einstein*   His papers on the Brownian movement, special relativity, matter–energy equivalence, and the photon theory of light were all published in 1905, the year in which he received his Ph.D. from the University of Zurich. Could he have been "not even a graduate student" and "without a doctorate" *both*?

Rothman's careful phrase "at the highest levels" lets him out. But, at lesser universities, Einstein's theories were received with loud cries of "mysticism" mixed with angry suspicions about his qualifications. The years reduced this to an apologetic murmur which died out before World War II.

*Engineers vs. Scientists*   Campbell is absolutely right on this point (though dead wrong on the other). I am glad to find something on which we agree, as I have been a great admirer of his since 1930. The distinction between scientists and engineers is, admittedly, somewhat blurred in academic circles. In industry, one gets a clearer picture. I claim that ninety percent of engineers could not be mistaken for scientists, and vice versa.

### Milton A. Rothman

John Campbell's main fallacy is that of the stereotype: he says "the scientist" is this and "the engineer" is that, disregarding the broad range of opinions which exist within both professions. Or he will take one or two examples in which *some* scientists have said stupid things, and he will then claim that this type of behavior categorizes the majority of scientists.

In the present discussion Campbell makes a claim which hits a high mark for sheer nonsense. He says: "Scientists won't admit a thing happens at all until they first are shown *why* it happens; no amount of evidence that it *does* happen suffices."

Now take the gravitational attraction between the earth and the sun. Scientists don't know why or how the sun can affect the motion of the earth 93 million miles away with nothing but empty space between. But they're willing to admit that something does happen. Oh yes, now they have a theory (or two), but that came very late in the game, and nobody really understands it.

Or take the phenomenon of superconductivity. Scientists didn't know why it happened for many years after it was discovered. But they knew it was there.

As a matter of fact, most of the phenomena of nature were observed before people could explain them on any kind of rational level: the radiation of energy by the sun, cosmic rays, electrical forces, magnetic forces, and—oh yes—the human brain. We don't know how that works, either.

To compound the confusion, the examples Campbell gives to prove his point don't even have anything to do with the point he is making. For example: the rejection of Christofilos' strong focusing principle by a small group of scientists. Notice carefully that Christofilos did not have a working model of a device to show them. He did not have evidence that something was *happening*. He just had a lot of calculations which nobody could understand. Whether or not these scientists were at fault is not the question here. The point is that this is NOT an example of scientists rejecting a physical phenomenon which had happened and which they could see with their own eyes. There was nothing to see except symbols written in a language they did not understand.

As for ball lightning, I wouldn't say that this subject has just now become fashionable *because* some people at Westinghouse calculated that it could happen. I know physicists who have been doing research on this subject for several years. It is one of the minor branches of plasma physics, and in fact it has proven of much interest because it represents a possibility of a system which is hydrodynamically stable. This is something we would like to see in plasma physics.

Campbell certainly has a backward idea about the relationship between theory and experiment. He has the impression that "scientists" hold theories to be sacred. If that is so, why are they overthrowing them all the time? Actually, those who really understand what is going on know that theories are simply models of nature which are no good until they are experimentally verified. The entire basis of science is observation and experiment. (Those interested in what the best scientists think should read Richard Feynman's Nobel Prize lecture, reprinted in the latest issue of *Physics Today*, and also in *Science*.)

Of course, I well understand what Campbell's basic beef is. He doesn't like the way scientists are skeptical toward his pet offbeat ideas such as ESP, UFO's, Dean drives, etc. But there, the question arises, how do we even prove that the phenomenon exists? I think I have a right to be skeptical toward phenomena which a few people can observe but which most people can't. If you have something like ESP that disappears when there is a skeptic in the crowd, then you have a hard time proving that there is anything to explain. It is on occasions such as this that scientists must fall back on their basic principles and on their (experimentally verified) theories. Then we can say that if telepathy exists it must propagate by something like electromagnetic waves, it can't go faster than light, it must follow the inverse-square law, and ought to be detectible by electronic equipment which is sensitive enough to receive waves from galaxies a billion light years away. So until you show me a causal relationship between the transmitter and the receiver, don't waste my time. Causality is perhaps the basic principle of science, and if you take that away you have nothing left.

### James V. McConnell

I trust that your readers won't pay too much attention to the comments Philip R. Geffe makes concerning the supposed absence of a "conservative Establishment" in science today. Geffe sounds like a bright Cal Tech engineer trained in the physical sciences but with little experience in the fields of biology, medicine, the social or behavioral sciences. I can't speak for physics or chemistry, about which I know almost nothing. But as far as the bio-social sciences are concerned, yes, Philip, there is indeed a reactionary and conservative Establishment and bright young scientists do get put down for espousing crazy ideas.

Two years ago I heard a pair of young biochemist-geneticists talking about the possibility of causing "directed mutations" in animals by training them in certain ways. "Aren't you being a little Lamarckian?" I asked, hiding my smirk. "Oh, come off it," one of them said. "Everybody knows the truth is halfway between Darwin and Lamarck." I burst out laughing. You see, a couple of weeks before, I had been thoroughly taken to task by a senior scientist because my own ideas on memory coding via RNA "smacked of Lamarckism." Smacked so much, in fact, that there were troubles with research funds. It's quite true that the scientific evidence has been around for decades showing that not all mutations were as "accidental" as the Morgan-Mendel position claimed, but the American Genetic Dogma was against such heresy, and still is. To the best of my knowledge, no government agency has ever given a single cent to research designed to "test the Lamarckian viewpoint." A few people I know are doing this type of work, but doing it strictly sub-rosa, "borrowing" funds from other more respectable projects, knowing that if they get the positive results they expect, they probably will have one helluva time publishing their findings. No Establishment? Don't make me laugh. For a detailed account of this very live battle, see Carl C. Lindegren's book *The Cold War in Biology*, published by Planarian Press. Lindegren, a noted geneticist but one who's never gone along with the American Establishment, was recently told by one of his friends that he'd never, never get elected to the National Academy "no matter what he found in the laboratory" because Lindegren's ideas were "just too radical."

Or take penicillin, which Geffe himself mentions. Anyone who wishes to read about the Establishment in action should look up the recent biography of Fleming. At the time he was putting the final touches on his experiments proving that penicillin was indeed an antibiotic, his colleagues were openly reviling him, asking that he be read out of his Society, doing their best to prevent him from finishing his work. Lovely chaps, and many of them are still alive today, probably in part because of penicillin!

One of the top administrators in the National Institutes of Health informed me a few months ago that Masters, the St. Louis M.D. who's been researching human sexual physiology, had just had his funds cut off from NIH. The research Masters was doing was considered excellent from a scientific point of view; the ax came because the work was considered "too controversial to merit further support." This same administrator and I had a long talk about such subjects, for it's one that I'm vitally interested in. As you may know, government research funds are usually given out by scientific panels or committees that judge the excellence of the proposals sent to the granting agencies. If the committee is against you, you can't get money. Which means you can't do research, for these agencies support the overwhelming bulk of scientific research these days. As the NIH chap pointed out, research done by social psychologists on the behavior of small groups (including committees) suggests that group decisions tend to be much more conservative than would be the personal, individual decisions of any single member of the group. In short, the Establishment can hardly be anything other than conservative. And, of course, only "highly respectable" individuals are named to the committees in the first place.

Last year a big shot in the National Science Foundation came to speak at the Institute where I do my research. For an hour he railed politely at the scientists assembled because we failed to submit any "exciting new research proposals" to NSF—the ones they got were pedestrian in the extreme. At the end of his talk, we reminded him of the facts of life. The brightest idea we ever had was not to send bright ideas to Washington to be funded. Several of us present had done so once or twice, to our dismay. We asked him in all honesty if NSF would have, a decade ago, supported research in several areas of science quite respectable today but highly controversial then. He admitted that it probably wouldn't have, then began asking us how we thought NSF could be changed so that it would support creative, oddball research during the early stages of such work (before it becomes a part of the Establishment's dogma). We didn't know, and still don't.

Geffe doesn't seem to realize that while there are differences between scientists and "ordinary folk," these differences are usually not as great as the similarities. There has always been an Establishment, even in times and places where a deliberate attempt has been made to do away with same. Probably there always will be. And the Establishment serves a very real purpose, meets real human needs perhaps too obvious to be mentioned here. Heresy is not a way of life in most quarters, is feared and distrusted now just as it always was and probably always will be. The way to become a departmental chairman and/or get huge government grants is almost always to play the Establishment's game, at least on the surface. Until you become a member in good standing yourself; at which time it's probably too late to change . . .


**John W. Campbell**

I was delighted to see Jim McConnell's letter anent the real existence of The Establishment.

Being an Inside Member of The Establishment is like being an air-breathing mammal—it's extremely difficult to become aware of the existence of air. The thing that will make you acutely aware that air exists is when somebody cuts you off from it.

Thus for Rothman, who's deep in the Inner Establishment, the fact of the existence of the Establishment is genuinely imperceptible. For McConnell who is one of those pushing like fury to get the Establishment to move its leaden tail, the existence of the Establishment and its rigid traditions is obvious. And for me, living outside the Establishment, and trying, like Jim, to get it to budge its ponderous pomposity, it is also obvious. ( . . . )

Re Christofilos' "calculations that no one could understand": Christofilos presented his strong focusing principle in the language of algebra. Any Scientist who can't read algebra is certainly incapable of handling calculus, differential equations, or tensor analysis. So why couldn't they read Christofilos' algebra? Because Christofilos, at the time, didn't have the Union card—the Guild Membership—a Ph.D. in physics, and that proved he couldn't have anything important to offer. Because *they wouldn't try to see* what he had to offer.

Rothman makes a great point of the "Show me a working model!" being the one necessary and sufficient requirement to convince a good Scientist that something new has been discovered. He also explains why, since he *knows* the Dean device couldn't possibly work, it was entirely unnecessary for him to go look at it to see if it worked.

My complaint in the original Dean Drive article was that Dean *couldn't get anybody to look.* No one would look-to-see, because they knew-without-looking that it wouldn't work. ( . . . )

Look, Dr. Rothman . . . how can I show you the moons of Jupiter if you positively refuse to look through my telescope?

You live and work in Princeton, New Jersey. O.K., Dr. Rothman—go out in the street, and watch the local water company use dowsing rods to locate underground pipes. You don't have to go far, or expend great effort, nor invest any capital—your local water company routinely *uses* on an *engineering* level of "it works—let's use it" an example of an ESP phenomenon that you "know" is nonsense.

You try demonstrating that TV really works, and I can guarantee to ruin your demonstration completely with a little electronic gimmick I can hide in my pack of cigarettes. What electronic circuits can do with great effort and sophistication, an electronic circuit of great simplicity can louse up to a fare-thee-well. All *it* has to do is make a white noise—an electronic Bronx cheer. In any communications technique, the problem is signal-to-noise ratio—and generating noise energy is extremely easy.

In like sense, what a mental circuit can learn to accomplish—a much simpler mental circuit can louse up completely, by just radiating a mental Bronx cheer. One brief spray with a can of Drylon, and I can louse up the finest watch ever made. One tablespoon of coarse emery in the oil filter, and a champion Ferrari race car won't win a Classic Car race at 15 miles per hour.

The trouble with Rothman, as a typical Pure Scientist, is his absolute refusal to look—with the consequence that he can, of course, truthfully say "I'll believe it only when I'm shown," and be perfectly safe.

Typical of my gripe at the "I know without having to look" attitude is Rothman's statement (italics mine), "Then we can say that if telepathy exists it *must* propagate by something like electromagnetic waves, it *can't* go faster than light, it *must* follow the inverse-square law, and *ought* to be detectible by electronic equipment which is sensitive enough to receive waves from galaxies a billion light-years away." For someone who has never studied ESP Rothman sure knows a lot about what it *must* be and what it *can't* do. By what right or evidence does he establish that it *must* be like electromagnetic waves?

It reminds me of the time during WW II when the Germans sent out specially equipped research submarines, to learn what the secret weapon the Allies were using to detect and destroy their submarines was. They took along radio receiving equipment capable of detecting any electromagnetic waves in the entire spectrum of generatable frequencies—from 10 kilocycles all the way to 2,000 megacycles. All three research submarines were detected and sunk thanks to the strange weapon. The researchers had found no activity over the entire radio spectrum, so they knew the Allied system depended on something else. Since their equipment didn't even come close to the 10,000 megacycles the Allied airborne radar used, they never detected that they were being pinged with kilowatts of RF energy at frequencies they were certain could not be generated. They had lousy klystrons, and didn't have magnetrons.

Because their equipment was inadequate *in a way they did not suspect*, they knew-for-certain that the detection system was not radar. And Rothman who knows-for-certain just how telepathy has to act is making an equal mistake—the characteristic mistake of the theory-oriented scientist. He's *sure* he knows what it *must* be and what it can't do.

Incidentally, that galaxy-detecting hypersensitive electronic equipment wouldn't even know that a kilowatt signal from a pseudo-random noise coded transmitter was blasting through it. It's very carefully designed to integrate signals over a period of time; a signal deliberately coded to resemble noise very closely would be completely suppressed by the integrator circuits.

So your equipment is hypersensitive . . . So what? It's sensitive to the wrong thing. It's like boasting that you have the most complete, sensitive, and perfect analytical equipment possible; it can detect one part in a billion of any chemical element in any combination or mixture. So how good is it at analyzing a magnetic field?

Moreover, Rothman wasn't really old enough to be interested back in the 1928–32 period when I was at M. I. T. and the scientists were beating me about the ears for being interested in my "pet off-beat ideas such as" commercial use of nuclear energy, spaceships capable of visiting the Moon, radio astronomy, and other such pseudo-science fantasies. And while it was true that stars were able to fuse hydrogen to release energy, the idea that Man could make some kind of a machine to do it—utter nonsense, stemming from a complete lack of knowledge of what physics was. Why, you'd have to confine the gas at temperatures of millions of degrees—which was clearly utterly impossible since nothing can exist in a solid state at that temperature.

Rothman better get out of that hydrogen-fusion research; it's clearly pseudo-scientific research—a crazy off-beat idea. And he certainly can't show anybody that it actually works!

Sure, we have more knowledge now than we did in 1930. But does that make you one whit wiser—more understandingly judicious—than were the professors at M. I. T. in 1930?

The only one of the M. I. T. professors who ever helped me with a science-fiction story was another fellow who had a lot of off-beat ideas. A guy who believed in pseudo-scientific fantasy ideas like robots and automatic self-operating machinery—Norbert Weiner.

For a man who's working on way-out ideas like hydrogen fusion to call my interest in the present-day, routine engineering application of a solidly useful technology like dowsing "off-beat" is kind of stretching things, isn't it? Your attitude implies "All my ancestors and my predecessors in Science were fools, and only I am wise." They said that what you're doing was pseudo-science and fantasy. Their best judgment was, we can now recognize, badly off. Are you intrinsically wiser—better able to judge the still-unknown areas of the Universe than they? How can you be so arrogantly and smugly certain that you're righter than they were? And can you suggest how I can show you something—when you positively refuse to dignify "such nonsense" by looking at it?

### Milton A. Rothman

I don't want to carry the argument to absurd lengths, but there are two small points I must make, in reply to Campbell's letter.

(1) Re looking at a working model of the Dean drive. Campbell forgets that when the first Dean article appeared I *did* write to him and asked to look at the device. He declined this offer, with the excuse that he was showing it to some other people. Furthermore, I read the original patent so was quite familiar with the technical details. In retrospect, the fact that Campbell never did have a model which got off the ground proves that I was right.

(2) I had sound reasons for my remarks about telepathy following the inverse square laws. Any signal which carries information must carry energy in order to activate a receiver. Any energy broadcast in all directions must follow the inverse square law in order for the flux of energy through the spherical surfaces to be constant as it goes away from the source. My bet is on the law of conservation of energy. Only time will tell who is right.

# V.
# HOW TO, IN FOUR
# TRICKY LESSONS

# ON THE WRITING OF
# SPECULATIVE FICTION

## Robert A. Heinlein

*There are nine and sixty ways
Of constructing tribal lays
And every single one of them is right!*

—RUDYARD KIPLING

There are at least two principal ways to write speculative fiction—write about people, or write about gadgets. There are other ways; consider Stapleton's *Last and First Men*, recall S. Fowler Wright's *The World Below*. But the gadget story and the human-interest story comprise most of the field. Most science fiction stories are a mixture of the two types, but we will speak as if they were distinct—at which point I will chuck the gadget story aside, dust off my hands, and confine myself to the human-interest story, that being the sort of story I myself write. I have nothing against the gadget story—I read it and enjoy it—it's just not my pidgin. I am told that this is a how-to-do-it symposium; I'll stick to what I know how to do.

The editor suggested that I write on "Science Fiction in the Slicks." I shan't do so because it is not a separate subject. Several years ago Will F. Jenkins said to me, "I'll let you in on a secret, Bob. *Any* story—science fiction, or otherwise—if it is well written, can be sold to the slicks." Will himself has proved this, so have many other writers—Wylie, Wells, Cloete, Doyle, Ertz, Noyes, many others. You may protest that these writers were able to sell science fiction to the high-pay markets because

---

FROM *Of Worlds Beyond*, Advent, 1964

they were already well-known writers. It just ain't so, pal; on the contrary they are well-known writers because they are skilled at their trade. When they have a science fiction story to write, they turn out a well-written story and it sells to a high-pay market. An editor of a successful magazine will bounce a poorly written story from a "name" writer just as quickly as one from an unknown. Perhaps he will write a long letter of explanation and suggestion, knowing as he does that writers are as touchy as white leghorns, but he will bounce it. At most, prominence of the author's name might decide a borderline case.

A short story stands a much better chance with the slicks if it is not more than 5,000 words long. A human-interest story stands a better chance with the slicks than a gadget story, because the human-interest story usually appeals to a wider audience than does a gadget story. But this does not rule out the gadget story. Consider "Note on Danger B" in a recent *Saturday Evening Post* and Wylie's "The Blunder," which appeared last year in *Collier's*.

Let us consider what a story is and how to write one. (Correction: how *I* write one—remember Mr. Kipling's comment!)

A story is an account which is not necessarily true but which is interesting to read.

There are three main plots for the human interest story: boy-meets-girl, The Little Tailor, and the man-who-learned-better. Credit the last category to L. Ron Hubbard; I had thought for years that there were but two plots—he pointed out to me the third type.

Boy-meets-girl needs no definition. But don't disparage it. It reaches from the "Iliad" to John Taine's *Time Stream*. It's the greatest story of them all and has never been sufficiently exploited in science fiction.[28] To be sure, it appears in most s-f stories, but how often is it dragged in by the hair and how often is it the compelling and necessary element which creates and then solves the problem? It has great variety: boy-fails-to-meet-girl, boy-meets-girl-too-late, boy-meets-too-many-girls, boy-loses-girl, boy-and-girl-renounce-love-for-higher-purpose. Not science fiction? Here is a throw-away plot; you can have it free: Elderly man meets very young girl; they discover that they are perfectly adapted to each other, perfectly in love, "soul mates." (Don't ask me how. It's up to you to make the thesis credible. If I'm going to have to write this story, I want to be paid for it.)

Now to make it a science fiction story. Time travel? Okay, what time theory—probable-times, classic theory, or what? Rejuvenation? Is this mating necessary to some greater end? Or vice versa? Or will you transcend the circumstances, as C. L. Moore did in that tragic masterpiece "Bright Illusion"?

I've used it twice as tragedy[29] and shall probably use it again. Go ahead and use it yourself. I did not invent it; it is a great story which has been kicking around for centuries.

The "Little Tailor"—this is an omnibus for all stories about the little guy who becomes a big shot, or vice versa. The tag is from the fairy story. Examples: "Dick Whittington," all the Alger books, *Little Caesar*, *Galactic Patrol* (but not *Grey Lensman*), *Mein Kampf*, David in the Old Testament. It is the Success story, or, in reverse, the story of tragic failure.

The man-who-learned-better; just what it sounds like—the story of a man who has one opinion, point of view, or evaluation at the beginning of the story, then acquires a new opinion or evaluation as a result of having his nose rubbed in some harsh facts. I had been writing this story for years before Hubbard pointed out to me the structure of it. Examples: my "Universe" and "Logic of Empire," Jack London's "South of the Slot," Dickens' "A Christmas Carol."

The definition of a story as something interesting-but-not-necessarily-true is general enough to cover all writers, all stories—even James Joyce, if you find his stuff interesting. (I don't!) For me, a story of the sort I want to write is still further limited to this recipe: a man finds himself in circumstances which create a problem for him. In coping with this problem, the man is changed in some fashion inside himself. The story is over when the inner change is complete—the external incidents may go on indefinitely.

People changing under stress:

A lonely rich man learns comradeship in a hobo jungle.

A milquetoast gets pushed too far and learns to fight.

A strong man is crippled and has to adjust to it.

A gossip learns to hold her tongue.

A hard-boiled materialist gets acquainted with a ghost.

A shrew is tamed.

This is the story of character, rather than incident. It's not everybody's dish, but for me it has more interest than the most overwhelming pure adventure story. It need not be unadventurous; the stress which produces the change in character can be wildly adventurous, and often is.

But what has all this to do with science fiction? A great deal! Much so-called science fiction is not about human beings and their problems, consisting instead of a fictionized framework, peopled by cardboard figures, on which is hung an essay about the Glorious Future of Technology. With due respect to Mr. Bellamy, *Looking Backward* is a perfect example of the fictionized essay. I've done it myself; "Solution Unsatisfactory" is a fictionized essay, written as such. Knowing that it would have to compete with real *story*, I used every device I could think of, some of them hardly admissible, to make it look like a story.

Another type of fiction alleged to be science fiction is the story laid in the future, or on another planet, or in another dimension, or sich, which could just as well have happened on Fifth Avenue, in 1947. Change the costumes back to now, cut out the pseudo-scientific double-talk and the blaster guns and it turns out to be straight adventure story, suitable, with appropriate facelifting, to any other pulp magazine on the newsstand.

There is another type of honest-to-goodness science fiction story which is not usually regarded as science fiction: the story of people dealing with contemporary science or technology. We do not ordinarily mean this sort of story when we say "science fiction"; what we do mean is the speculative story, the story embodying the notion "Just suppose—" or "What would happen if—" In the speculative science fiction story accepted science and established facts are extrapolated to produce a new situation, a new framework for human action. As a result of this new situation, new *human* problems are created—and our story is about how human beings cope with those new problems.

The story is *not* about the new situation; it is about coping with problems arising out of the new situation.

Let's gather up the bits and define the simon-pure science fiction story:

1. The conditions must be, in some respect, different from here-and-now, although the difference may lie only in an invention made in the course of the story.

2. The new conditions must be an essential part of the story.

3. The problem itself—the "plot"—must be a *human* problem.

4. The human problem must be one which is created by, or indispensably affected by, the new conditions.

5. And lastly, no established fact shall be violated, and, furthermore, when the story requires that a theory contrary to present accepted theory be used, the new theory should be rendered reasonably plausible and

it must include and explain established facts as satisfactorily as the one the author saw fit to junk. It may be far-fetched, it may seem fantastic, but it must *not* be at variance with observed facts, i.e., if you are going to assume that the human race descended from Martians, then you've *got* to explain our apparent close relationship to terrestrial anthropoid apes as well.

Pardon me if I go on about this. I love to read science fiction, but violation of that last requirement gets me riled. Rocketships should not make banked turns on empty space the way airplanes bank their turns on air. Lizards can't cross-breed with humans. The term "space warp" does not mean anything without elaborate explanation.

Not everybody talking about heaven is going there—and there are a lot of people trying to write science fiction who haven't bothered to learn anything about science. Nor is there any excuse for them in these days of public libraries. You owe it to your readers (a) to bone up on the field of science you intend to introduce into your story; (b) unless you yourself are well-versed in that field, you should also persuade some expert in that field to read your story and criticize it before you offer it to an unsuspecting public. Unless you are willing to take this much trouble, please, *please* stick to a contemporary background you are familiar with. Paderewski had to practice; Sonja Henie still works on her school figures; a doctor puts in many weary years before they will let him operate—why should you be exempt from preparatory effort?

The simon-pure science fiction story—examples of human problems arising out of extrapolations of present science:

Biological warfare ruins the farm lands of the United States; how is Joe Doakes, a used-car dealer, to feed his family?

Interplanetary travel puts us in contact with a race able to read our thoughts; is the testimony of such beings admissible as evidence in a murder trial?

Men reach the Moon; what is the attitude of the Security Council of the United Nations? (Watch out for this one—and hold on to your hats!)[30]

A complete technique for ectogenesis is developed; what is the effect on home, family, morals, religion? (Aldous Huxley left lots of this field unplowed—help yourself.)

And so on. I've limited myself to *my* notions about science fiction, but don't forget Mr. Kipling's comment. In any case it isn't necessary to know how—just go ahead and do it. Write what you like to read. If you have a yen for it, if you get a kick out of "Just imagine—," if you love to think up new worlds, then come on in, the water's fine and there is plenty of room.

But don't write to me to point out how I have violated my own rules in this story or that; I've violated all of them and I would much rather try a new story than defend an old one.

I'm told that these articles are supposed to be some use to the reader. I have a guilty feeling that all of the above may have been more for my amusement than for your edification. Therefore I shall chuck in as a bonus a group of practical, tested rules which, if followed meticulously, will prove rewarding to any writer.

I shall assume that you can type, that you know the accepted commercial format or can be trusted to look it up and follow it, and that you always use new ribbons and clean type. Also, that you can spell and punctuate and can use grammar well enough to get by. These things are merely the word-carpenter's sharp tools. He must add to them these business habits:

1. You must *write*.

2. You must *finish* what you start.

3. You must refrain from rewriting except to editorial order.

4. You must put it on the market.

5. You must keep it on the market until sold.

The above five rules really have more to do with how to write speculative fiction than anything said above them. But they are amazingly hard to follow—which is why there are so few professional writers and so many aspirants, and which is why I am not afraid to give away the racket! But, if you will follow them, it matters not how you write, you will find some editor somewhere, sometime, so unwary or so desperate for copy as to buy the worst old dog you, or I, or anybody else, can throw at him.

# HOW TO BUILD A PLANET


## Poul Anderson


One justification for the existence of science fiction—perhaps the main one—is that it can suggest to us the size, variety, and sheer wonder of the universe. It *can*; but how often does it do so? Far too many stories merely give us a planet exactly like Earth except for having neither geography nor history. Other stories, trying for the exotic, serve up an unbelievable mishmash. A background which is really different, but well thought out, detailed and self-consistent, creates an excitement and an illusion of verisimilitude that adds much to an otherwise bald and unconvincing narrative. Furthermore, the process of designing a world suggests innumerable story points. Though I don't pretend to bat in Hal Clement's league, I have long been using a few elementary principles of astronomy and physics to generate settings. Perhaps others would like to try their hands. All that's needed is some reference works, a slide rule, and a little patience.

We start by picking a star. Now the familiar ones such as Vega and Antares have not only been overworked, they are no longer plausible. The evidence is that they don't have planets.

Consider the diagram. It is a simplified version of the Russell-Hertzsprung diagram, which summarizes the results of many thousand observations. On the left side are the luminosities of the stars—one tenth as much output as Sol, ten times as much, etc. (The range is so vast that

FROM *SFWA Bulletin*, November 1966

the numbers have to be on a logarithmic scale.) On the bottom of the diagram is a row of letters. These indicate spectral types; for our purposes, we can say they indicate colors and surface temperatures. The O stars are the extremely hot blue giants. Continuing down the diagonal, you go through yellow (around G) to cool and red (M). Intermediate classes are indicated by a number between 0 and 9. For example, an A5 star lies halfway between an A0 and an F0. Sol is G2 (a recent reclassification from the former G0). In other words, color/temperature and luminosity are correlated; you find no cool blue dwarfs, for instance. [Since this was written, Zwicky has reported the discovery of "pygmy stars," some of which are indeed blue. However, they seem to be in the very last stages of their evolution.]

Below the letters are more figures. These are, very approximately, the corresponding masses, where Sol's = 1. Thus we can see that a typical F0 star is about twice as massive as Sol and puts out about ten times as much radiant energy.

The diagonal is called the main sequence. Most stars stay on it for most of their lives. Eventually they move to the right, becoming red giants like Betelgeuse, finally flaring up and then sinking to the white dwarf condition. See a good modern book on stellar astronomy for details. The important point here is that red giants, variables, and others not on the main sequence are generally dying stars. They will scarcely have any habitable planets. (I did recently do some fast footwork regarding Betelgeuse; and this rationalization in turn suggested a story.) Furthermore, all indications are that *no* stars above F5 or thereabouts have planets. (Figuring out a freakish way in which a blue giant could do so gave me another plot.) In general, writers should stick to the yellow and red suns. They are in the overwhelming majority anyway.

It is debatable whether double, triple, etc. stars can have planets. Orbits might or might not be too unstable. I suspect that many do, if only as Earth-sized satellites of supergiant worlds like 61 Cygni C. But the mechanics of this may be left to writers who are interested; and, once again, many a plot point will show up.

Let us here confine ourselves to a single star. At the risk of bragging, I'll use a recent construction of my own as an example. (Starkad, in the forthcoming novel *Ensign Flandry*, in case anyone cares.) The same principles can be applied to any number of star and planet types.

In this instance, I picked the upper end of the available main se-

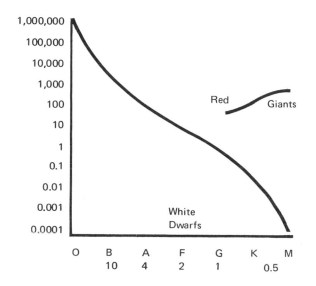

quence, making my star an F5. Its luminosity was therefore taken as 5.4 S. (The S stands for "times the corresponding quantity of Sol.") The mass was therefore in the neighborhood of 1.75 S, which is the value I specifically picked. Of course, these figures are somewhat arbitrary; there seems to be a good deal of variation in reality. Assuming that the density was about the same as Sol's, and applying the principle that mass is proportional to the cube of diameter, I got a diameter of 1.2 S. The star would look brighter than Sol, somewhat whiter in color, and emit more ultraviolet light and charged particles. Already, then, I could think of exotic touches like the color of objects and shadows on its planets, the spectacular auroras, and the deep tan acquired by humans.

But what about those planets? I needed one not too unlike Earth; therefore it had to get neither too much nor too little irradiation. Apply the inverse-square law. If $L$ = the luminosity (in toto) of the sun, $r$ the distance of the planet, and $i$ the irradiation it gets, then

$$i = \frac{L}{r^2}. \tag{1}$$

These quantities are all in terms of the Sol–Earth situation. That is, in the present example $L = 5.4$ and $r$ is expressed in astronomical units. (The a.u. is the average distance of Earth from Sol, about 93 million miles.)

Thus we get $i$ directly as so-and-so much times the irradiation Earth receives.

But what value should we pick for $r$? That depends on what we want $i$ to be. Solving equation (1), we get

$$r = \sqrt{\frac{L}{i}}. \tag{2}$$

So if we want the planet to receive just as much radiant energy as Earth does ($i = 1$), we need $r = 2.3$ a.u. It will be a little farther out than Mars is. To date, the theory of planetary formation is not so complete that anyone can call this an impossible choice. However, for the sake of being different, and on the assumption that planets will tend to form where stellar gravitational attraction has certain definite values, I decided to make my world a bit more remote than that: at such a distance that it would be in a gravitational field more or less equal to that in the middle of our asteroid belt. To be specific, I set $r = 3.28$. Gravitation, of course, also follows an inverse-square law, so that if $M$ is the mass of a body and $a$ the acceleration it produces on some other body,

$$a = \frac{M}{r^2} \tag{3}$$

—again taking some such values as Earth-Sol as unity.

Thus I had an $i = 0.5$ $E$ (where $E$ means "times the corresponding quantity for Earth"). To be sure, this will vary a little, since the orbit is almost certain to be an ellipse rather than a perfect circle. But the complication can be ignored, as long as you don't postulate a very eccentric ellipse.

The planet, then, gets only about half as much light as Earth does: slightly less, in fact, since a larger proportion of $i$ is in the ultraviolet. But the human eye is so adaptable that this wouldn't seem dim; there would simply be an absence of the glare we sometimes get on Earth. How big does the sun look in the sky of this world? We can answer that by trigonometry, since its diameter and distance are known. It comes out approximately 11 minutes of arc, about 0.37 Sol seen from Earth. Accordingly, on this planet, the sun is quite small, though extremely intense.

How long is the planet's year? Call this $P$, for period. Sticking with our Sol-Earth values as unity, we have

$$P^2 = \frac{r^3}{M} \tag{4}$$

and that's where you really need a slide rule. In this case, $P = 4.48\ E$. Its year is about four and a half times as long as ours. (The effect of that on biology, civilization, etc. is worth many plots.)

Now we come to the planet itself. If we make it too small, it won't retain much atmosphere; too big, and it will retain its primordial hydrogen and the atmosphere won't be breathable by men. Since $i =$ only 0.5, one reason I wanted a fairly thick atmosphere was for greenhouse effect to keep the surface reasonably warm. So I picked a mass of 1.81 $E$.

The size was somewhat problematical. But evidently, the more massive a planet, the denser it is, because gravity squeezes atoms at the core. (Jupiter, Saturn, etc. have low *apparent* densities because what we actually measure is their huge atmospheric envelopes.) I set the average density for the entire globe at 1.10 $E$. Now obviously the mass, which is given, equals overall density times volume, and volume is a cube function of diameter. Therefore the diameter comes out as 1.18 $E$. (This assumes the planet is a perfect sphere, which it won't be, but again the difference isn't enough to worry about except in extreme cases like Clement's Mesklin.)

Having worked this out, it's easy to find the surface gravity, $g$. On the good-enough assumption of sphericity, and taking Earth values as unity,

$$g = dD \tag{5}$$

where $d =$ average density and $D =$ diameter. In the present instance, $g = 1.30\ E$. A 200-pound man weighs 260 pounds. As it happened, this did not affect the plot; but mention of the fact, of how older men in particular were always aware of the extra drag on them, was another realistic touch.

But what about the atmosphere? Unfortunately, the principles governing this are complicated and not too well understood. It seemed reasonable to me, though, that the air could indeed be a lot thicker than Earth's. There is less irradiation to drive molecules into space, and there is more gravity to hold and compress them. (Gravitational potential is another factor, but not very important here since $D$ is not very different from Earth.) For reasons to be explained later, I made the surface concentration of air $= 6.67\ E$. (The pressure, the actual weight per square inch, is naturally still greater because of the greater gravity.) This is too much for humans. The composition can be all right, as far as proportions go, but you'd get unpleasant effects like nitrogen narcosis and carbon dioxide acidosis. Hence people need special equipment at sea level.

Many phenomena would be quite unlike what we are used to. Winds are slow, because a given amount of energy has to push a bigger air mass than here. Waves, on the other hand, move a little faster than on Earth, since wave velocity on deep water =

$$\sqrt{\frac{gw}{2\pi}}$$

where $w$ is the wavelength.

How far up would humans have to move before they could safely breathe? If an atmosphere has the same temperature throughout—it doesn't, but we don't need absolutely exact figures—then the pressure $p$ at any given altitude $h$ is

$$p = p_o e^{-kgh}$$

where $p_o$ = sea level pressure, $e$ = 2.72 approximately, and $k$ is a rather complicated constant depending on the composition of the air. It turns out that, on my planet, the pressure drops by one half for every 4.23 kilometers. Thus you get an Earth sea-level value at about 11.6 kilometers, or 38,000 feet. The men have their base on the highest available mountain. More opportunities to show how variegated a world can be!

The sea-level density I picked was not arbitrary. The more pressure, the more gas dissolves in water; and, since I wanted intelligent beings living in the sea as well as others living on the land, I had to provide the former with enough oxygen to support an active metabolism. At the pressure mentioned, the oxygen concentration in cool water is just about the same as that in Earth's sea-level air, give or take a few percent. Actually, what I did was to choose such values for planetary mass, etc., that the pressure and temperature I wanted sounded plausible. In fact, designing a planet is very much a cut-and-try process.

Having chosen your values, though, you should stick with their consequences. Sometimes these are not significant. For instance, how far off is the horizon on a level plain? Well, that quantity is proportional to the square root of $D$ (for small elevations) and thus doesn't vary fast. Had the world been twice as large as Earth, which it wasn't, the horizon distance would still only have been $\sqrt{2} \times 5$ miles (5 miles being roughly the value for Earth), or about 7 miles. What with haze, mountains, and such to clutter up vision, the difference would scarcely be noticeable.

Now, how long is the planet's day? Again, we don't know what the laws are that govern these things. But tidal action will tend to slow down rotation over billions of years. So what tidal action is there on this particular world? Well, it is proportional to the mass of the tide-producing object and inversely proportional to the *cube* of that object's distance. I checked, to make sure, and the star's tidal effect on this world turned out to be only 0.05 Sun-Earth. (We'll consider satellites later.) So it appeared likely that the planet would still be spinning rather fast. After all, our big outer planets do. I made the day 16 hours 30 minutes long. Hence the year is about 2,364 planetary days.

The axial inclination is also a matter of choice. One might have postulated a really rakish tilt and thus have gotten some extreme seasons. But here I already had so much local color that there wasn't room for this extra complication; so I made the tilt only slightly greater than Earth's and never got a chance to mention it. If you do want to play with a curious spin, you'll need trigonometry, again, to find out how much the seasons differ from each other and how the sun moves across the sky throughout the year.

What about satellites, though? Without any, the oceans would get pretty stagnant—remember how weak the solar tides are—and, while this has interesting possibilities, it didn't happen to be what I wanted. Trying for difference from Earth, though, I settled on two small moons. *Mutatis mutandis*, the formulas already given will tell you their angular diameters, periods, and tidal effects, once you have chosen quantities like mass and density. But don't forget that the planet rotates, and that this will affect a moon's period as seen from the ground.

To be specific, for one moon I picked a diameter of 720 kilometers— which, assuming a density about like Luna's, gave a mass of 0.009 Luna— and an average distance of 48,000 kilometers (from the planetary center; subtract one-half $D$ to get distance from the surface). The satellite couldn't be too close, you see, or it would break up because of unequal tidal pulls. The lower (Roche's) limit is, for more or less Earthlike worlds, about 2.5 times the radius of the planet. Nor can the moon be too distant, or perturbation will eventually make it wander away altogether.

Anyhow, from these chosen values everything else could be derived. The angular diameter came out as a little over one degree, about twice what Luna shows to Earth. The tidal effect was about 4.5 times Luna–Earth. Those would be some rough seas, especially when the other moon was taken into account! (But tidal friction wouldn't have lengthened the day too much, since I had comparatively little land for waves to rub against. This was due to the erosive effect of the dense atmosphere.) The sidereal period, the time to complete an orbit, was 21.8 hours. But because of the planet's rotation, the synodic period, the time which the moon needed to get back to the same place with respect to an observer on the ground, was 67.5 hours, or a bit more than four local days. Had the inclination of the orbit to the planet's equator been great, such computations would have been more complicated; and had any of my characters visited a high latitude, I'd have used trigonometry to learn whether he could still see the moon.

All of this may sound dull. It isn't, really. To me, at least, the process of planet-building is fascinating. But whether or not it is fun for the writer, it does provide him with a rich background. He finds innumerable exotic details—especially if he plays with quantities less conservative than in the present example—and they are not vague generalities but concrete data. His figures, the precise values of this and that, will rarely get into the story as such. But they will be there in his own mind. He will *know* his setting, and thus he will make it seem real to the reader.

Of course, these mechanics are only the beginning. He has to go on to develop geography, life forms, civilizations, and everything else. But much of this will be suggested by the homework he has already done.

I conclude with a grab bag of stuff which I have also found useful.

$$\text{Escape velocity} = 7\sqrt{\frac{M}{D}} \text{ miles per second.}$$

The orbital velocity close to the surface is this divided by 1.4. As you go further out, orbital velocity is inversely proportional to the square root of distance from the center of the planet.

If a spaceship is accelerating at $a$ gravities (1 gravity = 32.2 feet per second per second), then the time $t$ (in hours) to cover a distance $s$ (in millions of miles) is

$$t = 5.1\sqrt{\frac{s}{a}} \quad \text{and} \quad s = \frac{at^2}{25.7}.$$

The velocity $v$ achieved, in miles per second,

$$v = 22 \, at = 110 \sqrt{as}$$

The corresponding formulas for the metric system, with $s$ in millions of kilometers, and $v$ in kilometers per second, are

$$t = 4\sqrt{\frac{s}{a}} \qquad s = \frac{at^2}{16} \qquad v = 35.2 \, at = 141 \sqrt{as} \; .$$

As for time conversions, 1 hour = 3600 seconds, 24 hours = 86,400 seconds, 1 year = $3.15 \times 10^7$ seconds. In distance, 1 light-year = $5.9 \times 10^{12}$ miles = $9.45 \times 10^{12}$ kilometers = $6.35 \times 10^4$ astronomical units.

If you accelerate continuously at one gravity, you will be pushing the speed of light in 355 days. The mass ratio $R$ (ratio of ship-plus-reaction-mass to ship-plus-whatever-is-left) to reach a velocity $v$ depends on the exhaust velocity $k$. In the Newtonian case, correct for fairly small fractions of light velocity $c$,

$$R = e^{v/k}$$

but if you intend to crowd the speed of light you need the Einsteinian formula

$$R = \left( \frac{1 + \dfrac{v}{c}}{1 - \dfrac{v}{c}} \right)^{c/2k}$$

—and, if you plan to decelerate, the mass ratio is not merely doubled but squared. A little calculation of this sort gives the author a good idea of what his spaceship looks and acts like.

The well-known Einsteinian time contraction does not become important until one is traveling almighty fast. If $T$ is the time aboard ship (for a straight-line journey) and $T_o$ is the time as experienced by a stay-at-home observer,

$$T = T_o \sqrt{1 - \frac{v^2}{c^2}}$$

and the mass $m$ of a moving object as measured by a "stationary" observer is related to the mass $m_o$ measured by someone stationary with respect to that object (i.e., moving along with it) by

$$m = \frac{m_o}{\sqrt{1 - \frac{v^2}{c^2}}}$$

A star catalogue, or a good astronomy text, is a handy sourcebook but you have to know how to use it. Herewith we change the meaning of the symbols $m$ and $M$, to conform to astronomical usage. Let $m$ be the visual magnitude of a star and $M$ its absolute magnitude (what it would have at a standard distance of 10 parsecs, where 1 parsec = 3.26 light-years). The parallax $p$, in seconds of arc, is just the inverse of the distance in parsecs.

$$M = m + 5 + 5 \log p.$$

For a given $M$, the luminosity $L$ as compared to the sun

$$\log L = 0.4 \, (4.85 - M).$$

The visual magnitude of Sol seen from Earth is $-26.7$, the absolute magnitude is 4.85. Bright stars have visual magnitudes in the neighborhood of 1. An object with a visual magnitude of 6.0 is barely visible to the naked eye. Thus Sol ceases to be a naked-eye object at a distance of 55.5 light-years.

Now I had better sit back and wait for the whole SFWA to point out my goofs to me.

# HOW TO COLLABORATE WITHOUT GETTING YOUR HEAD SHAVED

## Keith Laumer

There are probably as many ways to go about collaborating as there are reasons for getting the idea in the first place. I've heard tell of those who divided the work evenly; one collaborator did all the adjectives, adverbs, and nouns, and the other handled prepositions, verbs, etc. I don't know how this worked out. The older boys have told me about joint efforts in which one writer took certain characters as his own, while his partner backed the others, and proceeded to work the thing out, with each writer trying to outwit the other from page to page. This may not be a good way to produce a murder mystery, but, handled right, it could work out in a pretty fair murder. Some of the motives behind collaborations are just as bad.

For an ambitious beginner to propose a dual authorship with an established name may be tempting for both parties: Junior gets his name on the cover along with Robert H. Asimov, and the old-timer gets to haul some clag out of a drawer where it has been gathering dust, and allow the neophyte to spread the milt of his youthful enthusiasm over it in the hope of hatching out a nest egg, if not a milestone in contemporary letters. Likewise, a writer tired of wrestling with an uninspired opus may be tempted to turn it over to good old George to finish; and George may agree, seeing visions of adding a few words to what looks like an almost completed novel and splitting the take. Unhappily, good books aren't

---

From *SFWA Bulletin*, October 1967

made this way. There is only one legitimate reason to undertake a project as soul-baring and ego-frustrating as writing a book in tandem: to produce a better book than you could do alone—perhaps a book which couldn't otherwise be written at all.

My first collaboration was unpremeditated. Nay, more, the whole idea of collaboration was a traumatic area with Rosel Brown on account of she once had a very unhappy experience with a name writer who shall be nameless just this once.[31] It ended (after Rosel had written endless tens of thousands of words of deathless prose, all set in medieval Germany, the technical details of which had been supplied by the collaborator) with his accusation, while in his cups, that she only wanted to use his name, whereupon Rosel hurled the entire bundle into the fire. Mr. —— suffered burned pinkies trying to rake it back out, but alas, it went on to *Brennschluss*.

Anyway, I was sitting at table one cold summer evening at Highfield Place, my manor in Ealing W.5, and suddenly this grand idea hit me: a sign nailed to a wall, reading, FOR SALE—VIABLE HUMAN EMBRYO, etc. I dashed to the phone, dialed Rosel, and said, "Hey, I've got this great idea: there's this sign, and it says: FOR SALE—VIABLE HUMAN EMBRYO, and this pair of evil aliens buy it for their nefarious purposes, and—"

"No they don't," Rosel interrupted without so much as a by-your-leave. "This nice old couple buy it, because they want a son, you see . . ."

Obviously, this collaboration was the way Destiny wanted it. We got together and talked over the general outline of the book (Terran seeks Terra) and worked out the ground to be covered in the opening canto. Then we both wrote same, met again, compromised on the inconsistencies (I'll trade my name for the villain for your name for the heroine, if you'll let me keep in the guy with hair on his teeth). Then one of us rewrote it, drawing on both versions.

That was a lot of work. Thereafter, we discussed the upcoming chapters in pairs, each picked one, and wrote it. We met about once a week and swapped chapters, resolved any discrepancies, and repeated the process. When we finished, each of us gave the ms. a final revision to put back in all the good stuff the other had axed. The result was *Earthblood*, which is a better book than it would have been had the idea been left to my tender mercies. (Rosel wrote all the sexy parts, of course. And some of the worst of the gore. And her a handsome southern gentlewoman. Tsk.)

My other collaboration came to pass in this wise: I wrote the first draft of a novel and wasn't satisfied with it. I liked the characters, the basic plot idea and situation, but something was missing. Rather than give some editor the chance to reject it—or worse yet, print it—I put it aside to cool and went on to other matters.

Many moons later, at Milford, I found myself telling my troubles to Gordon Dickson, a man who knows how to listen constructively where writing problems are concerned. He thought the book sounded good and offered to take a look at it. So I mailed it off, and lo! In due course I got a four page single-spaced critique showing me the complex interrelationships among the characters which I had inadvertently left out while I wasn't looking. By that time, Gordy knew more about the story than I did. So I suggested that he take the material in hand to do a rewrite, as a collaboration. This he did, adding and subtracting lines and paragraphs on virtually every page, and adding sixty pages of new material, along with a plot and some motivations, without which no book should be. This was *Planet Run*. (Available at $3.95 from Doubleday, or ask your friendly neighborhood pusher.)

From the above it will be seen that any method that works is a good method. Just be sure you're bringing something to the collaboration, not merely looking for the easy way out. A collaboration requires as much work as a solo book, if not more. On the other hand, the whole can turn out to be greater than the sum of the parts, if you're lucky in your choice of co-genius. Still, if you've got a good idea, why share all that glory and cash with somebody? If you possibly can, write it yourself. Collaborations, like marriages, should only be undertaken if any alternative is unthinkable.

# WRITING AND SELLING SCIENCE FICTION

## Damon Knight

Science fiction writers often point out with unassuming pride that their task is much harder than that of mundane writers, because they have to invent all the backgrounds. This is true, but it is also true that writers who make up their backgrounds are spared the trouble of looking them up. In this sense it can be said that science fiction is easier to write than mundane fiction, because if the author needs a detail he invents it on the spot, and nobody can call him a liar. Nevertheless, good science fiction is not easy to write. Inventing a self-consistent and plausible future society, for instance, is only the beginning. Even when the writer has imagined the people who live in that society and take it for granted, and can make them behave accordingly, he still faces the problem of making all this manifest in the story without lecturing the reader. Earlier writers felt free to stop the story dead in favor of long passages of exposition, but this is now considered crude. Another solution no longer in favor is to have one character tell another, with or without some flimsy pretext, whatever it is that the author wants the reader to know. Current practice requires that if, for instance, a nuclear war has taken place fifty years before the time of the story, this information must be brought out through casual references, or through scenes and incidents that advance the plot. In the short story especially, this calls for extreme economy of structure; everything that happens and is said in the story must carry three or four functions at once.

✽ ✽ ✽

Where does a science fiction writer get his ideas? They can come from almost anywhere. Some appear spontaneously and without warning; even these have probably been marinating in the author's unconscious for months or years. Some of them come from deliberate exercises in extrapolation, about which more later; some are corrections or inversions of other people's ideas. An example of a fruitful inversion is H. G. Wells's *The War of the Worlds*, in which the aliens invade *us*; another is my "The Dying Man," whose central character is the only man who ages and dies in a society of immortals.

In fiction as in science, the same ideas frequently occur to more than one writer, and some of them turn up repeatedly over a period of years, a fact ignored by certain critics, who often see influence or plagiarism where there is none. Contrary to most people's impression, ideas are the least of a writer's worries. They can come from reading, from observation, from a chance remark, a sound, a remembered dream, a memory of childhood. Making them into good stories is the hard part; getting them is easy.

To illustrate this, I looked around the room to see what ideas I could get from nearby objects. (Most of them happened to be books.) In about twenty minutes I made the following notes:

A biography of H. G. Wells makes me think of inverting his story "The Sea Raiders": an assault by land-dwellers on a deep-sea civilization. How would we discover such a civilization, if it exists? What technology would we need to fight a war on the bottom of the ocean? What motives would compel us to do that? If I could find answers to all those questions there would be a story in it.

A slight gastric distress makes me think of alien food—what about an intestinal parasite that makes it possible for humans to digest cellulose as termites do? Would slum dwellers tear down buildings for food? Would civilization collapse? Would people become grazing animals?

The chain on the outside door reminds me of the monkey bridge in one of the Dr. Doolittle books, and that makes me think of aliens combining into structures—what about aliens who can form larger organisms as slime-molds do?

Another book, part of the "Looking-Glass Library," makes me think of another inversion—fantasy-world characters come through the looking-glass into a Victorian household.

I don't want to write these stories, but the point is that I could, and that the ideas I got in twenty minutes would be more than enough to keep me occupied for a couple of months.

A story with me usually starts out with a fuzzy feeling that I can't put into words and that does not appear in my working notes. I generally have an idea of the background or the gadget, if it is a gadget story, and the problem is then to work out a series of scenes and incidents that use the material in such a way as to reinforce or embody the feeling I had to start with. I call it a feeling for lack of any better word, but it is not a sensation or emotion; it's more like an object perceived by something other than the classic five senses, and I call it fuzzy because it seems to have an indefinite surface. It is roughly spherical or ovoid, and is about as big as a fingernail. It is as nonverbal as a musical note; it carries with it a strong emotion, but I can't say what the emotion is—I mean, I could say "despair" or "anguish" or whatever, but that would be like defining a nickel by saying "smaller than a breadbox."

Then I have to try beginnings until one of them works. I can't do this by logic; I succeed only by throwing myself into space and catching myself in an impromptu net.

Once I have the beginning, the rest follows. Unlike my wife, Kate Wilhelm, who is a storyteller, I never know who my characters are until I see them created on paper. Sometimes I like them more than I expected to, sometimes less; they always turn out to be more interesting than the general idea I had of them before I began. Details then have to accrete to the growing story from all directions, like a crystal growing in a super-saturated solution; if they don't, if the story only moves in a linear fashion, I know something is missing and I have to try again.

I often make a short list of things that happen in a story, just to make sure I know how many there are and that they are all there. Individual scenes crystallize around a single vivid image of some kind—a dog's moist nose, or a figure falling silently down a canyon of buildings. Usually my people don't behave exactly as I intended them to (if they did, they wouldn't seem real to me or anybody), but if the structure is right, they move through it roughly in the way I intended, and the finished story gives me a feeling analogous to, but not the same as, the one I started with. It is stronger, more specific, and now so thoroughly embedded in the story that I could never get it out again.

✿    ✿    ✿

Elsewhere in this book, in an essay called "What Is Science Fiction?" I list seven elements which, found in various combinations, serve to identify s.f. Following are a few comments on each one.

1. *Science.* How much of it do you have to know to write science fiction? One answer is that you don't *have* to know any. There have been at least two highly successful s.f. writers, Ray Bradbury and Robert Sheckley, who neither knew nor wanted to know anything about science; it would be easy, though unrewarding, to cite lesser examples by the score. Few of the most successful s.f. writers have been scientists, and even these have almost never written about their own specialties.

A science fiction writer in the conventional mode ought to know something about astronomy and physics, at least enough to restrain him from giving asteroids breathable atmospheres or having his rocket ships make U-turns, etc. A good deal of this can be picked up from science fiction itself, but the writer who gets all his information from that source is bound to turn out pallid imitations of other stories, or, at best, trivial variations.

An alert science fiction writer can pick up from *Scientific American* and *Science Digest* ideas that are new to the general reader. If he wants to catch new ideas even earlier, he must follow the technical journals, something that few writers have the training or patience to do. Even this has its dangers, because new developments often become obsolete and new theories are exploded by the time the writer can get his story into print.

2. *Technology, invention.* The term "science fiction," invented by Hugo Gernsback (who earlier called it "scientifiction"), became so ingrained in our consciousness that it was not generally noticed, until P. Schuyler Miller pointed it out in the fifties, that most s.f. is really "invention fiction." Murray Leinster's story "Jezebel," for example, is about an amateur inventor who makes a substance he calls a "solid vacuum." This consists of a paint which, when it dries, violently repels any other substance—throws it off sideways. The inventor explains this by saying that the paint has "surface tension so high that it won't let anything touch it." Scientifically this may be nonsense, but the story isn't about science, it is about the consequences of an invention. All Leinster has to do is to detail these consequences logically and self-consistently—the invention itself is the "given" of the story, the one fantastic assumption the author is allowed to make.

Painted on the end of a dowel, the substance makes a drill that will go effortlessly through anything—wood, metal, glass. It can be painted on cloth, and the inventor, a Mr. Binder, thinks of making bullet-proof uniforms for the army, but he gives that idea up: " 'A man in a solid-vacuum suit couldn't sit down.' "

Another consequence: by flinging away air molecules that touch it, the substance creates a vacuum ahead of it and therefore tends to move forward. A friend, the owner of a decrepit charter boat (named *Jezebel*, whence the misleading title), suggests making a flying machine by painting the stuff on an umbrella. " 'Then you hold on to the handle and open the umbrella. You'll fly. Close the umbrella, and you'll come down. Just like that!' "

The inventor vetoes this too. If the umbrella somehow got turned upside down and ran into the solid earth, it would keep right on going. The stick with the substance painted on the end makes a perfect drink mixer—but if a careless bartender touched the bottom of the glass with it . . . The invention seems to have no practical application—until it occurs to Mr. Binder that he might paint his substance on canvas stretched over the bow of his friend's charter boat, to make it go faster. They try it. The ship, which has been on a marine railway waiting for a new engine, is lowered into the water:

When water tried to touch the canvas-covered bow, it was flung violently aside. It went in all directions in a thin, glistening, high-velocity sheet. When the *Jezebel* hit water, an appearance set up about her front parts which looked singularly like a liquid pinwheel twenty feet high. That was water getting away from before the boat, and leaving a vacuum there. Nature abhors a vacuum. So did the *Jezebel*. She tried to move into the vacuum and to fill it. The vacuum moved on before. The *Jezebel* hastened, flinging water higher and wider in her haste. The vacuum moved still faster, being fastened to her.

The *Jezebel* went out of the slip leading to the railway, exactly like a bat out of hell.

A story like this goes through three stages: getting the idea ("What if somebody discovered a substance which—" etc.); working out its consequences; applying them to specific human beings. Notice how Leinster has done this with comic effect by introducing the charter boat captain and his broken-down boat. Fiction, including science fiction, is about people.

3. *Future, past.* The remote past is seldom used in science fiction (and

perhaps too much neglected); most stories in this category are set in the future, and they make up the great bulk of science fiction.

Fashions in anticipation change; forty years ago most such stories were overoptimistic. More recently, and for good reason, stories set in the near future tend to be glum. Adventure writers usually skip over this inconvenient period to distant futures which they can make as jolly as they like.

Most stories set in the future contain some element of extrapolation, but some have none, for instance Jack Vance's "The Dragon Masters," about a world and a society which have no apparent connection with our own.

4. *Extrapolation* means extending a trend into the future, e.g., if you know that your weight has been increasing ten percent a year, and you weigh 150 now, you can predict that in ten years you will weigh 389. In its crudest form, as in the foregoing example, this leads to absurdities. To extrapolate plausibly, you must bear in mind that some processes are cyclical, that exponential growth must reach a ceiling somewhere, and that the future is determined by a number of processes occurring simultaneously, most of them interacting in subtle and complicated ways. If you want to extrapolate one trend into the world of fifty years from now, for instance the increasing use of automobiles for transportation, you can't leave everything else unaltered (as many early s.f. writers did), because your readers are too well aware that everything is changing at once. No matter what the principal concern of the story is, you must ask yourself, how have mores changed? speech patterns? dress? religion? architecture? and so on.

5. *The scientific method*, although Reginald Bretnor makes it central to his definition, is rarely found in s.f. and is the least important of the seven elements for diagnostic use. Briefly, the scientific method consists of gathering data, arranging it in logical or comprehensible form, formulating a hypothesis to explain it, then devising an experiment or gathering further data (in fields where experiment is impossible) to test the hypothesis, and so on. It is hard to make stories about people doing this seem dramatic or exciting. An exception is James Blish's story "The Box," in which New York City has been enclosed in a field of force, and the hero, who is inside, has to solve the problem before everybody smothers to death. He takes readings of the signal which generates the field (data gathering), concludes that it is an intermittent signal generated outside,

probably by a satellite in synchronous orbit (hypothesis), and by aiming a radio reflector straight up (experiment), burns out the generator by back EMF and saves the day. Such behavior is rare. When the scientific method is present in science fiction, it is usually only by implication—people in the story are doing science, therefore must be using the method.

6. *Other places.* Creating a genuinely alien race or culture is a task beyond the capacities of most people. Writers usually take the easy way out and populate their alien planets with bug men, cat people, giant squids, etc. This is one form of the "just like" fallacy. In the same way, alien planets and future Earths are given social and political structures copied from history—feudalism is the most popular because it is so conveniently simple, and because of all the jolly swords and armor. As a rule each of these stories has a beautiful princess who falls in love with the hero, whereupon they get married and raise a family, even if (like Burroughs' Dejah Thoris) she lays eggs. It often turns out that the local males are degenerate and/or infertile, and that the hero's vigorous sperm is needed to rejuvenate the race. This plot was standard in the thirties, and turned up as late as 1963 in Roger Zelazny's "A Rose for Ecclesiastes."

The fallacy referred to above takes another form in stories of new technology; in many early spaceflight stories, for instance (and in some recent ones, alas), the space liners were "just like" oceangoing passenger ships, and usually had Scottish engineers.

7. *Catastrophes,* a popular theme in the science fiction of the twenties and thirties, later fell into eclipse, but there have been occasional revivals: see, for instance, John Christopher's *No Blade of Grass* or George R. Stewart's *Earth Abides.* As a rule the interest of such stories centers not so much on the catastrophe itself as on the survivors and how they adapt to a changed world. One exception is *The Year of the Cloud,* by Ted Thomas and Kate Wilhelm, in which the Earth passes through a cosmic cloud containing a substance which forms a colloidal suspension in water, increasing its viscosity. The human consequences of this are followed carefully throughout the novel, including the effects of the stuff in the bloodstream, and even its effect on the male orgasm.

Now let's suppose you have written a science fiction story or novel and you want to get it published, preferably for money. The first thing you must know is how to prepare a manuscript for submission. It should be typed, double-spaced, in black ribbon only (meaning not black-and-red, and not gray), on opaque white paper. If you happen to be so poor a typist that you can't do this yourself without a lot of strikeovers and corrections, you should have it professionally done.

The first page of each manuscript should have your name and address (single-spaced) in the upper left-hand corner, and an approximate word-count (to the nearest hundred words) in the upper right. Do not put "All rights" or "First North American rights" or "Usual rates" or anything of that kind here, no matter how many writers'-magazine articles tell you to do so; if an editor buys your short story he will tell you what rights he wants and how much he will pay, and usually will not negotiate. Rights and payments are negotiable in a book contract, but you are expected to make your demands in correspondence, after you have been offered a contract, not on the manuscript.

The title should be centered about halfway down the page or a little less, with your by-line under it; then skip a few double spaces and begin the text. Following pages should have your name or the title of the story in the upper left corner, page number in the right.

There are good reasons for all this. First, and most important, this is the format in which editors are accustomed to receive manuscripts from professional writers, and if you violate it in any important particular you signal that you are an amateur. Messy or dim manuscripts are hard to read and hard to edit. The space above the title on the first page is convenient for notes, instructions to the printer, etc. Identifying the story on each page has a practical purpose—if a stack of mss. happens to fall on the floor, it helps to be able to tell which pages go together when the editor, cursing and red-faced, picks them up.

Every manuscript should be accompanied by a stamped, return-addressed envelope. (Some editors prefer to have the stamps paper-clipped to the envelope, so that in case they buy the story they can use or sell them; they really ought to return them, in fact, but this seldom happens.) It is unbelievable but true that some amateur writers submit stories without return envelopes or addresses on the manuscripts—I have a little stack of these.

Should you write a covering letter? Yes, probably, unless the idea embarrasses you intolerably. Even if the letter says only, "I enclose my story, (title), which I hope you will like," it gives the editor a sense that the manuscript comes from a fellow human being and not from a fiction-writing robot. If you have been lucky enough to get a personal reply from the editor (or have sold him something) it helps to refer to that in your letter, just to jog his memory. You should not synopsize the story or tell him how great it is—he will make up his own mind about that.

Generally speaking, science fiction can be divided into highbrow, middlebrow and lowbrow markets. The highbrow markets want literary writing and high quality, usually at the expense of hard science; the lowbrows want fast action and a lot of local color, and the middlebrows are in between. Presumably you have read enough to know which markets are which—if not, you are submitting at random and wasting everybody's time.

Before you send a story out, you should make up a list of all the markets to which you intend to submit it. On this list, or in a separate notebook, you should record the dates of submission and return (or sale), so that you will know when an editor has had a manuscript an unreasonable or unusual length of time, and can write a polite letter of inquiry. Once you begin to sell, you should begin keeping records of payment, for tax purposes and for your own information.

Slush-pile manuscripts (those from unknown writers) do get read, but not always all the way through. The editor may give up after a page or a paragraph, for any of the following reasons:

**1.** Incoherence. (The editor can't make heads or tails of the story; back it goes.)

**2.** Insanity. (The author has written an essay, more or less disguised as fiction, to prove that Martians are persecuting him, or that the Communists have infiltrated the Boy Scouts, or whatever.)

**3.** Bad grammar and spelling, mangled syntax, etc.

**4.** Ignorance. (The author is confused about the difference between stars and planets; or he has sent a fifty-line poem to a magazine that uses only prose.)

**5.** Triviality and superficiality. (The story is not about anything important or interesting, except perhaps to the author.)

**6.** Overfamiliarity. (There is nothing in the story that the editor hasn't already seen in a hundred others.)

**7.** Technical flaws—"technical" referring here to the technique of writing. The work is not a story but an incident or situation; the characters are stereotypes; the dialogue is wooden. Very often the story has a reasonably novel idea or background but nothing else—the author has not found a way to make it into a human drama. (James Blish has a useful formula: ask yourself, "Whom would this hurt?")

Most science fiction writers, never having had any instruction themselves, are inclined to believe that writing can't be taught. I think myself that the essential process of writing can only be learned, not taught, but that certain technical things—tricks of the trade—can be and have been taught. Among these are characterization, point of view, structure (including what is usually called "plot"), etc. Many colleges and even high schools now offer science fiction courses of various kinds; some are no more than appreciation courses, but others make some effort to help beginning writers.

The Clarion Workshop in Science Fiction and Fantasy, held every summer at Justin S. Morrill College, East Lansing, Michigan, is an intensive six-week course for writers; its graduates include Vonda N. McIntyre, Edward Bryant, George Alec Effinger, Robert Thurston, Kathleen M. Sidney, F. M. Busby, and Dave Skal.

The Milford Science Fiction Writers' Conference, on which Clarion was modeled, is an annual eight-day gathering for professional writers. Science Fiction Writers of America, also restricted to professionals (but if you sell one story, you're eligible for membership), is more concerned with safeguarding its members' rights and interests than with teaching them to write, but it publishes occasional helpful articles in its *Bulletin*, available by subscription to nonmembers.

Can you make a living writing science fiction? Yes, but it isn't easy. To make $4,000 a year at current rates, you would have to write and sell at least a hundred thousand words a year, the equivalent of about twenty short stories or two rather short novels. This is on the assumption that the stories will not be reprinted, and that all you will get is the original payment for the stories or the advance on the novels. Many short stories are reprinted again and again, however, and a successful novel can bring many times the advance. Even so, most science fiction writers have other occupations or sources of income.

From writing science fiction, as distinct from editing and anthologizing, I have seldom made much more than $5,000 in any year. Beginning in 1940, when my first story was accepted for publication, my annual income from this source (reconstructed, because it wasn't until 1956 that it occurred to me to keep proper records) was as follows: 0 (the editor, starting a new magazine, asked me to donate the story, and I was glad to get into print—I would have paid him a modest sum), $30, $10, $130, 0, 0, 0 (editorial interlude), $110, 0 (editing again), $220, $1,701 (writing full time), $657, $5,140 (most of this for *Captain Video* scripts), $1,835, $890, $1,223, and so on. If I had been entirely dependent on writing during this period I would have starved to death, and in fact I did starve a little from time to time.

In fairness to a profession that has kept me out of the labor market for more than twenty years and has richly rewarded me in other ways, I should add that I have spent a lot of time editing not merely through necessity but because I love it, and that for some years I have made a comfortable living from science fiction. When I was young I wanted to be either John W. Campbell or Robert A. Heinlein, and I have pursued both goals compulsively ever since.

## *Bibliography*

Aldiss, Brian W., and Harry Harrison, eds. *Hell's Cartographers.* New York: Harper & Row, 1976.

Atheling, William, Jr. (James Blish). *The Issue at Hand.* Chicago: Advent, 1964.

————. *More Issues at Hand.* Chicago: Advent, 1970.

De Camp, L. Sprague and Catherine C. *Science Fiction Handbook, Revised.* Philadelphia: Owlswick Press, 1975.

Eshbach, Lloyd Arthur, ed. *Of Worlds Beyond.* Chicago: Advent, 1964.

Knight, Damon. *In Search of Wonder.* Chicago: Advent, 1967 (second edition, revised).

# VI.
# S.F. AS PROPHECY

# CHEMICAL PERSUASION

## Aldous Huxley

In the Brave New World of my fable there was no whiskey, no tobacco, no illicit heroin, no bootlegged cocaine. People neither smoked, nor drank, nor sniffed, nor gave themselves injections. Whenever anyone felt depressed or below par, he would swallow a tablet or two of a chemical compound called soma. The original soma, from which I took the name of this hypothetical drug, was an unknown plant (possibly *Asclepias acida*) used by the ancient Aryan invaders of India in one of the most solemn of their religious rites. The intoxicating juice expressed from the stems of this plant was drunk by the priests and nobles in the course of an elaborate ceremony. In the Vedic hymns we are told that the drinkers of soma were blessed in many ways. Their bodies were strengthened, their hearts were filled with courage, joy and enthusiasm, their minds were enlightened and in an immediate experience of eternal life they received the assurance of their immortality. But the sacred juice had its drawbacks. Soma was a dangerous drug—so dangerous that even the great sky-god, Indra, was sometimes made ill by drinking it. Ordinary mortals might even die of an overdose. But the experience was so transcendently blissful and enlightening that soma drinking was regarded as a high privilege. For this privilege no price was too great.

The soma of *Brave New World* had none of the drawbacks of its Indian original. In small doses it brought a sense of bliss, in larger doses it

FROM *Brave New World Revisited*, Harper & Row, 1958

231

made you see visions and, if you took three tablets, you would sink in a few minutes into refreshing sleep. And all at no physiological or mental cost. The Brave New Worlders could take holidays from their black moods, or from the familiar annoyances of everyday life, without sacrificing their health or permanently reducing their efficiency.

In the Brave New World the soma habit was not a private vice; it was a political institution, it was the very essence of the Life, Liberty and Pursuit of Happiness guaranteed by the Bill of Rights. But this most precious of the subjects' inalienable privileges was at the same time one of the most powerful instruments of rule in the dictator's armory. The systematic drugging of individuals for the benefit of the State (and incidentally, of course, for their own delight) was a main plank in the policy of the World Controllers. The daily soma ration was an insurance against personal maladjustment, social unrest and the spread of subversive ideas. Religion, Karl Marx declared, is the opium of the people. In the Brave New World this situation was reversed. Opium, or rather soma, was the people's religion. Like religion, the drug had power to console and compensate, it called up visions of another, better world, it offered hope, strengthened faith and promoted charity. Beer, a poet has written,

> . . . *does more than Milton can*
> *To justify God's ways to man.*

And let us remember that, compared with soma, beer is a drug of the crudest and most unreliable kind. In this matter of justifying God's ways to man, soma is to alcohol as alcohol is to the theological arguments of Milton.

In 1931, when I was writing about the imaginary synthetic by means of which future generations would be made both happy and docile, the well-known American biochemist, Dr. Irvine Page, was preparing to leave Germany, where he had spent the three preceding years at the Kaiser Wilhelm Institute, working on the chemistry of the brain. "It is hard to understand," Dr. Page has written in a recent article, "why it took so long for scientists to get around to investigating the chemical reactions in their own brains. I speak," he adds, "from acute personal experience. When I came home in 1931 . . . I could not get a job in this field (the field of brain chemistry) or stir a ripple of interest in it." Today, twenty-seven years later, the non-existent ripple of 1931 has become a tidal wave of biochemical and psychopharmacological research. The enzymes which regulate the workings of the brain are being studied. Within the body, hitherto unknown chemical substances such as adrenochrome and serotonin (of which Dr. Page was a co-discoverer) have been isolated and their far-reaching effects on our mental and physical functions are now being investigated. Meanwhile new drugs are being synthesized—drugs that reinforce or correct or interfere with the actions of the various chemicals, by means of which the nervous system performs its daily and hourly miracles as the controller of the body, the instrument and mediator of consciousness. From our present point of view, the most interesting fact about these new drugs is that they temporarily alter the chemistry of the brain and the associated state of the mind without doing any permanent damage to the organism as a whole. In this respect they are like soma— and profoundly unlike the mind-changing drugs of the past. For example, the classical tranquillizer is opium. But opium is a dangerous drug which, from neolithic times down to the present day, has been making addicts and ruining health. The same is true of the classical euphoric, alcohol— the drug which, in the words of the Psalmist, "maketh glad the heart of man." But unfortunately alcohol not only maketh glad the heart of man; it also, in excessive doses, causes illness and addiction, and has been a main source, for the last eight or ten thousand years, of crime, domestic un-happiness, moral degradation and avoidable accidents.

Among the classical stimulants, tea, coffee, and maté are, thank good-ness, almost completely harmless. They are also very weak stimulants. Unlike these "cups that cheer but not inebriate," cocaine is a very power-ful and a very dangerous drug. Those who make use of it must pay for their ecstasies, their sense of unlimited physical and mental power, by spells of agonizing depression, by such horrible physical symptoms as the sensation of being infested by myriads of crawling insects and by para-noid delusions that may lead to crimes of violence. Another stimulant of more recent vintage is amphetamine, better known under its trade name of Benzedrine. Amphetamine works very effectively—but works, if abused, at the expense of mental and physical health. It has been re-ported that, in Japan, there are now about one million amphetamine addicts.

Of the classical vision-producers the best known are the peyote of Mexico and the southwestern United States and *Cannabis sativa*, con-sumed all over the world under such names as hashish, bhang, kif and marijuana. According to the best medical and anthropological evidence, peyote is far less harmful than the White Man's gin or whiskey. It permits the Indians who use it in their religious rites to enter paradise, and to feel at one with the beloved community, without making them pay for the privilege by anything worse than the ordeal of having to chew on something with a revolting flavor and of feeling somewhat nauseated for an hour or two. *Cannabis sativa* is a less innocuous drug—though not nearly so harmful as the sensation-mongers would have us believe. The Medical Committee, appointed in 1944 by the Mayor of New York to investigate the problem of marijuana, came to the conclusion, after careful investigation, that *Cannabis sativa* is not a serious menace to society, or even to those who indulge in it. It is merely a nuisance.

From these classical mind-changers we pass to the latest products of psychopharmacological research. Most highly publicized of these are the three new tranquillizers, resperine, chlorpromazine and meprobamate. Administered to certain classes of psychotics, the first two have proved to be remarkably effective, not in curing mental illnesses, but at least in temporarily abolishing their more distressing symptoms. Meprobamate (alias Miltown) produces similar effects in persons suffering from various forms of neurosis. None of these drugs is perfectly harmless; but their cost, in terms of physical health and mental efficiency, is extraordinarily low. In a world where nobody gets anything for nothing tranquillizers offer a great deal for very little. Miltown and chlorpromazine are not yet soma; but they come fairly near to being one of the aspects of that mythical drug. They provide temporary relief from nervous tension without, in the great majority of cases, inflicting permanent organic harm, and without causing more than a rather slight impairment, while the drug is working, of intellectual and physical efficiency. Except as narcotics, they are probably to be preferred to the barbiturates, which blunt the mind's cutting edge and, in large doses, cause a number of undesirable psychophysical symptoms and may result in a full-blown addiction.

In LSD-25 (lysergic acid diethylamide) the pharmacologists have recently created another aspect of soma—a perception-improver and vision-producer that is, physiologically speaking, almost costless. This extraordinary drug, which is effective in doses as small as fifty or even twenty-five millionths of a gram, has power (like peyote) to transport people into the other world. In the majority of cases, the other world to which LSD-25 gives access is heavenly; alternatively it may be purgatorial or even infernal. But, positive or negative, the lysergic acid experience is felt by almost everyone who undergoes it to be profoundly significant and enlightening. In any event, the fact that minds can be changed so radically  at so little cost to the body is altogether astonishing.

Soma was not only a vision-producer and a tranquillizer; it was also (and no doubt impossibly) a stimulant of mind and body, a creator of active euphoria as well as of the negative happiness that follows the release from anxiety and tension.

The ideal stimulant—powerful but innocuous—still awaits discovery. Amphetamine, as we have seen, was far from satisfactory; it exacted too high a price for what it gave. A more promising candidate for the role of soma in its third aspect is Iproniazid, which is now being used to lift depressed patients out of their misery, to enliven the apathetic and in general to increase the amount of available psychic energy. Still more promising, according to a distinguished pharmacologist of my acquaintance, is a new compound, still in the testing stage, to be known as Deaner. Deaner is an amino-alcohol and is thought to increase the production of acetyl-choline within the body, and thereby to increase the activity and effectiveness of the nervous system. The man who takes the new pill needs less sleep, feels more alert and cheerful, thinks faster and better—and all at next to no organic cost, at any rate in the short run. It sounds almost too good to be true.

We see then that, though soma does not yet exist (and will probably never exist), fairly good substitutes for the various aspects of soma have already been discovered. There are now physiologically cheap tranquillizers, physiologically cheap vision-producers and physiologically cheap stimulants.

That a dictator could, if he so desired, make use of these drugs for political purposes is obvious. He could ensure himself against political unrest by changing the chemistry of his subjects' brains and so making them content with their servile condition. He could use tranquillizers to calm the excited, stimulants to arouse enthusiasm in the indifferent, hallucinants to distract the attention of the wretched from their miseries. But how, it may be asked, will the dictator get his subjects to take the pills that will make them think, feel and behave in the ways he finds desirable? In all probability it will be enough merely to make the pills available. Today alcohol and tobacco are available, and people spend considerably more on these very unsatisfactory euphorics, pseudostimulants and sedatives than they are ready to spend on the education of their children. Or consider the barbiturates and the tranquillizers. In the United States these drugs can be obtained only on a doctor's prescription. But the demand of the American public for something that will make life in an urban-industrial environment a little more tolerable is so great that doctors are now writing prescriptions for the various tranquillizers at the rate of forty-eight million a year. Moreover, a majority of these prescriptions are re-filled. A hundred doses of happiness are not enough: send to the drugstore for another bottle—and, when that is finished, for another. . . . There can be no doubt that, if tranquillizers could be bought as easily and cheaply as aspirin, they would be consumed, not by the billions, as they are at present, but by the scores and hundreds of billions. And a good, cheap stimulant would be almost as popular.

Under a dictatorship pharmacists would be instructed to change their tune with every change of circumstances. In times of national crisis it would be their business to push the sale of stimulants. Between crises, too much alertness and energy on the part of his subjects might prove em-barrassing to the tyrant. At such times the masses would be urged to buy tranquillizers and vision-producers. Under the influence of these soothing syrups they could be relied upon to give their master no trouble.

As things now stand, the tranquillizers may prevent some people from giving enough trouble, not only to their rulers, but even to themselves. Too much tension is a disease; but so is too little. There are certain occasions when we *ought* to be tense, when an excess of tranquillity (and especially of tranquillity imposed from the outside, by a chemical) is entirely inappropriate.

At a recent symposium on meprobamate, in which I was a participant, an eminent biochemist playfully suggested that the United States gov-ernment should make a free gift to the Soviet people of fifty billion doses of this most popular of the tranquillizers. The joke had a serious point to it. In a contest between two populations, one of which is being constantly stimulated by threats and promises, constantly directed by one-pointed propaganda, while the other is no less constantly being distracted by television and tranquillized by Miltown, which of the opponents is more likely to come out on top?

As well as tranquillizing, hallucinating and stimulating, the soma of my fable had the power of heightening suggestibility, and so could be used to reinforce the effects of governmental propaganda. Less effectively and at a higher physiological cost, several drugs already in the pharmacopoeia can be used for the same purpose. There is scopolamine, for example, the active principle of henbane and, in large doses, a powerful poison; there are pentothal and sodium amytal. Nicknamed for some odd reason "the truth serum," pentothal has been used by the police of various countries for the purpose of extracting confessions from (or perhaps suggesting confessions to) reluctant criminals. Pentothal and sodium amytal lower the barrier between the conscious and the subconscious mind and are of great value in the treatment of "battle fatigue" by the process known in England as "abreaction therapy," in America as "narcosynthesis." It is said that these drugs are sometimes employed by the Communists, when preparing important prisoners for their public appearance in court.

Meanwhile pharmacology, biochemistry and neurology are on the march, and we can be quite certain that, in the course of the next few years, new and better chemical methods for increasing suggestibility and lowering psychological resistance will be discovered. Like everything else, these discoveries may be used well or badly. They may help the psychiatrist in his battle against mental illness, or they may help the dictator in his battle against freedom. More probably (since science is divinely impartial) they will both enslave and make free, heal and at the same time destroy.

# PANDORA'S BOX

# Robert A. Heinlein

Once opened, the Box could never be closed. But after the myriad swarming Troubles came Hope.

Science fiction is not prophecy. It often reads as if it were prophecy; indeed the practitioners of this odd genre (pun intentional—I won't do it again) of fiction usually strive hard to make their stories sound as if they were true pictures of the future. Prophecies.

Prophesying is what the weatherman does, the race track tipster, the stock market adviser, the fortune-teller who reads palms or gazes into a crystal. Each one is predicting the future—sometimes exactly, sometimes in vague, veiled, or ambiguous language, sometimes simply with a claim of statistical probability, but always with a claim seriously made of disclosing some piece of the future.

This is not at all what a science fiction author does. Science fiction is almost always laid in the future—or at least in a fictional possible-future —and is almost invariably deeply concerned with the shape of that future. But the method is not prediction; it is usually extrapolation and/or speculation. Indeed the author is not required to (and usually does not) regard the fictional "future" he has chosen to write about as being the events most likely to come to pass; his purpose may have nothing to do with the *probability* that these storied events may happen.

"Extrapolation" means much the same in fiction writing as it does in

From *The Worlds of Robert A. Heinlein*, Ace, 1966

mathematics: exploring a trend. It means continuing a curve, a path, a trend into the future, by extending its present direction and continuing the *shape* it has displayed in its past performance—i.e., if it is a sine curve in the past, you extrapolate it as a sine curve in the future, not as an hyperbola, nor a Witch of Agnesi, and *most certainly not* as a tangent straight line.

"Speculation" has far more elbowroom than extrapolation; it starts with a "What if?"—and the new factor thrown in by the what-if may be both wildly improbable and so revolutionary in effect as to throw a sine-curve trend (or a yeast-growth trend, or any trend) into something unrecognizably different. What if little green men land on the White House lawn and invite us to join a Galactic union?—or big green men land and enslave us and eat us? What if we solve the problem of immortality? What if New York City really does go dry? (And not just the present fiddlin' shortage tackled by fiddlin' quarter-measures—can you imagine a man being lynched for wasting an ice cube? Try Frank Herbert's *Dune World* saga, which is not—I judge—prophecy in any sense, but is powerful, convincing, and most ingenious speculation. Living, as I do, in a state which has just two sorts of water, too little and too much—we just finished seven years of drought with seven inches of rain in two hours, and one was about as disastrous as the other—I find a horrid fascination in *Dune World*, in Charles Einstein's *The Day New York Went Dry,* and in stories about Biblical-size floods such as S. Fowler Wright's *Deluge.*)

Most science fiction stories use both extrapolation and speculation. Consider "Blowups Happen." It was written in 1939, updated very slightly for book publication just after World War II by inserting some words such as "Manhattan Project" and "Hiroshima," but not rewritten, and is one of a group of stories published under the pretentious collective title of *The History of the Future* (!)—which certainly sounds like prophecy.

I disclaim any intention of prophesying; I wrote that story for the sole purpose of making money to pay off a mortgage and with the single intention of entertaining the reader. As prophecy the story falls flat on its silly face—any tenderfoot Scout can pick it to pieces—but I think it is still entertaining as a *story*, else it would not be here; I have a business reputation to protect and wish to continue making money. Nor am I ashamed of this motivation. Very little of the great literature of our heritage arose solely from a wish to "create art"; most writing, both great and not-so-great, has as its proximate cause a need for money combined with an aversion to, or an inability to perform, hard "honest labor." Fiction writing offers a legal and reasonably honest way out of this dilemma.

A science fiction author may have, and often does have, other motivations *in addition to* pursuit of profit. He may wish to create "art for art's sake," he may want to warn the world against a course he feels to be disastrous (Orwell's *1984*, Huxley's *Brave New World*—but please note that each is intensely entertaining, and that each made stacks of money), he may wish to urge the human race toward a course which he considers desirable (Bellamy's *Looking Backward*, Wells' *Men Like Gods*), he may wish to instruct, or uplift, or even to dazzle. But the science fiction writer —*any* fiction writer—must keep entertainment consciously in mind as his prime purpose . . . or he may find himself back dragging that old cotton sack.

If he succeeds in this purpose, his story is likely to remain gripping entertainment long years after it has turned out to be false "prophecy." H. G. Wells is perhaps the greatest science fiction author of all time—and his greatest science fiction stories were written around sixty years ago . . . under the whip. Bedfast with consumption, unable to hold a job, flat broke—he had to make money somehow, and writing was the heaviest work he could manage. He was clearly aware (see his autobiography) that to stay alive he must be entertaining. The result was a flood of some of the most brilliant speculative stories about the future ever written. As prophecy they are all hopelessly dated . . . which matters not at all; they are as spellbinding now as they were in the Gay 'Nineties and the Mauve Decade.

Try to lay hands on his *The Sleeper Awakes*. The gadgetry in it is ingenious—and all wrong. The projected future in it is brilliant—and did not happen. All of which does not sully the story; it is a great story of love and sacrifice and blood-chilling adventure set in a matrix of mind-stretching speculation about the nature of Man and his Destiny. I read it first forty-five years ago, plus perhaps a dozen times since . . . and still reread it whenever I get to feeling uncertain about just how one does go about the unlikely process of writing fiction for entertainment of strangers—and again finding myself caught up in the sheer excitement of Wells' story.

"Solution Unsatisfactory" is a consciously Wellsian story. No, no, I'm not claiming that it is of H. G. Wells' quality—its quality is for you to judge, not me. But it was written by the method which Wells spelled out for the speculative story: Take one, just one, basic new assumption, then examine all its consequences—but express those consequences in terms of human beings. The assumption I chose was the "Absolute Weapon"; the speculation concerns what changes this forces on mankind. But the "history" the story describes simply did not happen.

However, the problems discussed in this story are as fresh today, the issues just as poignant, for the grim reason that we have not reached even an "unsatisfactory" solution to the problem of the Absolute Weapon; we have reached *no* solution.

In the twenty-five years that have passed since I wrote that story the world situation has grown much worse. Instead of one Absolute Weapon there are now at least five distinct types—an "Absolute Weapon" being defined as one against which there is no effective defense and which kills indiscriminately over a very wide area. The earliest of the five types, the A-bomb, is now known to be possessed by at least five nations; at least twenty-five other nations have the potential to build them in the next few years.

But there is a possible sixth type. Earlier this year I attended a seminar at one of the nation's new think-factories: One of the questions discussed was whether or not a "Doomsday Bomb" could be built—a single weapon which would destroy all life of all sorts on this planet; *one* weapon, not an all-out nuclear holocaust involving hundreds or thousands of ICBMs. No, this was to be a world-wrecker of the sort Dr. E. E. Smith used to use in his interstellar sagas back in the days when S-F magazines had bug-eyed monsters on the cover and were considered lowbrow, childish, fantastic.

The conclusions reached were: Could the Doomsday Machine be built?—yes, no question about it. What would it cost?—quite cheap.

A seventh type hardly seems necessary.

And that makes the grimness of "Solution Unsatisfactory" seem more like an Oz book in which the most harrowing adventures always turn out happily.

"Pandora's Box" was the original title of an article researched and written in 1949 for publication in 1950, the end of the half-century. Inscrutable are the ways of editors: it appeared with the title "Where To?" and purported to be a non-fiction prophecy concerning the year 2000 A.D. as seen from 1950. (I agree that a science fiction writer should avoid marijuana, prophecy, and time payments—but I was tempted by a soft rustle.)

Our present editor [1966] decided to use this article, but suggested that it should be updated. Authors who wish to stay in the business listen most carefully to editors' suggestions, even when they think an editor has been out in the sun without a hat; I agreed.

And reread "Where To?" and discovered that our editor was undeniably correct; it needed updating. At least.

But at last I decided not to try to conceal my bloopers. Below is reproduced, unchanged, my predictions of fifteen years back. But here and there through the article I have inserted signs for footnotes—like this: ($z$)—and these will be found at the end of the 1950 article . . . calling attention to bloopers and then forthrightly excusing myself by rationalizing how anyone, even Nostradamus, would have made the same mistake . . . hedging my bets, in other cases, or chucking in brand-new predictions and carefully laying them farther in the future than I am likely to live . . . and, in some cases, crowing loudly about successful predictions.

So—

## WHERE TO?
### (And Why We Didn't Get There)

Most science fiction consists of big-muscled stories about adventures in space, atomic wars, invasions by extra-terrestrials, and such. All very well —but now we will take time out for a look at ordinary home life half a century hence.

Except for tea leaves and other magical means, the only way to guess at the *future* is by examining the *present* in the light of the *past*. Let's go back half a century and visit your grandmother before we attempt to visit your grandchildren.

1900: Mr. McKinley is President and the airplane has not yet been invented. Let's knock on the door of that house with the gingerbread, the stained glass, and the cupola.

The lady of the house answers. You recognize her—your own grandmother, Mrs. Middleclass. She is almost as plump as you remember her, for she "put on some good, healthy flesh" after she married.

She welcomes you and offers coffee cake, fresh from her modern kitchen (running water from a hand pump; the best coal range Pittsburgh ever produced). Everything about her house is modern—hand-painted china, souvenirs from the Columbian Exposition, beaded portieres, shining baseburner stoves, gas lights, a telephone on the wall.

There is no bathroom, but she and Mr. Middleclass are thinking of putting one in. Mr. Middleclass's mother calls this nonsense, but your grandmother keeps up with the times. She is an advocate of clothing reform, wears only one petticoat, bathes twice a week, and her corsets are guaranteed rust proof. She has been known to defend female suffrage—but not in the presence of Mr. Middleclass.

Nevertheless, you find difficulty in talking with her. Let's jump back to the present and try again.

The automatic elevator takes us to the ninth floor, and we pick out a door by its number, that being the only way to distinguish it.

"Don't bother to ring," you say? What? It's *your* door and you know exactly what lies beyond it—

Very well, let's move a half century into the future and try another middle class home.

It's a suburban home not two hundred miles from the city. You pick out your destination from the air while the cab is landing you—a cluster of hemispheres which makes you think of the houses Dorothy found in Oz.

You set the cab to return to its hangar and go into the entrance hall. You neither knock, nor ring. The screen has warned them before you touched down on the landing flat and the autobutler's transparency is shining with: PLEASE RECORD A MESSAGE.

Before you can address the microphone a voice calls out, "Oh, it's you! Come in, come in." There is a short wait, as your hostess is not at the door. The autobutler flashed your face to the patio—where she was reading and sunning herself—and has relayed her voice back to you.

She pauses at the door, looks at you through one-way glass, and frowns slightly; she knows your old-fashioned disapproval of casual nakedness. Her kindness causes her to disobey the family psychiatrist; she grabs a robe and covers herself before signaling the door to open.

The psychiatrist was right; you have thus been classed with strangers, tradespeople, and others who are not family intimates. But you must swallow your annoyance; you cannot object to her wearing clothes when you have sniffed at her for not doing so.

There is no reason why she should wear clothes at home. The house is clean—not somewhat clean, but *clean*—and comfortable. The floor is warm to bare feet; there are no unpleasant drafts, no cold walls. All dust is precipitated from the air entering this house. All textures, of floor, of couch, of chair, are comfortable to bare skin. Sterilizing ultra-violet light floods each room whenever it is unoccupied, and, several times a day, a "whirlwind" blows house-created dust from all surfaces and whisks it out. These auto services are unobtrusive because automatic cut-off switches prevent them from occurring whenever a mass in a room is radiating at blood temperature.

Such a house can become untidy, but not dirty. Five minutes of straightening, a few swipes at children's fingermarks, and her day's house-keeping is done. Oftener than sheets were changed in Mr. McKinley's day, this housewife rolls out a fresh layer of sheeting on each sitting surface and stuffs the discard down the oubliette. This is easy; there is a year's supply on a roll concealed in each chair or couch. The tissue sticks by pressure until pulled loose and does not obscure the pattern and color.

You go into the family room, sit down, and remark on the lovely day. "Isn't it?" she answers. "Come sunbathe with me."

The sunny patio gives excuse for bare skin by anyone's standards; thankfully she throws off the robe and stretches out on a couch. You hesitate a moment. After all, she is your own grandchild, so why not? You undress quickly, since you left your outer wrap and shoes at the door (only barbarians wear street shoes in a house) and what remains is easily discarded. Your grandparents had to get used to a mid-century beach. It was no easier for them.

On the other hand, their bodies were wrinkled and old, whereas yours is not. The triumphs of endocrinology, of cosmetics, of plastic surgery, of figure control in every way are such that a woman need not change markedly from maturity until old age. A woman can keep her body as firm and slender as she wishes—and most of them so wish. This has produced a paradox: the United States has the highest percentage of old people in all its two and a quarter centuries, yet it seems to have a larger proportion of handsome young women than ever before.

("Don't whistle, son! That's your grandmother—")

This garden is half sunbathing patio, complete with shrubs and flow-ers, lawn and couches, and half swimming pool. The day, though sunny, is quite cold—but not in the garden, nor is the pool chill. The garden appears to be outdoors, but is not; it is covered by a bubble of transparent plastic, blown and cured on the spot. You are inside the bubble; the sun is outside; you cannot see the plastic.

She invites you to lunch; you protest. "Nonsense!" she answers, "I like to cook." Into the house she goes. You think of following, but it is deliciously warm in the March sunshine and you are feeling relaxed to be away from the city. You locate a switch on the side of the couch, set it for gentle massage, and let the couch knead your troubles away. The couch notes your heart rate and breathing; as they slow, so does it. As you fall asleep it stops.

Meanwhile your hostess has been "slaving away over a hot stove." To be precise, she has allowed a menu selector to pick out an 800-calory, 4-ration-point luncheon. It is a random-choice gadget, somewhat like a slot machine, which has in it the running inventory of her larder and which will keep hunting until it turns up a balanced meal. Some housewives claim that it takes the art out of cookery, but our hostess is one of many who have accepted it thankfully as an endless source of new menus. Its choice is limited today as it has been three months since she has done grocery shopping. She rejects several menus; the selector continues patiently to turn up combinations until she finally accepts one based around fish disguised as lamb chops.

Your hostess takes the selected items from shelves or the freezer. All are prepared; some are pre-cooked. Those still to be cooked she puts into her—well, her "processing equipment," though she calls it a "stove." Part of it traces its ancestry to diathermy equipment; another feature is derived from metal enameling processes. She sets up cycles, punches buttons, and must wait two or three minutes for the meal to cook. She spends the time checking her ration accounts.

Despite her complicated kitchen, she doesn't eat as well as her great-grandmother did—too many people and too few acres.

Never mind; the tray she carries out to the patio is well laden and beautiful. You are both willing to nap again when it is empty. You wake to find that she has burned the dishes and is recovering from her "exertions" in her refresher. Feeling hot and sweaty from your nap you decide to use it when she comes out. There is a wide choice offered by the 'fresher, but you limit yourself to a warm shower growing gradually cooler, followed by warm air drying, a short massage, spraying with scent, and dusting with powder. Such a simple routine is an insult to a talented machine.

Your host arrives home as you come out; he has taken a holiday from his engineering job and has had the two boys down at the beach. He kisses his wife, shouts, "Hi, Duchess!" at you, and turns to the video, setting it to hunt and sample the newscasts it has stored that day. His wife sends the boys in to 'fresh themselves, then says, "Have a nice day, dear?"

He answers, "The traffic was terrible. Had to make the last hundred miles on automatic. Anything on the phone for me?"

"Weren't you on relay?"

"Didn't set it. Didn't want to be bothered." He steps to the house phone, plays back his calls, finds nothing he cares to bother with—but the machine goes ahead and prints one message; he pulls it out and tears it off.

"What is it?" his wife asks.

"Telestat from Luna City—from Aunt Jane."

"What does she say?"

"Nothing much. According to her, the Moon is a great place and she wants us to come visit her."

"Not likely!" his wife answers. "Imagine being shut up in an air-conditioned cave."

"When you are Aunt Jane's age, my honey lamb, and as frail as she is, with a bad heart thrown in, you'll go to the Moon and like it. Low gravity is not to be sneezed at—Auntie will probably live to be a hundred and twenty, heart trouble and all."

"Would *you* go to the Moon?" she asks.

"If I needed to and could afford it." He turns to you. "Right?"

You consider your answer. Life still looks good to you—and stairways are beginning to be difficult. Low gravity is attractive, even though it means living out your days at the Geriatrics Foundation on the Moon. "It might be fun to visit," you answer. "One wouldn't have to stay."

Hospitals for old people on the Moon? Let's not be silly—

Or is it silly? Might it not be a logical and necessary outcome of our world today?

Space travel we will have, not fifty years from now, but much sooner. It's breathing down our necks. As for geriatrics on the Moon, for most of us no price is too high and no amount of trouble is too great to extend the years of our lives. It is possible that low gravity (one sixth, on the Moon)

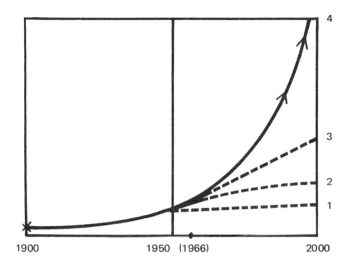

may not lengthen lives; nevertheless it *may* —we don't know yet—and it will most certainly add greatly to comfort on reaching that inevitable age when the burden of dragging around one's body is almost too much, or when we would otherwise resort to an oxygen tent to lessen the work of a worn-out heart.

By the rules of prophecy, such a prediction is *probable*, rather than impossible.

But the items and gadgets suggested above are examples of *timid* prophecy.

What are the rules of prophecy, if any?

Look at the graph shown here. The solid curve is what has been going on this past century. It represents many things—use of power, speed of transport, numbers of scientific and technical workers, advances in communication, average miles traveled per person per year, advances in mathematics, the rising curve of knowledge. Call it the curve of human achievement.

What is the correct way to project this curve into the future? Despite everything, there is a stubborn "common sense" tendency to project it along dotted line number one—like the patent office official of a hundred years back who quit his job "because everything had already been invented." Even those who don't expect a slowing up at once, tend to expect us to reach a point of diminishing returns (dotted line number two).

Very daring minds are willing to predict that we will continue our present rate of progress (dotted line number three—a tangent).

But the proper way to project the curve is dotted line number four—for there is no reason, mathematical, scientific, or historical, to expect that curve to flatten out, or to reach a point of diminishing returns, or simply to go on as a tangent. The correct projection, by all facts known today, is for the curve to go on up indefinitely with *increasing* steepness.

The timid little predictions earlier in this article actually belong to curve one, or, at most, to curve two. You can count on changes in the next fifty years at least *eight times* as great as the changes of the past fifty years.

The Age of Science *has not yet opened.*

AXIOM: A "nine-days' wonder" is taken as a matter of course on the tenth day.

AXIOM: A "common sense" prediction is sure to err on the side of timidity.

AXIOM: The more extravagant a prediction sounds the more likely it is to come true.

So let's have a few free-swinging predictions about the future.

Some will be wrong—but cautious predictions are *sure* to be wrong.

**1.** Interplanetary travel is waiting at your front door—C.O.D. It's yours when you pay for it. (*a*)

**2.** Contraception and control of disease is revising relations between sexes to an extent that will change our entire social and economic structure. (*b*)

**3.** The most important military fact of this century is that there is no way to repel an attack from outer space. (*c*)

**4.** It is utterly impossible that the United States will start a "preventive war." We will fight when attacked, either directly or in a territory we have guaranteed to defend. (*d*)

**5.** In fifteen years the housing shortage will be solved by a "breakthrough" into new technology which will make every house now standing as obsolete as privies. (*e*)

**6.** We'll all be getting a little hungry by and by.

**7.** The cult of the phony in art will disappear. So-called modern art will be discussed only by psychiatrists.

**8.** Freud will be classed as a pre-scientific, intuitive pioneer and psychoanalysis will be replaced by a growing, changing "operational psychology" based on measurement and prediction.

**9.** Cancer, the common cold, and tooth decay will all be conquered; the revolutionary new problem in medical research will be to accomplish "regeneration," i.e., to enable a man to grow a new leg, rather than fit him with an artificial limb. (*f*)

**10.** By the end of this century mankind will have explored this solar system, and the first ship intended to reach the nearest star will be abuilding. (*g*)

**11.** Your personal telephone will be small enough to carry in your handbag. Your house telephone will record messages, answer simple queries, and transmit vision.

**12.** Intelligent life will be found on Mars. (*h*)

**13.** A thousand miles an hour at a cent a mile will be commonplace; short hauls will be made in evacuated subways at extreme speeds. (*i*)

**14.** A major objective of applied physics will be to control gravity. (*j*)

**15.** We will not achieve a "world state" in the predictable future. Nevertheless, Communism will vanish from this planet. (*k*)

**16.** Increasing mobility will disenfranchise a majority of the population. About 1990 a constitutional amendment will do away with state lines while retaining the semblance.

**17.** All aircraft will be controlled by a giant radar net run on a continent-wide basis by a multiple electronic "brain."

**18.** Fish and yeast will become our principal sources of proteins. Beef will be a luxury; lamb and mutton will disappear. (*l*)

**19.** Mankind will *not* destroy itself, nor will "civilization" be destroyed. (*m*)

Here are things we *won't* get soon, if ever:

Travel through time.

Travel faster than the speed of light.

"Radio" transmission of matter.

Manlike robots with manlike reactions.

Laboratory creation of life.

Real understanding of what "thought" is and how it is related to matter.

Scientific proof of personal survival after death.

Nor a permanent end to war. (I don't like that prediction any better than you do.)

Prediction of gadgets is a parlor trick anyone can learn; but only a fool would attempt to predict details of future history (except as fiction, so labeled); there are too many unknowns and no techniques for integrating them even if they were known.

Even to make predictions about overall trends in technology is now most difficult. In fields where before World War II there was one man working in public, there are now ten, or a hundred, working in secret. There may be six men in the country who have a clear picture of what is going on in science today. *There may not be even one.*

This is in itself a trend. Many leading scientists consider it a factor as disabling to us as the nonsense of Lysenkoism is to Russian technology. Nevertheless there are clear-cut trends which are certain to make this coming era enormously more productive and interesting than the frantic one we have just passed through. Among them are:

*Cybernetics:* The study of communication and control of mechanisms and organisms. This includes the wonderful field of mechanical and electronic "brains"—but is not limited to it. (These "brains" are a factor in themselves that will speed up technical progress the way a war does.)

*Semantics:* A field which seems concerned only with definitions of words. It is not; it is a frontal attack on epistemology—that is to say, *how* we know *what* we know, a subject formerly belonging to long-haired philosophers.

*New tools of mathematics and logic,* such as calculus of statement, Boolean logic, morphological analysis, generalized symbology, newly invented mathematics of every sort—there is not space even to name these enormous fields, but they offer us hope in every other field—medicine, social relations, biology, economics, anything.

*Biochemistry:* Research into the nature of protoplasm, into enzyme chemistry, viruses, etc., give hope not only that we may conquer disease, but that we may someday understand the mechanisms of life itself. Through this, and with the aid of cybernetic machines and radioactive isotopes, we may eventually acquire a rigor of chemistry. Chemistry is not a discipline today; it is a jungle. We know that chemical behavior depends on the number of orbital electrons in an atom and that physical and chemical properties follow the pattern called the Periodic Table. We don't

know much else, save by cut-and-try, despite the great size and importance of the chemical industry. When chemistry becomes a discipline,
mathematical chemists will design new materials, predict their properties,
and tell engineers how to make them—without ever entering a laboratory.
We've got a *long* way to go on that one!

*Nucleonics:* We have yet to find out what makes the atom tick. Atomic
power?—yes, we'll have it, in convenient packages—when we understand
the nucleus. The field of radioisotopes alone is larger than was the entire
known body of science in 1900. Before we are through with these problems, we may find out how the universe is shaped and *why.* Not to
mention enormous unknown vistas best represented by ?????

Some physicists are now using two time scales, the T-scale, and the
*tau*-scale. Three billion years on one scale can equal an incredibly split
second on the other scale—and yet both apply to you and your kitchen
stove. Of such anarchy is our present state in physics.

For such reasons we must insist that *the Age of Science has not yet
opened.*

The greatest crisis facing us is not Russia, not the Atom Bomb, not
corruption in government, not encroaching hunger, nor the morals of the
young. It is a crisis in the *organization* and *accessibility* of human knowledge. We own an enormous "encyclopedia"—which isn't even arranged
alphabetically. Our "file cards" are spilled on the floor, nor were they ever
in order. The answers we want may be buried somewhere in the heap, but
it might take a lifetime to locate two already known facts, place them side
by side and derive a third fact, the one we urgently need.

Call it the Crisis of the Librarian.

We need a new "specialist" who is not a specialist, but a synthesist.
(*n*) We need a new science to be the perfect secretary to all other
sciences.

But we are not likely to get either one in a hurry and we have a
powerful lot of grief before us in the meantime.

Fortune-tellers can always be sure of repeat customers by predicting
what the customer wants to hear . . . it matters not whether the prediction
comes true. Contrariwise, the weatherman is often blamed for bad
weather.

Brace yourself.

In 1900 the cloud on the horizon was no bigger than a man's hand—

but what lay ahead was the Panic of 1907, World War I, the panic following it, the Depression, Fascism, World War II, the Atom Bomb, and Red Russia.

Today the clouds obscure the sky, and the wind that overturns the world is sighing in the distance.

The period immediately ahead will be the roughest, cruelest one in the long hard history of mankind. It will probably include the worst World War of them all. It might even end with a war with Mars, God save the mark! Even if we are spared that fantastic possibility, it is certain that there will be no security anywhere, save what you dig out of your own inner spirit.

But what of that picture we drew of domestic luxury and tranquility for Mrs. Middleclass, style 2000 A.D.?

*She* lived through it. She survived.

Our prospects need not dismay you, not if you or your kin were at Bloody Nose Ridge, at Gettysburg—or trudged across the Plains. You and I are here because we carry the genes of uncountable ancestors who fought—and won—against death in all its forms. We're tough. We'll survive. Most of us.

We've lasted through the preliminary bouts; the main event is coming up.

But it's not for sissies.

The last thing to come fluttering out of Pandora's box was Hope— without which men die.

The gathering wind will not destroy everything, nor will the Age of Science change everything. Long after the first star ship leaves for parts unknown, there will still be outhouses in upstate New York, there will still be steers in Texas, and—no doubt—the English will still stop for tea.

Afterthoughts, fifteen years later—

(*a*) And now we are paying for it and the cost is high. But, for reasons understandable only to bureaucrats, we have almost halted development of a nuclear-powered spacecraft when success was in sight. Never mind; if we don't, another country will. By the end of this century space travel will be cheap.

(*b*) This trend is so much more evident now than it was fifteen years ago that I am tempted to call it a fulfilled prophecy. Vast changes in sex relations are evident all around us—with the oldsters calling it "moral decay" and the youngsters ignoring them and taking it for granted. Surface signs: books such as *Sex and the Single Girl* are smash hits; the formerly taboo four-letter words are now seen both in novels and popular magazines; the neologism "swinger" has come into the language; courts are conceding that nudity and semi-nudity are now parts of the mores. But the end is not yet; this revolution will go much farther and is now barely started.

The most difficult speculation for a science fiction writer to undertake is to imagine correctly the *secondary* implications of a new factor. Many people correctly anticipated the coming of the horseless carriage; some were bold enough to predict that everyone would use them and the horse would virtually disappear. But I know of no writer, fiction or non-fiction, who saw ahead of time the vast change in the courting and mating habits of Americans which would result primarily from the automobile—a change which the diaphragm and the oral contraceptive merely confirmed. So far as I know, no one even dreamed of the change in sex habits the automobile would set off.

There is some new gadget in existence today which will prove to be equally revolutionary in some other way equally unexpected. You and I both know of this gadget, by name and by function—but we don't know which one it is nor what its unexpected effect will be. This is why science fiction is *not* prophecy—and why fictional speculation can be so much fun both to read and to write.

( *c* ) I flatly stand by this one. True, we are now working on Nike-Zeus and Nike-X and related systems and plan to spend billions on such systems—and we know that others are doing the same thing. True, it is possible to hit an object in orbit or trajectory. Nevertheless this prediction is as safe as predicting tomorrow's sunrise. Anti-aircraft fire never stopped air attacks; it simply made them expensive. The disadvantage in being at the bottom of a deep "gravity well" is very great; gravity gauge will be as crucial in the coming years as wind gauge was in the days when sailing ships controlled empires. The nation that controls the Moon will control the Earth—but no one seems willing these days to speak that nasty fact out loud.

( *d* ) Since 1950 we have done so in several theaters and are doing so as this is written, in Viet Nam. "Preventive" or "pre-emptive" war seems as unlikely as ever, no matter who is in the White House. Here is a new prediction: World War III (as a major, all-out war) will not take place at least until 1980 and could easily hold off until 2000. This is a very happy prediction compared with the situation in 1950, as those years of grace may turn up basic factors which (hopefully!) might postpone disaster still longer. We were *much* closer to ultimate disaster around 1955 than we are today—much closer indeed than we were at the time of the Cuban confrontation in 1962. But the public never knew it. All in all, things look pretty good for survival, for the time being—and that is as good a break as our ancestors ever had. It was far more dangerous to live in London in 1664–5 than it is to live in a city threatened by H-bombs today.

(*e*) Here I fell flat on my face. There has been no breakthrough in housing, nor is any now in prospect—instead the ancient, wasteful methods of building are now being confirmed by public subsidies. The degree of our backwardness in this field is hard to grasp; we have never seen a modern house. Think what an automobile would be if each one were custom-built from materials fetched to your home—what would it look like, what would it do, and how much would it cost? But don't set the cost lower than $100,000, nor the speed higher than 10 m/h, if you want to be realistic about the centuries of difference between the housing industry and the automotive industry.

I underestimated (through wishful thinking) the power of human stupidity—a fault fatal to prophecy.

(*f*) In the meantime spectacular progress has been made in organ transplants—and the problem of regeneration is related to this one. Biochemistry and genetics have made a spectacular breakthrough in "cracking the genetic code." It is a tiny crack, however, with a long way to go before we will have the human chromosomes charted and still longer before we will be able to "tailor" human beings by gene manipulation. The possibility is there—but not by year 2000. This is probably just as well. If we aren't bright enough to build decent houses, are we bright enough to play God with the architecture of human beings?

(*g*) Our editor suggested that I had been too optimistic on this one—but I still stand by it. It is still thirty-five years to the end of the century. For perspective, look back thirty-five years to 1930—the American Rocket Society had not yet been founded then. Another curve, similar to the one herewith in shape but derived entirely from speed of transportation, extrapolates to show faster-than-light travel by year 2000. I guess I'm chicken, for I am not predicting FTL ships by then, if ever. But the prediction still stands without hedging.

(*h*) Predicting intelligent life on Mars looks pretty silly after those dismal photographs. But I shan't withdraw it until Mars has been *thoroughly* explored. As yet we really have no idea—and no data—as to just how ubiquitous and varied life may be in this galaxy; it is conceivable that life as we *don't* know it can evolve on *any* sort of a planet . . . and nothing in our present knowledge of chemistry rules this out. All the talk has been about life-as-we-know-it—which means terrestrial conditions.

But if you feel that this shows in me a childish reluctance to give up thoats and zitidars and beautiful Martian princesses until forced to, I won't argue with you—I'll just wait.

(*i*) I must hedge number thirteen; the "cent" I meant was scaled by the 1950 dollar. But our currency has been going through a long steady inflation, and no nation in history has ever gone as far as we have along this route without reaching the explosive phase of inflation. Ten-dollar hamburgers? Brother, we are headed for the hundred-dollar hamburger— for the barter-only hamburger.

But this is only an inconvenience rather than a disaster as long as there is plenty of hamburger.

(*j*) This prediction stands. But today physics is in a tremendous state of flux with new data piling up faster than it can be digested; it is anybody's guess as to where we are headed, but the wilder you guess, the more likely you are to hit it lucky. With "elementary particles" of nuclear physics now totaling about half the number we used to use to list the "immutable" chemical elements, a spectator needs a program just to keep track of the players. At the other end of the scale, "quasars"—quasi-stellar bodies—have come along; radio astronomy is now bigger than telescopic astronomy used to be; and we have redrawn our picture of the universe several times, each time enlarging it and making it more complex—I haven't seen this week's theory yet, which is well, as it would be out of date before this gets into print. Plasma physics was barely started in 1950; the same for solid-state physics. This is the Golden Age of physics—and it's an anarchy.

(*k*) I stand flatly behind prediction number fifteen.

(*l*) I'll hedge number eighteen just a little. Hunger is not now a problem in the USA and need not be in the year 2000—but hunger *is* a world problem and would at once become an acute problem for us if we were conquered . . . a distinct possibility by 2000. Between our present status and that of subjugation lies a whole spectrum of political and economic possible shapes to the future under which we would share the worldwide hunger to a greater or lesser extent. And the problem grows. We can expect to have to feed around half a billion Americans circa year 2000—our present huge surpluses would then represent acute shortages even if we never shipped a ton of wheat to India.

(*m*) I stand by prediction number nineteen.

I see no reason to change any of the negative predictions which follow the numbered affirmative ones. They are all conceivably possible; they are all wildly unlikely by year 2000. Some of them are debatable if the terms are defined to suit the affirmative side—definitions of "life" and "manlike," for example. Let it stand that I am not talking about an amino acid in one case, nor a machine that plays chess in the other.

(*n*) Today the forerunners of these synthesists are already at work in many places. Their titles may be anything; their degrees may be in anything—or they may have no degrees. Today they are called "operations researchers," or sometimes "systems development engineers," or other interim tags. But they are all interdisciplinary people, generalists, not specialists—the new Renaissance Man. The very explosion of data which forced most scholars to specialize very narrowly created the necessity which evoked this new non-specialist. So far, this "unspecialty" is in its infancy; its methodology is inchoate, the results are sometimes trivial, and no one knows how to train to become such a man. But the results are often spectacularly brilliant, too—this new man may yet save all of us.

I'm an optimist. I have great confidence in Homo sapiens.

We have rough times ahead—but when didn't we? Things have always been "tough all over." H-bombs, Communism, race riots, water shortage—all nasty problems. But not basic problems, merely current ones.

We have three basic and continuing problems: The problem of population explosion; the problem of data explosion; and the problem of government.

Population problems have a horrid way of solving themselves when they are not solved rationally; the Four Horsemen of the Apocalypse are always saddled up and ready to ride. The data explosion is now being solved, mostly by cybernetics and electronics men rather than by librarians—and if the solutions are less than perfect, at least they are better than what Grandpa had to work with. The problem of government has not been solved either by the "Western Democracies" or the "People's Democracies," as of now. (Anyone who thinks the people of the United States have solved the problem of government is using too short a time scale.) The peoples of the world are now engaged in a long, long struggle with no end in sight, testing whether one concept works better than another; in that conflict millions have already died and it is possible that hundreds of millions will die in it before year 2000. But not all.

I hold both opinions and preferences as to the outcome. But my personal preference for a maximum of looseness is irrelevant; what we are experiencing is an evolutionary process in which personal preference matters, at most, only statistically. Biologists, ecologists in particular, are working around to the idea that natural selection and survival of the fittest is a notion that applies more to groups and how they are structured than it does to individuals. The present problem will solve itself in the cold terms of evolutionary survival, and in the course of it both sides will make changes in group structure. The system that survives might be called "Communism" or it might be called "Democracy" (the latter is my guess)—but one thing we can be certain of: it will not resemble very closely what either Marx or Jefferson had in mind. Or it might be called by some equally inappropriate neologism; political tags are rarely logical.

For Man is rarely logical. But I have great confidence in Man, based on his past record. He is mean, ornery, cantankerous, illogical, emotional—and amazingly hard to kill. Religious leaders have faith in the spiritual redemption of Man; humanist leaders subscribe to a belief in the perfectibility of Man through his own efforts; but I am not discussing either of these two viewpoints. My confidence in our species lies in its past history and is founded quite as much on Man's so-called vices as on his so-called virtues. When the chips are down, quarrelsomeness and selfishness can be as useful to the survival of the human race as is altruism, and pigheadedness can be a trait superior to sweet reasonableness. If this were not true, these "vices" would have died out through the early deaths of their hosts, at least a half million years back.

I have a deep and abiding confidence in Man as he is, imperfect and often unlovable—plus still greater confidence in his potential. No matter how tough things are, Man copes. He comes up with adequate answers from illogical reasons. But the answers work.

Last to come out of Pandora's Box was a gleaming, beautiful thing—eternal Hope.

# GOURMET DINING IN OUTER SPACE

## Alfred Bester

In the stone age of science fiction, back in the twenties, nobody thought much about cooking in space. Those were the early days of vitamins, and writers who imagined what the future would be like thought in terms of pills. They loaded their spaceships with scientists, laboratories and death rays; and then, as an afterthought, threw in a handful of pills which would feed the crew for a year.

In the thirties, science fiction dropped the pills and went in for extra-terrestrial menus. What this amounted to was a meal in Joe's Diner with an exotic name. The intrepid spacemen would knock off work in the fourth dimension for a dinner consisting of Venusian *grzzb* (grapefruit), Martian *schlumphh* (meat and potatoes), Juniper pandowdy and Andromeda coffee. Authors never specified how these goodies were prepared, or how you cleaned up afterward. You simply lit a Neptunian *Wmphz* (the cigarette with the spaceman's filter) and chucked the garbage into the rocket engines. Presumably you not only ate off paper plates but cooked in paper pots as well.

By the forties, science fiction was making a valiant attempt at realism, and every spaceship was equipped with giant hydroponic tanks in which vegetables were grown. This meant that spaceships had to be imagined bigger. Some authors made their spaceships a couple of miles long and fitted them out with dirt farms under sun lamps. They also took over the

From *Holiday*, May 1960

newfangled freezer, and any spaceship could boast of lockers stocked with thousands of prime steaks.

But it's interesting to note that the authors of science fiction have never bothered about the serious business of cooking in space. This attitude is understandable in stories dealing with long, lean, bronzed heroes sworn to wipe out the space pirates swarming in the rings of Saturn—*that* breed never sleeps, much less eats. But what about the short, fat, pasty tourists of A.D. 2060 who plank down their $2060 for a first-class seven-day round trip to the moon, including a three-day stopover at the Lunar Hilton Hotel? This breed demands luxury accommodations, and would raise hell with the Matson-Moon Line if they were served pills or parsnips or even *schlumphh*.

Let's take a tourist on a luxury trip to the moon and see what may happen. In this case the tourist is you.

You have paid for your ticket and are packing on the morning of the take-off. You are packing very carefully because the Matson-Moon has warned you that weight is the critical problem in space flight, and the weight allowance is 200 pounds per passenger, *including* the passenger. If you are a big man, weighing around 185 pounds, you are allowed fifteen pounds of baggage. If you are a small woman, you may be able to take ninety pounds of baggage with you. Matson-Moon has kindly given you a list of your fellow passengers with their telephone numbers, and all of you have been phoning back and forth, trying to locate lightweights willing to include something of yours in their allowance.

You weigh in at International Spaceport. You are wearing featherweight clothing and carrying your gear in a transparent plastic wrap bag. No one can afford to waste weight even on the lightest of valises. Passengers stand around hugging bundles of clothes, linen and toilet articles to their bosoms, looking like old-clothes dealers.

When the officials put you on the scales you are not permitted to pay an extra fee for overweight. You discard something then and there. There are agonizing last-minute decisions to be made. Tempers are short because everybody has been dieting frantically for weeks to increase his baggage allowance. This means trouble for the chef.

You board the ship and are greeted by the maintenance engineer, who immediately confiscates all tobacco. Smoking will be permitted only at specified hours, after meals and before bedtime. This is not only a question of oxygen supply; engineers have discovered that the chemicals in tobacco smoke are dangerous to the delicate electronic equipment aboard spaceships.

You are packed into your coffin-sized cabins and strapped down. The ship takes off with the roar of a Niagara, crushing you deep into your berth with its frightful acceleration. Then you burst into outer space. The sky turns from atmospheric blue to vacuum black; the stars appear in the sky; the sun is a diamond glory; the rocket thrust is cut off; there is a stark silence, broken only by the sounds of you and your fellow passengers being very sick.

This is the result of being in free fall, of being cut loose from the bonds of gravity. When you unstrap yourself from your berth, you float in the air. Everything inside you seems to be floating too. The sensation is strange and unpleasant at first, but then you begin to enjoy the weightlessness. Without gravity straining at you, you breathe easier, your heart beats gently, you feel wonderfully carefree.

You float out of your cabin to the narrow corridor and wriggle and push yourself forward to the salon which serves as lounge, observation room and dining room. It has no furniture. Since there is no gravity, no up or down in free fall, this makes no difference. No one can sit or stand anyway. Everybody simply floats. The salon is walled all the way around with portholes. You and your fellow passengers float around the portholes like fish in an aquarium, staring, exclaiming, photographing.

The chef appears from the galley. He is a small man with a fierce mustache and a savage expression. The mustache is French; the expression is savage because he must be his own waiter, and this galls the artist in him even though he is paid a fabulous salary. His colleagues, anchored on earth, kid him about the job.

They call him espaçon, which is a combination of espace and garçon with overtones of assassin.

The chef carries a net bag filled with plastic globes the size of baseballs. From each globe protrudes a plastic straw. "Hot!" he warns. "Hot!" And he demonstrates how the hot globe should be picked out of the bag by its straw. Each globe contains steaming bouillon, and you have your first snack in space, intended to settle your stomach and teach you the vagaries of eating without benefit of gravity.

It's a strange sensation. The soup must be sucked through the straw into your mouth. Then an effort must be made to swallow the mouthful, rather like deliberately swallowing a large pill. There is no gravity to trickle the broth down your throat. You can feel the muscular action of your throat doing the job all by itself, gently pressing the food down into your stomach.

Experienced space travelers are expert at eating without benefit of gravity, and you can spot your fellow first-timers by their clumsiness. Like you, they sputter the hot soup, which does not stain their clothes but rather floats around their heads in tiny droplets. The old-timers advise you to chase the droplets and lick them back into your mouth.

"Can't have the lounge swimming with soup," they tell you.

The chef collects the empty plastic globes and takes them back into the galley with him. Let's follow and watch him prepare dinner.

There is no floor in the kitchen. The chef floats in midair, surrounded on all sides by his kitchen equipment. He can stand on his head, as it were, and reach up to tend the stove. He can kick open the refrigerator, stir a sauce behind his back and crack eggs over one shoulder. He never has to worry about spilling things: nothing ever spills in free fall. On the other hand he has a hell of a problem getting eggs out of their shells once they're cracked. Nothing ever pours in free fall. Everything has to be shaken, pushed, nudged, coaxed.

IIis stove is a battery of hot plates set in the sun side of the spaceship. The naked sun in space is incredibly hot, far hotter than gas flame or electric coils. In fact, the entire ship must be insulated against it. The stove is a solar stove. By adjusting regulators, the chef can open the insulation masking the undersides of the hot plates and allow the sun to heat them from lukewarm to broiling hot.

On the shadow side of the spaceship, the temperature is the absolute zero of outer space, and the chef's refrigerator and freezer are built into this dark wall. Space does his chilling for him, just as the sun does his cooking. These conditions are the source of continual warfare between chef and pilot.

If the ship rotates a few feet in the course of its flight, it may slowly revolve the stove out of the direct glare of the sun, cool it, and ruin the cooking. The chef picks up the intercom phone and howls at the pilot: "Imbecile! You are assassinating my soufflé!" The same rotation brings the refrigerator out of the ice shadow into the sunlight and warms it. The chef phones again: "Bandit! You are sabotaging my aspic!"

The first night's menu is characteristic of the meals served on this de luxe trip:

*Caviar Beluga*
*La Tortue Verte*
*La Mousse de Brocheton Homardine*
*Accompagnée de Petites Bouchées*
*La Coeur de Charolais Beaugency*
*Endives Meunière*
*Beurre Noisette*
*Fond d'Artichaut Châtelaine*
*La Pèche Flambée au Feu d'Enfer*
*Café Noir très Chaud*

Just to be sure you're not under the impression that this is more Venusian *grzzb* and Martian *schlumphh*, and to enable you to understand how the chef goes about cooking all this in space, I translate:

*Sturgeon Roe*
*The Green Turtle*
*The froth of lobstered baby*
*pickerels accompanied by little*
*greedy mouthfuls*
*Beef filet from Charol with a sauce*
*in a state of beauty*
*Endive as the miller's wife would cook it*
*Nut butter*
*The bottoms of artichokes as served*
*by the lady of the manor*
*A peach enflamed by the fire of hell*
*Black coffee, very hot*

The sturgeon roe presents no problem. The chef has stocked a quart can of "Super-Pressed" caviar. It looks and operates exactly like a can of aerated shaving cream. The chef presses the button and, *phht!*—out comes the caviar. A quart can is good for one hundred servings.

The green-turtle soup is a powder packed in single-portion capsules. Each capsule is the size of a sleeping pill. Not only is the powder the quintessence of concentrated turtles but it has been treated so that it can absorb water from the atmosphere. Nothing need be added. The chef opens each capsule and taps the powder into an empty plastic globe. In five minutes each globe is full of *la tortue verte*. Since the process of water absorption produces heat, the soup is hot. Add straw and serve. *Voilà!*

The froth of lobstered baby pickerels is a sore point with the chef. It is essential for the dish (and his reputation as an artist) to enhance it with a hint of garlic. The maintenance engineer has absolutely prohibited the use of garlic in cooking; he finds it almost impossible to remove all traces of garlic from the air in his atmospheric reprocessing plant. But in this age of caffein-free coffee and nicotineless tobacco, the chef has located "No-Gar," a garlicless garlic, and smuggled a few *fleurettes* aboard. He tries a clove. The intercom shrills.

"*Allo? Allo?*"

"Damn it, chef, are you using garlic again? I've told you a hundred times—"

"*Non! Non! Mais non!*" The chef hastily shakes pepper over one shoulder into the ventilator grille. Still protesting his innocence, he is gratified to hear the engineer sneezing, and gently hangs up.

The preparation of the beef filets is perhaps the most fascinating aspect of cooking in free fall. The chef removes them from his freezer and poises them half an inch above the hot plates of his stove.

There they float while he adjusts the heat of the sun to sear them at exactly the right temperature and speed. No gravity, remember? No pots or pans are needed for cooking. Everything can be poised over the stove, even liquids.

For example, to *meunière* the endives, the chef removes a one-pound block of butter from the freezer and sets it above a plate. It heats, melts and becomes a large golden globe, hanging in midair. Then it sizzles and browns. At the precise moment, the chef thrusts the endive into the butter and gives the globe a gentle turn. It hangs over the hot plate, slowly revolving like a miniature planet, deliciously cooking its contents.

No plates or tableware are used to serve or eat the food. Gravity is required to keep food on a plate. Gravity is required to keep food on a fork. You can't cut food without gravity; you don't even dare spear it. The risk of food sailing into midair after the slightest miscalculation is too great. The dining room aboard a spaceship would be turned into a goulash.

No, the chef serves the food in midair directly before you, using ladles and tongs. He floats half a dozen *blinis* under your nose. *Phht! Phtt! Phtt!* He covers each one with caviar. You and the caviar are floating in space, confronting each other. You poke the *hors d'oeuvres*, one by one, into your mouth.

Next, the green-turtle soup in plastic globes with plastic straws. Easy.

You've already practiced on the bouillon. Next the froth of lobstered pickerels, looking like a foam in space, for the liquid sauce hangs in bubbles around the little greedy mouthfuls.

Then come the beef filets with sauce, the endive and the artichokes. All these are gently coaxed out of serving baskets and floated before you. And there you are, thirty passengers, floating in every possible corner of the dining room, upside-down and downside-up, with your gourmet dinner floating before you; and all of you are eating in the old barbarian manner, with the fingers, but with a new space-age skill and delicacy.

Three wines and a cognac are served with the meal: Dry Sack with the soup; Montrachet 2053 with the fish; Pommard Grands Epenots Domaine Gaunoux 2047 with the filet. Marc à la Cloche is served with the coffee. All of them are the products of Instant Wine, Ltd., and Sonny Boy Wine-Qwik of California, Inc. I will not break your hearts by describing how these beverages are prepared. All I will say is that Instant Wine's slogan is "Think Small!" and Sonny Boy Wine-Qwik's products are packaged in what look like toothpaste tubes.

The foregoing may well take place in the next century, but as one moves farther into the future and deeper into space, space cookery itself may become farther out. The time may come when the chef is no longer on board ship, but remains on earth, cooking by remote control via tele-robot, much the way scientists in nuclear laboratories today handle radio-active materials. The chef will never burn himself, but he can administer a bad short circuit to his robot slave if he isn't careful with the controls.

Or cooking may become altogether automatic with menus for 750 meals punched into the robot kitchen's instruction tape. The kitchen itself will look like an IBM computer, and the meals will pop out of its maw with distressing punctuality, whether you feel like eating or not.

Three hundred years from now, General Foods and Continental Can may merge and electrify the Space Age by crossing spinach with plastics (don't ask me how), producing an edible food container in fruit, fish, meat, fowl and vegetable flavors.

The label will be printed with Wine-Qwik ink, of course, and the top of the can, not necessarily edible, will be microgrooved on the inside so that you can listen to Bach, Beethoven and Brubeck while you are dining.

In this case there won't be any kitchen. Each cabin will have affixed to the wall the food equivalent of a cigarette machine; or aboard one-class cruise ships it may be a combination vending machine and juke box in the main salon, and you'll pay for your meals as you eat them, with coins in a slot.

Five hundred years from now the space lanes will be fairly well cluttered with debris—garbage, containers, bottles, nonedible plastics—all jettisoned by spaceships and floating in nowhere. Space, unlike the ocean, has no convenient bottom to which garbage can sink. Somewhere around A.D. 2460 the final miracle may take place. Exposed to cosmic rays and undiluted sunlight and proton bombardment, seeds and stems, leaves and fruit stones may mutate and begin to grow in the vacuum.

Can you imagine the spaceways slowly filling with spreading fields of new species of flowers, fruits, vegetables and grains; living in vacuum like orchids living on air; thriving in the light of the distant sun, feeding, perhaps, on the stray electrons, protons and stardust that pervade every inch of the universe? Can you see spaceships on long journeys stopping alongside these fields to replenish supplies, like adventuring Vikings? Can you conceive of the taste of these new foods of the future, and the strange new ways they may be cooked in space? Beyond this, the imagination can't go.

# VII.

# CONFESSIONS

# WHY SO MUCH SYZYGY?

## Theodore Sturgeon

Recent remarks about my apparent preoccupation with syzygy came as something of a jolt. One needs to be told about such things. No one knows what he thinks until it's crystallized for shipment, unspoken thoughts being the formless, tintless things they are.

My first reaction was to deny such an allegation and say loftily that you guys haven't been reading enough Sturgeon or you never could say such a thing. One gets strange and wonderful impressions from fanzines from time to time, like the science fiction historian a couple years back who said I was a discovery in 1940 and in the next paragraph said that *Astounding* had a dull year in 1941, no one there but the old regulars like Sturgeon. Or the knowing note identifying William Tenn as Robert Heinlein; and that magnificent tarfu explaining that H. B. Fyfe was of course H. Beam Piper, and since only vhf researchers know that ultra-short waves are led through plumbing, that the guy was obviously J. J. Coupling—followed by the informative parenthesis: (Dr. John Clark). So me and syzygy, this is just one more of those things.

My first-and-a-half reaction was to list some recent stories just to show you how wrong you are, and when I did, I found by God you have something there. It wasn't the something you state, but it *is* something, and I hadn't realized it before.

I've been accused (or reminded) of a number of other thematic rep-

From *Skyhook*, Summer 1953

etitions. Horace Gold asked me for a story over the phone recently and begged me not to make it another of these multiple personality things. Someone wrote to me not long ago and said my story in *Suchnsuch Stories* was fine, but when am I going to quit writing about children? And you would be surprised at the reaction I received from my yarn "The World Well Lost" in the first issue of *Universe Science Fiction*. ( I won't quote it because I wouldn't want to spoil a narrative switch for those who haven't read it, but if all authors wrote from source, as charged, then Bob Tucker is a murderer and Isaac Asimov is a mule. )

Fourteen years ago I wrote a story out of sheer self-defense; I knew it was unsalable but the damn thing got between me and everything I tried to do. For ten years it kicked around from market to market, and finally sold. It won a prize ( $1,000) in an English magazine and had a Graham Greene short for the runner-up. Groff Conklin reprinted it last year in his Permabook *In the Grip of Terror*, in case anyone wants to look it up. It's called "Bianca's Hands."

Now, that story had a peculiar effect on people. One editor I took it to called me up in a quaking rage and said he was sending it back using his own postage (that was really something in those days) because he wouldn't have it in his office. An agent I wanted to hook up with pushed it and a pile of other manuscripts across his desk to me and told me he wouldn't touch anything written by a guy who wrote such a story as that.

Recently in *Skyhook* you took somebody to task for a remark about "there is no reason for sex except for the purpose of procreation," and drew an eloquent analogy with the statement that sex is here for the purpose of a balanced economy: "Without sexual pleasure there would be no passionate attachments between humans." I think that in "Bianca's Hands" and "The Perfect Host" (*Weird Tales*, November 1948) and in the *Universe* story mentioned above, and in the remarks just quoted, we have sufficient material for the tentative establishment of that denominator. Mind you, I'm the least qualified of all Sturgeon critics to make this analysis; on the other hand I do have a bit more material on the subject than most people. I've read more Sturgeon than anybody.

It has to do with the enormously complex field of passionate human attachments. There are passionate lovers of women and passionate lovers of new panties and old shoes. There are also passionate lovers of music, Shakespeare, sports cars, and smorgasbord, and all these passions have their areas of sharing, of direct involvement of other human beings. It would seem easy to make two clear-cut divisions: this one is sexual and that one is not, but it isn't that simple. Then one might shade the matter off and say this is clearly sexual, that is also sexual but sublimated. You'll bog down on that one, too.

I think what I have been trying to do all these years is to investigate this matter of love, sexual and asexual. I investigate it by writing about it because, as stated above, I don't know what the hell I think until I tell somebody about it. And I work so assiduously at it because of a conviction that if one could understand it completely, one would have the key to cooperation itself: to creative inspiration: to self-sacrifice and that rare but real anomaly, altruism: in short, to the marvelous orchestration which enables us to keep ahead of our own destructiveness.

In order to do this I've had to look at the individual components. In "The Deadly Ratio" (the "definitive" syzygy story; its original title was "It Wasn't Syzygy") I had two lovers, only one of whom was real. In "Bianca's Hands" only one of them was human. In "Rule of Three" and "Synthesis" I had (in reverse order) a quasi-sexual relationship among three people, and one among six so it could break down into three couples and be normal. In "The Stars Are the Styx" I set up several (four, as I remember) different kinds of love motivations for mutual comparisons. In "Two Percent Inspiration" it was hero worship, a kid and a great scientist. In "Until Death Do Us Join" it was the murderous jealousy between two personalities in a schizophrenic,[32] both in love with the same girl. In "Cactus Dance" (upcoming in *Zane Grey's Western*) it is non-physical, perhaps even non-substitute physical love, as represented in several symbiotic relationships between humans and yucca plants. In "Killdozer" it was a choked-up worship for the majesty of a machine. By this time you get the idea.

"Bianca's Hands" and "The World Well Lost" cause the violently extreme reactions they do because of the simple fact that the protagonist was happy with the situation. No one was churned up (in these areas) by "Until Death Do Us Join" because the crazy mixed-up little guy was killed in the end. "Killdozer" didn't bother anyone, because love for a machine (as expressed) is too remote from most readers' ability to identify. But write a story well enough to force identification, and have the protagonist indulging in something weird, and let the guy be happy about it, and people explode all over the place. It is fashionable to overlook the fact that the old-shoe lover *loves* loving old shoes. Write that, and all the old-shoe lovers will love the story; all the deviates who equate their specialty with old-shoe loving will love the story; all the aberrates who so specialize or so equate but feel guilty about it will hate the story and you too.

Now if we can wrench this discussion out of the appetizing areas of pathology, and return to the original question: why so much syzygy?—well, it's pretty obvious why a clear-cut method of non-reproductive exchange should be so useful in such an overall investigation. It's beautifully open to comparison and analog. It handles all sorts of attachments felt by any sensitive person which could not conceivably be sexually based. It does this almost as well as the general theme of symbiosis, of which I think you'll find more in my stuff than syzygy.

If you can understand non-reproductive love you'll be able to understand—and convey—those two kinds of awe, the one for Boulder Dam or an atom bomb, and the other for Grand Canyon or a nova. You'll understand *why* Casals and Segovia and Landowska work with such exquisite devotion, and what's with the GI who falls on the live grenade to save his squad. A guy who could understand things like that could get to be a pretty fair writer.

Oh yes, before some of you supersophisticates knock down *all* of the pins I've set up: I *know* there's a temptation to translate all of love into sexual terms or transferences and sublimations thereof. But I have a deep conviction that it's a little like saucer sightings: you can explain away item after item in known terms, but always you'll find that damned percentage that just won't yield.

And those are the ones worth writing stories about.

# THERE'S NOTHING LIKE A
# GOOD FOUNDATION

## Isaac Asimov

During the 1940s, I was avidly engaged in writing two series of stories—the Foundation Series and the Positronic Robot Series. I had no intention in either case of writing a series when I started.

The Foundation Series had its origin in 1941, in the course of a subway ride to see John W. Campbell, Jr., editor of *Astounding Science Fiction*. In those days, I visited him frequently and always brought with me the plot of a new s.f. story. We discussed it and I went home and wrote it. Then he would sometimes accept it and sometimes not.

On this subway ride, I had no story idea to present him with so I tried a trick I still sometimes recommend. I opened a book at random, read a sentence, and concentrated on it till I had an idea. The book was a collection of the Gilbert and Sullivan plays which I just happened to have with me. I opened it to *Iolanthe* and my eye fell on the picture of the fairy queen kneeling before Private Willis of the Grenadier Guards.

I let my mind wander from the Grenadiers, to soldiers in general, to a military society, to feudalism, to the breakup of the Roman Empire. By the time I reached Campbell I told him that I was planning to write a story about the breakup of the Galactic Empire.

He talked and I talked and he talked and I talked and when I left I had the Foundation series in mind. It lasted for seven years, during which I wrote eight stories, ranging in length from a short story to a three-part serial.

From *SFWA Bulletin*, January 1967

The Positronic Robot Series began less oddly. I had written a robot story which I liked but which Campbell rejected so that I was forced to sell it elsewhere. In it, however, I had a kind of rudimentary notion of what have since become known as the Three Laws of Robotics. I had a character say in it, concerning my nursemaid robot: "He just can't help being faithful and loving and kind. He's a machine—*made* so!"

That reference to the First Law of Robotics interested Campbell even though the story did not, and we discussed it till we had the Three Laws worked out. Over the next ten years, I wrote nine short stories based on those Three Laws. (Since then I have written others, too, and two novels as well.)

There is no question but that writing those series was a Good Thing for me. The individual stories in a successful series have a cumulative effect. Readers who have liked the first story are pleased to see a second story and wait for the third story eagerly. They welcome the familiar situation and/or characters and are sold on each new story in the series even before they begin it.

The author benefits personally. The reader is grateful to him for each new installment of the series and is keenly aware of the author's power to grant or withhold the favor. The author begins to gain fans, to collect reader-loyalty, and when this is evidenced in the letters he receives, he begins to think better of himself. (And never underestimate the power of a satisfied ego to minimize the dangers of that most horrible of all diseases —writer's block.)

And writing the series can be pleasant too. The writer has a familiar background to deal with so that part of his work is done for him before he as much as starts the story. He has the satisfying feeling that people are waiting for the story (and that the editor is, too, with a check all written out).

Besides, a writer can be as pleased as a reader to meet a familiar and loved character or idea. *I* always was. I was in love with Susan Calvin of my Positronic Robot Series, and was delighted to meet her every time she showed up in my typewriter.

Then, too, the writer, working on a series, has the opportunity to develop ideas in depth and variety. What he misses in one story, he can catch in the next.

But there are disadvantages, too. There is, for one thing, the bugaboo of self-consistency. It is annoying to be hampered, in working out a story, by the fact that some perfectly logical development is ruled out since, three stories before, you had to make such a development impossible because of the needs of the plot of *that* story.

Of course, you might take the attitude that too much self-consistency is bad, and I tried not to worry about it in my Positronic Robot Series. Yet in 1950, when I put the stories into book form, I found that I had to straighten out a few things and that my easy-going attitude had just made work for me in the long run. For instance, I had to kill off one of my continuing characters who would otherwise have been about 150 years old by the end of the book.

Matters were much worse in the Foundation Series because here the stories were told consecutively, with one story leading directly to the next, and with the plots of all very intricate and closely knit.

Before I could write a new Foundation story I had to sit down and reread all the preceding ones, and by the time I got to the eighth story that meant rereading some 150,000 words of very complicated material. Even so, my success was limited. In April 1966, a fan approached me with a carefully made out list of inconsistencies in dates, names and events that he had dug out of the series by dint of close reading and cross-reference.

Furthermore, in designing each new Foundation story, I found I had to work within an increasingly constricted area, with progressively fewer and fewer degrees of freedom. I was forced to seize whatever way out I could find, without worrying about how difficult I might make the next story. Then, when I came to the next story, those difficulties arose and beat me over the head.

Then again, I had to start each story with some indication of what had gone before, for those readers who had never read any of the earlier stories. When I wrote the eighth story, I was forced to begin with a long introduction which I had to disguise as an essay my adolescent girl heroine was writing for class. It was not at all easy to make such an essay interesting. I had to introduce a number of human-interest touches and interrupt it by action at the first possible opportunity.

Finally, time passes for the author, and he changes. I was 21 when I started the Foundation Series and 28 when I wrote the eighth story. I was no longer very enthusiastic at the end about some of the ideas I had had at the start. I was also coming to be afraid that I was over-specializing myself and working myself into a situation where I could write *only* Foundation stories.

The eighth story had carried me only one-third of the way through the original plan of describing one thousand years of future history. However, to write a ninth story meant rereading the first eight, starting with a longer prologue than ever, working in a narrower compass than ever, and so on. So, I quit—permanently.

The Positronic Robot Series is much looser and it is still alive. I will undoubtedly write additional stories in the future—if I live.

On the whole, the series stories have much more in their favor than against them and I recommend the notion to those writers who find it congenial.

The years I spent on the Foundation Series were the most rewarding of my writing life—professionally, if not financially. They placed my name before the public in a way that an equal number of disconnected stories would not have succeeded in doing. They gave me a sense of success (very important!)—and kept me working at an increasingly difficult task that helped develop my writing technique. And they gave me indefinite insurance into the future.

The Foundation Series were first published in book form in three volumes in the early 1950's and they have never gone out of print. As book club selections, in paperback form, in foreign editions, in hardcover reissues and paperback reissues, they seem to have an indefinite number of lives. Even as I write, Avon Books is putting them out once again in paperback form.

No week passes without some piece of fan-mail referring to the Foundation stories, and usually asking for more. And at the 24th World Science Fiction Convention, held in Cleveland in 1966, the Foundation Series was awarded a Hugo as the All-Time Best Series.

What more can I ask for having opened a book in the subway twenty-five years ago?

# SON OF DR. STRANGELOVE

*Or, How I Learned to Stop Worrying and
Love Stanley Kubrick*

## Arthur C. Clarke

The first steps on the rather long road to *2001: A Space Odyssey* were taken in March 1964, when Stanley Kubrick wrote to me in Ceylon, saying that he wanted to do the proverbial "really good" science-fiction movie. His main interests, he explained, lay in these broad areas: "(1) The reasons for believing in the existence of intelligent extraterrestrial life. (2) The impact (and perhaps even lack of impact in some quarters) such discovery would have on Earth in the near future."

As this subject had been my main preoccupation (apart from time out for World War II and the Great Barrier Reef) for the previous thirty years, this letter naturally aroused my interest. The only movie of Kubrick's I had then seen was *Lolita*, which I had greatly enjoyed, but rumors of *Dr. Strangelove* had been reaching me in increasing numbers. Here, obviously, was a director of unusual quality, who wasn't afraid of tackling far-out subjects. It would certainly be worthwhile having a talk with him; however, I refused to let myself get too excited, knowing from earlier experience that the mortality rate of movie projects is about ninety-nine percent.

Meanwhile, I examined my published fiction for film-worthy ideas and very quickly settled on a short story called "The Sentinel," written over the 1948 Christmas holiday for a BBC contest. (It didn't place.) This story developed a concept that has since been taken quite seriously by the

FROM *Report on Planet Three*, Harper & Row, 1972

scientists concerned with the problem of extraterrestrials, or ETs for short.

During the last decade, there has been a quiet revolution in scientific thinking about ETs; the view now is that planets are at least as common as stars—of which there are some 100 billion in our local Milky Way galaxy alone. Moreover, it is believed that life will arise automatically and inevitably where conditions are favorable; so there may be civilizations all around us which achieved space travel before the human race existed, and then passed on to heights which we cannot remotely comprehend. . . .

But if so, why haven't they visited us? In "The Sentinel," I proposed one answer (which I now more than half believe myself). We may indeed have had visitors in the past—perhaps millions of years ago, when the great reptiles ruled the Earth. As they surveyed the terrestrial scene, the strangers would guess that one day intelligence could arise on this planet; so they might leave behind them a robot monitor, to watch and to report. But they would not leave their sentinel on Earth itself, where in a few thousand years it would be destroyed or buried. They would place it on the almost unchanging Moon.

And they would have a second reason for doing this. To quote from the original story:

They would be interested in our civilization only if we proved our fitness to survive—by crossing space and so escaping from the Earth, our cradle. That is the challenge that all intelligent races must meet, sooner or later. It is a double challenge, for it depends in turn upon the conquest of atomic energy, and the last choice between life and death.

Once we had passed that crisis, it was only a matter of time before we found the beacon and forced it open. . . . Now we have broken the glass of the fire-alarm, and have nothing to do but to wait. . . .

This, then, was the idea which I suggested in my reply to Stanley Kubrick as the take-off point for a movie. The finding—and triggering—of an intelligence detector, buried on the Moon aeons ago, would give all the excuse we needed for the exploration of the Universe.

By a fortunate coincidence, I was due in New York almost immediately, to complete work on the Time-Life Science Library's *Man and Space*, the main text of which I had written in Colombo. On my way through London I had the first chance of seeing *Dr. Strangelove*, and was happy to find that it lived up to the reviews. Its impressive technical virtuosity certainly augured well for still more ambitious projects.

It was strange, being back in New York after several years of living in the tropical paradise of Ceylon. Commuting—even if only for three stations on the IRT—was an exotic novelty, after my humdrum existence among elephants, coral reefs, monsoons, and sunken treasure ships. The strange cries, cheerful smiling faces, and unfailingly courteous manners of the Manhattanites as they went about their affairs were a continual source of fascination; so were the comfortable trains whispering quietly through the spotless subway stations; the advertisements (often charmingly adorned by amateur artists) for such outlandish products as Levy's bread, the New York *Post*, Piel's beer, and a dozen fiercely competing brands of oral carcinogens. But you can get used to anything in time, and after a while (about fifteen minutes) the glamour faded.

My work in the Time-Life Book Division was not exactly onerous, since the manuscript was in good shape and whenever one of the researchers asked me, "What is your authority for this statement?" I would look at her firmly and reply, "*I* am." So while *Man and Space* progressed fairly smoothly thirty-two floors above the Avenue of the Americas, I had ample energy for moonlighting with Stanley Kubrick.

Our first meeting took place at Trader Vic's, in the Plaza Hotel. The date—April 22, 1964—happened to coincide with the opening of the ill-starred New York World's Fair, which might or might not be regarded as an unfavorable omen. Stanley arrived on time, and turned out to be a rather quiet, average-height New Yorker (to be specific, Bronxian) with none of the idiosyncrasies one associates with major Hollywood movie directors, largely as a result of Hollywood movies. (It must be admitted that he has since grown a full-fledged beard, which is one of his few concessions to modern orthodoxy.) He had a night-person pallor, and one of our minor problems was that he functions best in the small hours of the morning, whereas I believe that no sane person is awake after 10 P.M. and no law-abiding one after midnight. The late Peter George, whose novel *Red Alert* formed the basis of *Dr. Strangelove*, once told me that Stanley used to phone him up for discussions at 4 A.M., desisting only when his bleary-eyed collaborator threatened to retreat to England. I am glad to say that he never tried this on me; in fact I would put consideration for other people as one of his most engaging characteristics—though this does not stop him from being absolutely inflexible once he has decided on some course of action. Tears, hysterics, flattery, sulks, threats of lawsuits will not deflect him one millimeter. I have tried them all: well, most of them. . . .

Another characteristic that struck me at once was that of pure intelligence; Kubrick grasps new ideas, however complex, almost instantly. He also appears to be interested in practically everything; the fact that he never came near entering college, and had a less-than-distinguished high-school career, is a sad comment on the American educational system.

On our first day together, we talked for eight solid hours about science fiction, *Dr. Strangelove*, flying saucers, politics, the space program, Senator Goldwater—and, of course, the projected next movie.

For the next month, we met and talked on an average of five hours a day—at Stanley's apartment, in restaurants and automats, movie houses and art galleries. Besides talking endlessly, we had a look at the competition. In my opinion there have been a number of good—or at least interesting—science-fiction movies in the past. They include, for example, the Pal-Heinlein *Destination Moon, The War of the Worlds, The Day the Earth Stood Still, The Thing,* and *Forbidden Planet.* However, my affection for the genre perhaps caused me to make greater allowances than Stanley, who was highly critical of everything we screened. After I had pressed him to view H. G. Wells's 1936 classic *Things to Come,* he exclaimed in anguish, "What *are* you trying to do to me? I'll never see anything you recommend again!"

Eventually, the shape of the movie began to emerge from the fog of words. It would be based on "The Sentinel" and five of my other short stories of space exploration; our private title for the project was "How the Solar System Was Won." What we had in mind was a kind of semi-documentary about the first pioneering days of the new frontier; though we soon left that concept far behind, it still seems quite a good idea. Later, I had the quaint experience of buying back—at a nominal fee—my unused stories from Stanley.

Stanley calculated that the whole project, from starting the script to the release of the movie, would take about two years, and I reluctantly postponed my return to Ceylon—at least until a treatment had been worked out. We shook hands on the deal during the evening of May 17, 1964, went out onto the penthouse veranda to relax—and at 9 P.M. saw, sailing high above Manhattan, the most spectacular of the dozen UFOs I've observed during the last twenty years.

It was the only one I was not able to identify fairly quickly, which put me on the spot as I'd tried to convince Stanley that the wretched things had nothing to do with space. *This* one looked exactly like an unusually brilliant satellite; however, the *New York Times*'s regular listing gave no transit at 9 P.M.—and, much more alarming, we felt convinced that this object came to rest at the zenith and remained poised vertically above the city for the best part of a minute before slowly sinking down into the north.

I can still remember, rather sheepishly, my feelings of awe and excitement—and also the thought that flashed through my mind: "This is altogether too much of a coincidence. *They* are out to stop us from making this movie."

What to do? When our nerves had ceased jangling, I argued that there must be a simple explanation, but couldn't think of one. We were reluctant to approach the Air Force, which was still smarting from *Strangelove* and could hardly be blamed if it regarded a report by two such dubious characters as a gag or a publicity stunt. But there was no alternative, so we apologetically contacted the Pentagon and had even gone to the trouble of filling in the standard sighting form—when the whole affair fizzled out.

My friends at the Hayden Planetarium set their computer to work, and discovered that we had indeed observed an Echo 1 transit. Why this spectacular appearance wasn't listed in the *Times*, which gave two later and less impressive ones for the same night, was the only real mystery involved. The illusion that the object had hovered at the zenith almost certainly resulted from the absence of reference points in the brilliantly moonlit sky.

Of course, if it had been a *real* flying saucer, there would have been no movie. Some time later, Stanley tried to insure MGM against this eventuality with Lloyd's of London, asking them to draw up a policy which would compensate him if extraterrestrial life was discovered and our plot was demolished. How the underwriters managed to compute the premium I can't imagine, but the figure they quoted was appropriately astronomical and the project was dropped. Stanley decided to take his chances with the Universe.

This was typical of Stanley's ability to worry about possibilities no one else would think of. He always acts on the assumption that if something *can* go wrong, it will; ditto if it can't. There was a time, as the Mariner 4 space probe approached Mars, when he kept worrying about alternative story lines—just in case signs of life were discovered on the red planet. But I refused to cross that bridge until we came to it; whatever happened,

I argued, we would be in fine shape. If there *were* Martians, we could work them in somehow—and the publicity for the movie would be simply wonderful.

Once the contracts had been signed, the actual writing took place in a manner which must be unusual, and may be unprecedented. Stanley hates movie scripts; like D. W. Griffith, I think he would prefer to work without one, if it were possible. But he had to have *something* to show MGM what they were buying; so he proposed that we sit down and first write the story as a complete novel. Though I had never collaborated with anyone before in this way, the idea suited me fine.

Stanley installed me, with electric typewriter, in his Central Park West office, but after one day I retreated to my natural environment in the Hotel Chelsea, where I could draw inspiration from the company of Arthur Miller, Allen Ginsberg, Andy Warhol, and William Burroughs— not to mention the restless shades of Dylan and Brendan. Every other day Stanley and I would get together and compare notes; during this period we went down endless blind alleys and threw away tens of thousands of words. The scope of the story steadily expanded, both in time and space.

During this period, the project had various changes of title: it was first announced as "Journey Beyond the Stars"—which I always disliked because there have been so many movie Voyages and Journeys that confusion would be inevitable. Indeed, *Fantastic Voyage* was coming up shortly, and Salvador Dali had been disporting himself in a Fifth Avenue window to promote it. When I mentioned this to Stanley, he said, "Don't worry—we've already booked a window for you." Perhaps luckily, I never took him up on this.

The merging of our streams of thought was so effective that, after this lapse of time, I am no longer sure who originated what ideas; we finally agreed that Stanley should have prime billing for the screenplay, while only my name would appear on the novel. Only the germ of the "Sentinel" concept is now left; the story as it exists today is entirely new—in fact, Stanley was still making major changes at a very late stage in the actual shooting.

Our brainstorming sessions usually took place in the Kubrick Eastside penthouse off Lexington, presided over by Stanley's charming artist wife Christiane, whom he met while making *Paths of Glory*. (She appears in its moving final scene—the only woman in the entire film.) Underfoot much of the time were the three—it often seemed more—Kubrick daughters, whom Stanley is in the process of spoiling. Very much of a family man, he has little social life and begrudges all time not devoted to his home or his work.

He is also a gadget lover, being surrounded by tape recorders and cameras—all of which are well used. I doubt if even the most trigger-happy amateur photographer takes as many snapshots of his children as does Stanley—usually with a Pen D half-frame camera, which makes a slight contrast to the Cinerama–Panavision 70-millimeter monster he is maneuvering most of the day. This would seem to suggest that he has no hobbies; it might be more true to say that they are integrated into his work.

He certainly has one absorbing recreation—chess, which he plays brilliantly; for a while he made a modest living at it, challenging the pros in Washington Square. Very fortunately, I long ago decided not even to learn the rules of this seductive game; I was afraid of what might happen if I did. This was very wise of me, for if we had both been chess players I doubt if *2001* would ever have been completed. I am not a good loser.

The first version of the novel was finished on December 24, 1964; I never imagined that two Christmases later we would *still* be polishing the manuscript, amid mounting screams of protest from publishers and agents.

But the first version, incomplete and undeveloped though it was, allowed Stanley to set up the deal. Through 1965, he gathered around him the armies of artists, technicians, actors, accountants, and secretaries without whom no movie can be made; in this case, there were endless additional complications, as we also needed scientific advisers, engineers, genuine space hardware, and whole libraries of reference material. Everything was accumulated during the year at MGM's Borehamwood Studios, some fifteen miles north of London; the largest set of all, however, had to be built just six miles south of the city, at Shepperton-on-Thames.

Seventy years earlier, in the twelfth chapter of his brilliant novel *The War of the Worlds*, H. G. Wells's Martians had destroyed Shepperton with their heat ray. *This* year, man had obtained his first close-up of Mars, via Mariner 4. As I watched our astronauts making their way over the lunar surface toward the ominously looming bulk of the Sentinel, while Stanley directed them through the radios in their space suits, I remembered that within five years, at the most, men would *really* be walking on the Moon.

Fiction and fact were indeed becoming hard to disentangle. I hope that in *2001: A Space Odyssey* Stanley and I have added to the confusion, but in a constructive and responsible fashion. For what we are trying to create is a realistic myth—and we may well have to wait until the year 2001 itself to see how successful we have been.

# JOURNEY WITH A LITTLE MAN

## Richard McKenna

If I have learned anything in the process of becoming a professional writer, it is that there are as many ways of becoming a writer as there are writers. I am going to talk only about the way that worked for me. The thought of becoming a writer first came to me as an occasional idle fancy during World War II. It did not become a firm decision until about 1950. Then I planned it rather carefully. I planned first to get a formal education and then to serve my writing apprenticeship in science fiction. That field pays poorly, so I thought I would not meet much skilled competition. It would also allow me to indulge the very great interest I had in all areas of science. My plan became my excuse for taking far more science courses than my major in English literature would conventionally accommodate.

Often on my way through school I was tempted to give up my plan. I read everything and listened to everything with a perpetual "What if?" before me. Many answers which suggested themselves fascinated me. By each science in turn I was tempted to forego writing and take to asking "What if?" directly of nature. It seemed to me then and does still that science is as much a creative activity as art. Both are concerned with discovery and fabrication. Science is the art of the intellect.

What held me back each time was the conviction that only as a writer would I remain free to range across the whole of human experience and to mix intellect with feeling. I wanted to present new and fascinating

From *The Sons of Martha and Other Stories*, Harper & Row, 1967 ideas from science in the form of stories. I always assumed that when the time came to write the stories I would find it as simple a matter as writing term papers. Seldom have I been more wrong.

I had one experience in a science course which, if I had understood it fully, might have spared me much anguish when I began writing. It was an experiment in a psychology lab which took me through what I now consider to be a learning process of the same kind as learning creative writing. It is worth recounting in some detail.

That morning in class the instructor had told us that between any conscious intention and the completed act lies an apparatus of nerves and primitive brain centers not under control of the conscious mind. I understood and accepted the statement.

The lab was in the afternoon. It was a fine summer day, and several of the girls came to the lab barefoot. The lab instructor formed us into teams of two, and one of the barefoot girls fell to me as partner. She was to be the experimenter and I the subject. My task was to trace a pencil over a large five-pointed star printed on a sheet of paper while I saw my hand and the star only in a mirror. The girl would time me and record how often and how widely my pencil strayed from the printed line.

I always tried to do well in that psych lab. I think I wanted to prove that my reflexes had not slowed down. That day in particular I wanted to do well. While we waited for the signal to begin, I thought out carefully the principles of mirror-reversal. I was going to use my knowledge of optics and geometry to give me an advantage over the other subjects. The girl smiled what I took to be encouragement at me. We were facing each other across a table, and all around the large room other couples were similarly awaiting the signal.

"Go!" the instructor said.

The girl clicked her stopwatch. My pencil went wildly off. I paused and thought quickly again through the geometry. When I knew exactly how my hand should move, I so moved it. Again it went skating awry with a will all its own. That happened again and again as I tried to reason my way through and to make my hand obey me. I felt a most peculiar, dismayed frustration at the disobedience of my hand. It began to seem like an entity separate from myself. It would rush clear off the paper. If only the girl had not been there, I could have cursed it. All around me the other subjects were finishing their first trial. I knew I was sweating and red-faced. The girl was plainly sorry for me, and that made it worse. I was her team and I was failing her.

Finally, in despair, I simply went at it by trial and error. That was not much better. I seesawed painfully along. When I had to change direction, my whole arm would freeze. I would will it to move and it would not. I could start the pencil tracing again only by moving my whole body from the waist. I was the last one in the class to finish the first trial, and my trace was eleven times longer than the line I was trying to follow. I was ashamed to look at the girl.

I did better on succeeding trials. I found I could set up a random tremor in the pencil point and somehow simply *wish* it along in the right direction. I began feeling better, and on each trial the tremor became less pronounced. At the end of the period the girl gave me a difficult pattern to trace, a complex affair of straight and curved lines. I yawed wildly off when I began it, but I did not call upon any optics or geometry. I just steadied on the course and wished my way on around it, and my score on it was one of the best in the class.

When I wrote up the experiment I said it demonstrated that the neural complex below the level of conscious awareness can be trained to a new mode of action only by trial and error. If a general principle is involved, the complex will, with enough trials, learn that also and be able to apply it in a new situation. The conscious mind may already know the principle perfectly and still be unable to apply it until it is also learned, slowly and painfully, by the unconscious part.

I should have written "unconscious partner." I should have pondered the implications of that experience more deeply than I did.

When I finished school I married, with a clear understanding between my wife and me that I was going to become a writer, and I settled in to write. My attitude was very matter-of-fact. I was going to set words end to end as methodically as masons lay bricks end to end. I studied books and articles about writing and abstracted from them all a list of rules by which to write. Then I sat down at the dining-room table to apply what I knew.

I found I could not. The words simply would not come. With all those rules in my mind I was like the fabled centipede who could not run for worrying which leg came after which. What little I wrote had about as much life in it as a brick wall. I scorned it myself. However, when I laid aside the rules, the writing went the opposite way. What was planned to be a neat 5,000 words would explode to 30,000 and leave me feeling like the sorcerer's apprentice.

The writing I did the second way pleased me too much. When I would try to apply the rules in rewriting, I felt distinctly that I was maiming living literature in favor of dead rule books. I applied them rather too gently, as I know now. I would send beautiful manuscripts fluttering off to the marketplace. They would come creeping back to me out of the dust and heat with printed rejection slips clamped in their ugly beaks.

That went on for more than a year. I became increasingly grim. I refused to believe that I could not write. I felt intolerably exasperated at my powerlessness to do as I willed. My plan had gone wrong, somehow. Originally I had meant to live in the Nevada desert, alone except for books, and to write there. I will not expand on the painful months during which the conviction grew in me that I would have to go to the desert. At last I could bear it no longer, and I proposed to my wife a trial separation both from her and from Chapel Hill.

I stood at that moment in the greatest danger of my life. I know now that no writer can have a better wife than I have nor a better place in which to write than Chapel Hill, where I found her. What I really had to have is what I have since come to call "creative isolation." I would have found that in the desert and misinterpreted it. But I will always be grateful that I gained it in a much less drastic way.

I took an office downtown. It had no telephone. Neither my wife nor anyone else was ever to come there and disturb me. Every morning before eight o'clock I would lock myself in with a thermos of coffee and a sandwich. I would not come out again until after five o'clock. I did that seven days a week.

From the first day, much of my anguish left me. I recognized it as the same I had felt in the psychology lab. My confidence and drive came back. I could read stories that were the best I could do six months before and see flaws all through them. I realized that all the while I had thought I was stopped cold I had really been making progress. I was midway in just such a process of unconscious learning as tracing that star had been.

*Learning to write creatively is a process of training the unconscious,* I decided. We all have an unconscious personality component, a silent partner in all we think we do alone. In some learning situations that silent partner can lag far behind his conscious partner. Mirror drawing is one such situation, and learning to write creatively is another.

That insight into my work saved me from a disastrous mistake in the other part of my life. It remained to act upon it in a way which would forward my work. Isolation was a necessary but not a sufficient condition. Fortunately, the others were easier to discover.

The first step was to attain and hold what I came to call "the writing mood." I had never experienced it before I began working in that office. It was a kind of inner excitement, a bit like waiting for a curtain to rise upon something unknown and wonderful. I learned to evoke it in various ways: wandering idly about the office and trying not to think at all; sitting at my desk toying with my pencil and a blank sheet of paper; reading poetry aloud to myself. At first it always took me several hours to evoke it, and distressingly often I could not evoke it all day long.

I learned not to fret about that. The one certain way not to attain the mood was to grasp for it with grim resolution. I had to *not-care* before it would come. Once attained, it was most precarious. A knock on my door and the necessity to speak even a few words would banish it for hours. A trip to the barbershop would destroy a whole day for me. Sometimes I became quite shaggy while I strove to finish a short story, and I could almost envy a bald man.

I wrote only when I was in the mood. Certain strange aspects of it came to my attention. I would write half a page and realize with a start that an hour or more had passed in what seemed like a few minutes. An observer would no doubt have seen me sitting frozen for minutes at a time, but I never had the sense of it. Often I would be up and away from my desk before I realized that I was pacing. At first, with the lingering conviction that one would never get a brick wall built that way, I would sit resolutely down again. That always broke the mood. But if I simply went on pacing I would before long find myself back at my desk and writing with no memory of having first willed it.

On days when I could not reach the mood I would do research for my stories. I read through many a science textbook, making notes and stopping to reflect and feeling the same pleasant excitement as when I was in school. That was a different excitement, more of an intellectual excitement. The writing mood was visceral; I could feel it vaguely across my midriff. Sometimes I would try to study Maugham or Kipling or some other master of the short story to learn technique. I could not deal with them as with the textbooks. After a paragraph or two I would be swept away by the story and only catch myself shirking duty after several pages. The trouble, and the familiar frustration, I knew how to explain to myself.

By then, strictly for my own purposes, I had postulated an unconscious part of myself which I personified and named "the little man in the subbasement." It was a game, and I played it as children do, only half-believing and half aware in delightful balance that it was only make-believe. I was not being scientific; I was simply trying very hard to learn to write. I never thought then that someday I would talk about it publicly. I find now, however, that I cannot tell how I became a professional writer without giving the little man his share of blame and credit. *He* was the one who was shirking duty when we read Maugham together.

Whatever I wrote when I was "in the mood" was better than I had done before. I began getting a few scrawled words and initials on the printed rejection slips. Then I began getting handwritten notes of rejection. Six months after I began work in my office, just as the Christmas holidays of 1957 set in, I received a formal letter of rejection. It pushed me across what I now consider to be the barrier between amateur and professional writing.

The rejected manuscript ran to 14,000 words. The editor told me that I had story enough for only 7,000 words. If I could compress it to that, he would be willing to read it again. It was not a promise of a sale. But it was the first expression of interest I had gotten in almost two years of steady work, and it energized me powerfully.

I reviewed all my rules for cutting wordage, and over the holidays I squeezed lifeblood out of that story in four rewrites. Each night I would count up the words I had eliminated that day. At first they were hundreds. Then they dwindled to tens. It grew progressively more painful. At the last I was pulling out single words and phrases that shrieked like mandrakes. But I told myself that it was the little man's pain, not mine, and he could learn only by suffering. With rules like razors I vivisected him unmercifully, cut the manuscript exactly in half, and sent it off again.

The little man should have hated me for it, but he did not. The day after his ordeal ended he handed up to me complete in one session a new story of only 3,500 words, shorter by half than anything I had done before. To this day I wonder whether he was not drawing in it a portrait of himself. The opening line read: "You can't just die; you got to do it by the book," and it was the little man speaking, all right.

That story, entitled "Casey Agonistes," sold at once and became my first published work. In his letter of acceptance the editor called it "admirably terse," and I could feel the little man glow when we read that.

The editor went on to ask that the story be expanded by several hundred words. I felt the little man glower. We expanded it by about fifty words and begrudged every one of them.

"Casey Agonistes" moved me from amateur to professional. The distinction is hard to define. Its salient characteristic, to me at that time and in my own terms, was that the little man had finally grasped the *idea* of learning. He began learning of his own volition. I found I could no longer read a short story purely for entertainment even if I wished to. I would note the technique as I went along, and it seemed an added dimension to the entertainment. I wonder now whether editors do not develop an intuition that tells them when a writer has crossed that invisible line and become professional. Only then, when it can be used effectively, do they offer help. In any case, 1958 became for me a year of rapid unfolding.

The story I had cut in half also sold. I began selling stories regularly. Editors would ask for revisions, and I would make them and learn by doing so. A literary agent named Rogers Terrill heard about me and "Casey" at a cocktail party and remarked casually, "Sounds like that guy might have a book in him." A mutual friend brought us together in correspondence. Terrill did not want to handle science fiction. He made a deal between us contingent upon my writing a sample straight fiction short story from which he could judge my potentiality. I set the little man searching for a suitable story idea.

Also through "Casey" I was invited to the annual science fiction writers' conference in June at Milford, Pennsylvania. It is restricted to professionals. I accepted and was hard put to get my sample short story written and off to Rogers Terrill beforehand. I was to meet him in New York after the conference for an interview. All through those days I lived in a sense of portent. My wife went to Milford with me, and all night on the bus we did not sleep a wink.

At Milford I met writers who for years had been only names to me. They treated me as another professional, without the slightest condescension. I wish I had time today to describe Milford more fully. The writers work in isolation during the year and come from many states to gather at Milford in June. It is something like a trappers' rendezvous in the old fur-trading days. Magazine and book editors attend; sales are made, book contracts talked about, another year's work planned. The work is strangely compounded of carnival and hardheaded practicality. The latter is the tone of the workshop, which takes up most of each day, and which had the greatest influence on me.

No one can be present in the workshop but the writers themselves, and each must have one or more stories in the pool. The stories are usually ones written during the year which would not sell but which the writers are reluctant to scrap. For each, it seemed to me, the problem was how to suit the story to the mass market without sacrifice of artistic integrity. And here were men and women who wrote for a precarious living at a few cents a word, who could see both requirements clearly without setting one above the other, and who were working out a solution with all the resources of their pooled experience. I was very proud to be one of them. There was a rapport quality to it. I felt distinctly upon me that "writing mood" which I had never before been able to attain in the presence of another human being.

We came down to New York in a daze. My wife walked with me to the interview with Rogers Terrill. She was going to leave me at the door. As a sailor I had known New York quite well, but now as we walked along it looked different. It *loomed* all around me, heavy with portent. As always, nameless people thronged along endlessly in both directions. Now they all had faces, strange faces. Now they were the people for whom I wished to write. As we approached the busiest corner, with a shock of pleased surprise I saw a familiar face. It was Dr. Bill Poteat, in whose philosophy classes at Chapel Hill I had probed more directly into the secret of existence than perhaps in any others. We talked for only a moment, but I went along strangely reassured, as if I had been granted a favorable omen.

I talked a long while with Rogers Terrill. He was a small man with a seamed face that could crinkle into a warmly infectious smile. He said he could sell my short story if I would revise it, and he asked me if I had any plans to write a novel. I said no, that I wanted to learn as much as I could by doing short stories before I thought about novels. He agreed, and I was encouraged to tell him the thought that had crystallized in me during those workshop sessions at Milford. I said I wanted to combine literary excellence with popular appeal, without sacrifice of either, no matter how relatively unproductive I might be of marketable manuscripts. Terrill jumped up and came smiling around his desk and we shook hands on that. The handshake was our contract.

I came home to Chapel Hill feeling that I had been through something very conclusive. I found that I could get more quickly into the writing mood each morning. It was much less vulnerable to distractions. Then I began hitting a new kind of block. I would start a short story, and it would go well the first day and less well on each succeeding day until the words would stop altogether. The mood would be strongly on me and yet the words would not come. When I tried to write just anything, in order to bull through a first draft, my handwriting would go all awry. It would become large and awkward and trembly, as if I were writing with my left hand. The first time that happened I was frightened, and I stopped work for that day.

Quite soon I discovered that if I would only start the story over from the beginning, my hand would be free and the words would come smoothly again. I would have to start a short story seven or eight times, each time getting a little further along with it, before I had a first draft. In terms of the game I was playing, it meant that something not apparent to me consciously went wrong with those stories along the way. The little man knew what was wrong, and the only way he could remedy it was to force a new start. With each new start there were changes, and sometimes, but not always, I thought I could see a reason for them. It made me feel floating and helpless, and I would figuratively hold my breath until I had a complete first draft. Then, however, I would have it nailed down. I could rewrite straight through as often as I wished and with more confidence than I had ever had.

The sample short story I had written for Rog Terrill was based on a yarn I had heard in China as a boy. My story did not quite reach to that yarn, but it set the stage for it. So I wrote a second story with the same characters and setting, and again I fell short of the germinal yarn. Rog sold both stories, after I had made extensive revisions, but he began telling me that I really had a novel in that material. He urged me to write it. I was reluctant to take the plunge.

However, I developed a great urge to read books on China, any book on China. The dryest book on China would hold my interest. I said that I was going to mine that material for short stories. I wrote them and Rog sold them, but in every letter he nudged me toward a novel. He said that with a few sample chapters and a synopsis he could get me a book contract. Thus I could be assured of publication before making the full investment of time and energy. By the end of 1958 he had persuaded me.

By June of 1959, in close consultation with Rog, I had written Part I of the novel at least six times. It ran well over a hundred pages. Rog arranged for some quick readings while I attended my second Milford conference. I had moved clear out of science fiction and into the men's magazines, but they still welcomed me at Milford. I went down to New York and spent a week reading files of old Chinese newspapers in the Public Library while Rog angled for a book contract. He tried three publishers and failed. Then he said I would have to rewrite. We talked over how I would do it, in the light of the editorial reactions.

Home in Chapel Hill, I seemed to lack the heart to go on with it. Probably in an effort to escape, and with a kind of false and feverish zeal, I explored the Spanish-American War, oil tankers, and early nineteenth-century pirates. Nothing I wrote was much good. Sometime about September I developed an urge to read Hemingway. I considered such capricious urges to be signals from the little man. For some reason he wanted to read Hemingway.

We had studied Hemingway before, but this was different. We stopped writing and read everything of Hemingway in print in a state of sustained, nonanalytical excitement. We came out of it with the concept of the "clean, well-lighted story." I will not try to explain it. It is the little man's concept, a matter of pure feeling, and the most he can do is grimace and point to "Big Two-hearted River." The experience had the feeling of a change in kind, as with "Casey Agonistes." Thereafter, in a manner impossible to convey, I wrote from a different posture, with a kind of spiritual body-English unknown to me until then. The first story I wrote from that posture, and very clumsily, sold to the *Saturday Evening Post*.

In the fall of that year, 1959, I had a chance to buy the house I now live in on Cobb Terrace. I bought it with misgivings. The down payment took the last of my Navy savings, and I was fearful of what economic insecurity might do to my writing. I would no longer be able to rent the office. But the house had an extra room which I could hedge about with the same tabus as my office, and I gambled that my work habits had become dependable enough to stand the transfer. The last story I wrote in my office was the *Post* sale, and it furnished our new kitchen.

The *Post* sale eased my feelings of insecurity. I decided that I would stay on short stories until the house was paid for and I had a small cash reserve again, before starting the long pull on the novel. For the next several years I was going to write primarily for money.

I stopped reading about China. I studied scores of *Post* stories, and I tailored every line I wrote specifically for the *Post*—and the *Post* would not buy any more stories. They always found something wrong with them too vague to remedy. When Rog tried them at other slick magazines the editors would say: "This is so obviously a *Post* story that I wonder you haven't given it to them." Rog told me it was just a symptom of what was happening to the magazine market and the reason he was urging all his clients who could do so to shift to novels. He wanted me to take up the China novel again.

I still held back. I gave up on the *Post* and tried stories for the men's magazines and even science fiction again. There was more desperation than pleasure in the work. By July, nine months had passed and I had made only one small sale. I realized I might just as well have been working on the novel all that while. With a sudden and angry resolution, I burned my bridges. I went back to the novel with a vow as solemn as marriage that I would write it through to the end. I did not care whether I had a book contract or how many years it took.

At once the work went well and smoothly. My thirst for China reading came back redoubled. I rewrote Part I several times and sent it to Rog just before Christmas. I had built up a kind of momentum, and I went right on with Part II while I was waiting to hear from Rog. Very soon I began to get the signal that the little man wanted to start over again, but with Part II. A feeling grew in me that the novel properly started with Part II. Late in January, with a curious kind of relief, I heard from Rog that Part I and my synopsis had again been rejected. I wrote Rog that I was scrapping Part I and that I was going to take the novel through a complete draft before I again showed anything to anyone. The next day I started afresh on Part II with the sense that I was at last really beginning a novel.

Thus began for me still another phase. My life began to contract wholly into my work. I became increasingly reluctant to go out evenings. I wanted the time for reading. But I could read nothing that did not, in some way not always known to me, relate to my work. When I tried to read simply for pleasure, I could not. Several times I hurled a book across the room and was astonished at myself afterward. I gave up reading newspapers on the plea to myself that I would keep up with the world by reading *Time* magazine every week. Then every Wednesday, when *Time* came blundering in like a Person from Porlock, I grew to hate the sight of it. Once I could not have imagined myself not reading the *Scientific American* avidly on its day of arrival, but now I was letting months of it pile up unread. Yet all the while I was reading voraciously, with the feeling that the demands of society would not let me read nearly as much as I needed.

My choice of reading was very whimsical. Sometimes I would read just the beginnings of novels and sometimes just the endings. For one stretch I read China novels and for another stretch I read dozens of military novels. I read a lot in the social sciences. All the while I read all the nonfiction China books I could find. When I did not know what I wanted to read next, I learned to go along the shelves of my library and leaf into books at random until one would engage my interest. When it did, I could almost feel the gears click into place. The cutoff would be equally abrupt. One night *Middlemarch* clicked into place for me and an hour later clicked off. I don't know what I wanted of it.

That was how it went for me. I wrote seven days a week and read every evening that I could. I became almost completely secluded. I would not answer letters. I let them pile up for months and then, resentfully, I would take a day off and answer them all at once. June neared, and I wrote to my friends at Milford that I could not come that year. I was afraid that if I broke my stride even for a few days I would not be able to pick it up again. As I neared the end of the first draft in July, a kind of superstitious terror grew in me, a haunting fear that some malignity of fate would stop me short. But nothing did, and I completed the first draft. I knew I had the novel nailed down.

Without loss of a day I began a second draft. In September I sent eight chapters and a synopsis up to Rog. I went right on working. In November Rog phoned me that Harper & Brothers were going to give me a contract for it. The news thrilled me and brought a tremendous exultation. I could not work any more that day. Nothing since has quite touched again the glory of that afternoon. After that, if possible, I worked with even more drive. The first half of the advance reached me just before Christmas. For my wife and me that was the happiest Christmas since our marriage six years before. On Christmas Day I wrote three thousand words.

In February I finished the second draft and went up to New York to confer with my editor, Marion S. Wyeth, Jr., on revisions. Rog joined us, and we talked through a long afternoon in a rapport very like that of the workshop at Milford. I came home and worked on revisions at the same pace. I kept in close touch with Rog and with Buz Wyeth, and our working rapport intensified. I no longer had the sense of being alone at my desk. It was a genuine group mind that worked out the final form of *Sand Pebbles*. Although I wrote all the words, I know I could not possibly have taken the novel to finished form in isolation.

A few days before June I finished the work. Milford for my wife and me that year was almost all carnival.

The story of my development as a writer properly ends here. For almost a year now I have not written anything of large scope. But I will recount briefly what has happened during the past year, because it is part of the larger story of my life in Chapel Hill.

Through July and August I worked up a quite detailed plot outline for another novel. In August the good news began, first the book club sale and then magazine serialization. In September I went to New York for the *Times* interview that was to break the story of the Harper Prize. While I was in New York the movie sale went through. And Rog went to the hospital with a heart attack and pulmonary complications.

I had brought the plot outline of the new novel with me to New York. Rog and Buz and I talked it over. From his hospital bed Rog negotiated a contract for it without a word of it yet written. I promised Rog that I would go right to work writing it. I said that when I came up in January for the publication of *Sand Pebbles* I would bring him one chapter of the new novel as a token.

I did not write a word of it. My correspondence had increased very greatly, and I seemed to spend much of each day answering letters. Rog came out of the hospital, but my health faltered and I went in for several weeks. I had still not fully recovered when I had to go back to New York in January. How I survived those three weeks in New York still amazes me. I promised Rog that I would bring him three chapters when I came up in February. Then I escaped home to Chapel Hill as if to a sanctuary.

It was no longer a sanctuary. I had a mountain of accumulated correspondence. I had to write speeches for delivery in Washington and New York. When I reached New York again in mid-February, I did not have even one chapter of the new novel. Through all that stay Rog chided me gently about my delay in getting back to my own proper work. He warned me at length of the difficulty of writing a second novel when the first has scored heavily. On my last night in New York we and our wives went out to dinner together, and all evening he kept on that theme. When we said goodbye, I slapped him on the shoulder and told him: "Rog, for sure now, I'm going home and go to work. We're going to do it again."

In Chapel Hill two days later I learned of his sudden death.

That brings my story up to date. Since last June I have not developed at all as a writer, although I have gained some competence at being a public figure of sorts. There is something frighteningly seductive about it. In another month I will have been idle for a full year, and I hardly know where the time has gone. So for my own salvation as a writer I am going once again to burn my ships on the coast of Mexico. I have set June 1 as an absolute cut-off date for all engagements which will work to delay or distract me from going to work full time on the new novel.

Let me in conclusion summarize what up to this point I think I have learned about professional writing. What I will say is not necessarily valid for anyone other than myself. And I speak from out the dust of continuing battle, so I may interpret my experience somewhat differently ten years from now. But here is how it seems to me today.

Learning creative writing is a process of training the unconscious. We all have in us a living something independent of that which thinks it says, "I" for the whole man. It is not enough to know it intellectually; one must also learn it through lived experience, which is a quite different way of knowing. What I did was to grant it a separate "I," to personify it as "the little man." I reached out my hand to him, and we clasped hands, to give help and to receive help.

At first the little man can learn only by doing, by blind trial and corrected error. It may take him years to learn on his level what the conscious mind can learn in a month of hard study. But the creative quality of what is written cannot improve any faster than the little man can learn. For that little man is the powerhouse of all creative writing.

He it is who explores the caverns measureless to man and therein listens to ancestral voices. He is the sole author, the scenarist, and all of the actors in our private dreams. His original media are visual imagery and feeling tones and only a few spoken words. Until a few years ago, my little man was illiterate. Sometimes printed matter would appear in my dreams, and when I tried to focus down and read it he would snatch it away. When I gained enough power over him to hold it in place, the presumed letters would turn out to be blurs and squiggles. There was great tension in the dream at such moments. But the time came when the letters were genuine and did not dissolve.

My theory for the moment is that the little man must' learn how to change himself from a private to a public dreamer. He must learn how to transmute his original media into words in such a way that the story will induce in readers something resembling the unconscious, nonverbal complex of imagery and feeling tones he began with. The professionally written story may be a kind of collective and public dream. From the start, my little man tried hard. I found my unsalable first stories so deeply satisfying that it was very painful to cut and revise. I wanted just to reread them and glow with pleasure. In that phase the dreams were fully verbalized but still private. To make them collective and public demanded a subtle but equally as radical a change in verbal structuring as mirror drawing demands in hand-eye coordination. Now I take professional pride and find considerable pleasure in rewriting. I have little pleasure in reading the published work.

For me I think the preliminary movement was best and soonest made in painful isolation. Perhaps there had to be pain, to make the little man start learning. Along the way that I was going solicitous critical help too early might have been a hindrance; at least I felt it so. So would have been premature publication in any subsidized or coterie outlet. Both would have seemed to me a kind of substitute gratification, whereas the gratification I sought lay in breaking through to Everyman in the dust and heat of the common marketplace.

For me the breakthrough came in two critical junctures. I think with "Casey Agonistes" the little man first grasped the principle of public dreaming and thereafter set himself to learn and apply it more fully. I believe, however, that he still thought he was the only little man in the universe and that he was still working for the familiar single spectator, who had suddenly grown outrageously demanding. Not until well over a year later did he learn from Hemingway that the theater was really public and all the seats were filled with other little men just like himself.

That, I think, was the source of the strange excitement with which he and I read Hemingway that time. My little man was learning that he was not alone. The clean, well-lighted story has in it a quality of deep calling to deep which will not yield to critical analysis. It can never be imposed upon or demanded of the little man by the intellect. It is the treasure that he must alone and voluntarily bring up from the deep waters. When he can bring it safely to shore, he breaks free of the solitary confinement into which the evolving human condition has plunged all the little men. Momentarily he can permit the other little men to feel that they are not alone either.

They say Leonardo was ambidextrous from infancy and could write in mirror-reversal without ever having had to practice it. Maybe he painted Mona Lisa in some looking-glass way that makes her a universal public dream-image. Possibly Leonardo remained a whole man from birth. I know that I did not. But more and more I find the little man and myself tending to coexist in the same "I." Perhaps the measure of artistic maturity is the degree of that coexistence and the calm joy it brings is the true reward of writing.

# NOTES

7     1. Lewis himself certainly would not have claimed that *Out of the Silent Planet* is realistic science fiction (see his essay "On Science Fiction" in this volume), but it is not the surface of Mars in his novel which has "conditions . . . much like those of Earth" but the bottoms of deep chasms; the surface is a world not unlike that of Heinlein's *Red Planet*.

8     2. For another view, see "Science in S.F.: A Debate," in this volume.

10     3. There is a persistent story that the inventor of the periscope couldn't patent it because Jules Verne had already described it in *Twenty Thousand Leagues Under the Sea*. In fact, as Ted Thomas has pointed out, there is no mention of the periscope in that book; the *Nautilus* didn't have one.

13     4. Raymond Z. Gallun used all these ideas in a story called "The Scarab," published in 1936.

13     5. "If This Goes On—"

14     6. The real names behind these pseudonyms, in order, are: Robert S. Richardson, John W. Campbell, Jr., Will F. Jenkins, Eric Temple Bell, and G. Harry Stine.

14     7. I asked Heinlein what this gadget was; he replied that as far as he knows it is still classified.

15     8. Alas, Hamilton never described his spacesuits; what Heinlein remembers are the cover and black-and-white illustrations by H. Wessolowski, an unsung contributor to the space program.

25     9. I can't help being reminded of a line from Thorne Smith's *Rain in the Doorway*: " 'Could Abe Lincoln change a tire? No. Very well, then. The man was a washout.' "

36     10. *The Shape of Things to Come* is not fiction. Asimov may have been thinking of the film loosely based on it, *Things to Come*, for which Wells wrote the screenplay.

42     11. Campbell flunked out of M.I.T., later got his degree in physics from Duke.

52     12. Schizophrenia is not the same thing as multiple personality, but if Guin had known that he wouldn't have had any story. "Schizoid per-

sonality" is not even the same thing as schizophrenia. Asimov and I, along with most science fiction writers and readers, would probably be classed as schizoid personalities.

102    13. "His mind, like so many minds of his generation, was richly furnished with bogies. He had read his H. G. Wells and others. His universe was peopled with horrors such as ancient and medieval mythology could hardly rival. No insect-like, vermiculate or crustacean Abominable, no twitching feelers, rasping wings, slimy coils, curling tentacles, no monstrous union of superhuman intelligence and insatiable cruelty seemed to him anything but likely on an alien world."—C. S. Lewis, *Out of the Silent Planet*.

103    14. "Nightmare Island," by Douglas Drew, *Astounding*, October 1936.

104    15. The only story of this title listed in the Day Index is by Nelson S. Bond; it appeared in *Fantastic Adventures*, July 1939.

105    16. By Henry Slesar.

109    17. "The Big Front Yard."

109    18. Rog Phillips.

109    19. "Paul Ash" (Pauline Ashwell).

110    20. By Randall Garrett.

110    21. By Jay Williams.

113    22. Seabury Quinn, a *Weird Tales* writer. De Camp tells this story in his biography of Lovecraft.

128    23. "By His Bootstraps," by Robert A. Heinlein.

163    24. Included in *More Soviet Science Fiction* (as "Heart of the Serpent"), Collier Books, 1962.

164    25. A close reading of "First Contact," aided by more knowledge of s.f. literary conventions than is available to French and Russian readers, will show that what Versins and Yefremov say is untrue. When Leinster's ship goes out of "overdrive," as it does on sighting the alien ship, it loses its faster-than-light speed—an assumption not much different from that implicit in Yefremov's "pulse-ships" ("warp ships" in the English version). The alien having done the same, the two ships are motionless relative to the universe and each other, and can maneuver freely.

165    26. Versins ends this sentence, "*sans aucune chance pour nous de leur rendre la pareille*," "without any chance for us to do the same to them," which is not in Leinster's original.

181    27. A device patented by a Washington, D.C., real estate dealer which, its inventor claimed, would produce net momentum within a closed system by using eccentric weights rotating on shafts. The inventor